"Political economy" has been the term used for nearly three hundred years to express the interrelationship between the political and the economic affairs of the state. In *Theories of Political Economy*, James A. Caporaso and David P. Levine explore some of the more important frameworks for understanding the relation between politics and economics, including the classical, Marxian, Keynesian, neoclassical, state-centered, power-centered, and justice-centered. The book emphasizes understanding both the differences among these frameworks and the issues common to them. Discussion is organized around two main themes: The first is that the competing theories use significantly different criteria for determining how society should assign tasks to market and government. The second is that the growing interest in political economy poses a challenge to the traditional idea that economics and politics deal with separable concerns and terrains or may even employ different methods. The authors examine the implications of weakening the lines that traditionally distinguished between what was political and what was economic. In the last chapter, they consider an alternative framework for political economy that is more sensitive to the integrity and distinctiveness of economic and political processes without ignoring or underemphasizing the relations between them.

Theories of political economy

Theories of
political economy

JAMES A. CAPORASO
University of Washington

DAVID P. LEVINE
University of Denver

CAMBRIDGE
UNIVERSITY PRESS

Published by the Press Syndicate of the University of Cambridge
The Pitt Building, Trumpington Street, Cambridge CB2 IRP
40 West 20th Street, New York, NY 10011-4211, USA
10 Stamford Road, Oakleigh, Victoria 3166, Australia

First published 1992
Reprinted 1993

Printed in the United States of America

Library of Congress Cataloging-in-Publication Data is available.

A catolog record for this book is available from the British Library.

ISBN 0-521- 41561-6 hardback
ISBN 0-521-42578-6 paperback

Contents

Preface

When we began work on this project, we intended to write a book that could be used as a text in political economy courses, at least those with more than a passing concern for theoretical frameworks and the structure of arguments. We planned to produce a text that surveyed those frameworks with a critical spirit. As we wrote the book, our task became more complicated. Even those approaches explicitly using the term "political economy" rarely presented fully explicit theories connecting politics to economics. Often an approach presented us with a picture of only economics or politics. We had to draw out the linkages ourselves. Because of this, the term "survey" may not be as accurate a description of the book we wrote as it was of the book we intended to write.

Our task was complicated in a second way. As our work progressed, something of a shared concern with the direction of work in political economy emerged. Those reading the manuscript strongly encouraged us to make that concern an integrating theme, and we have tried to do so. Still, the book remains largely what it was intended to be: a critical survey and elaboration of approaches.

The term "survey" naturally raises questions about coverage. Because so many disparate activities fall under the heading of political economy, no survey can be both coherent and comprehensive. You have to cut somewhere. Our first cut was to exclude approaches without a substantial theoretical grounding. Our second cut was to rule out approaches we judged to be without broad significance. Finally, we included approaches we found interesting and important even if not immediately recognizable within current literature.

This book is the result of two authors working separately and together. Caporaso had primary responsibility for Chapter 6 and the Conclusion, Levine for Chapters 2, 3, 5, 9, and the Introduction. Chapters 1, 4, 7, and 8 contain substantial contributions from both.

*   *   *

We would like to thank several people for their contributions to the project. Robert O. Keohane, Stephen D. Krasner, Margaret Levi, and Theda Skocpol read particular chapters. Pamela Wolfe contributed suggestions to and provided assistance with several chapters. Emily Loose, editor for Cambridge University Press, encouraged and facilitated completion of the project. Our greatest thanks go to two anonymous referees who provided extensive and constructive comments on the entire manuscript.

James Caporaso would like to acknowledge the support of Harvard's Center for International Affairs for the 1987–8 year, the Andrew W. Mellon Chair at the University of Denver from 1984 to 1987, and the Virginia and Prentice Bloedel Chair of the University of Washington from 1988 to the present. Finally, he would like to express appreciation to Daryll J. Caporaso for her support throughout.

Introduction

When political economy emerged in the eighteenth century, it did so to help people understand and cope with a dramatic change in the system of want satisfaction, both in the nature of wants and in the manner of production and distribution of goods for satisfying them. The shift from the older term "economy" to the newer term "political economy" marked this change. Economy, taken from the Greek usage, referred to household management. It had relevance to a society in which, to an important degree, wants emerged and the things that satisfied them were produced in the household. Political economy referred to the management of the economic affairs of the state.

The term "political" refers us to two interrelated qualities of the system of want satisfaction. First this system links persons otherwise independent: strangers rather than relatives. To satisfy our wants we now depend on persons not our relatives, whom we might not even know. Second, the boundaries of want satisfaction are now political; responsibility for the system of want satisfaction devolves onto a public authority: the head of state rather than the head of the household. In its earliest period, political economy sought to advise the statesman on how he could best manage the economic affairs of the state so that the wants of the citizens would be met.

The emergence of political economy brought with it a debate over the responsibilities of the state (or statesman) with regard to the economy. This debate still goes on. It continues to occupy a central place in political economy. Is the state responsible for determining which wants will be satisfied, and for mobilizing resources to ensure their satisfaction? Or will wants be better satisfied if the mobilization of resources is left in the hands of individuals acting as private agents, motivated by their private interest? Should, for example, housing, medical care, education, welfare be provided by private citizens using the resources they have available to them? Or should they be provided by the state?

This debate poses a number of problems addressed by the different approaches to political economy covered in this book. The most important of

1

these fall into two groups. The first includes problems posed by the idea of a self-regulating market. To what extent will a system of private, self-interested agents interacting through exchange contracts succeed in satisfying their wants within the limits of the resources available to them? In modern terms, does political intervention into the economy enhance or impede want satisfaction?

The second group of problems involves the notion of a public agenda. What is the relationship between public ends and private interests? Is the purpose of the state primarily to respond to private interests and thus to regulate the economy only so far as it fails to satisfy private interests when the resources to do so are available? How do private interests become relevant to and bear upon the setting of public goals?

Different theories pose and answer these questions in different ways. Our purpose in this book is to survey the most important approaches employed to define and answer these questions. The approaches surveyed vary along a number of dimensions. We have chosen to take these differences seriously rather than treat them as variations on a single theme or attempt to encompass them within a single methodology. At root the differences run deep, involving opposing judgments regarding the nature and ends of private interest, the meaning and extent of the autonomy of persons, the nature of freedom implied in exchange contracts, the meaning and significance of public or collective life, and, fundamentally, the kinds of bonds that connect persons into larger groups.

Because differences between approaches are fundamental, and because we have chosen not to subsume them under a single method, we have tried to be sensitive to nuances in the way they use the terms politics and economics. We cannot treat these approaches simply as variations in concrete hypotheses, for example, concerning the likelihood of market failure of one sort or another. Such differences exist, of course, and are important. They often provide us with a window into the more fundamental differences of conceptual and analytical structure underlying the approaches. Yet, judgments about the world embedded in these hypotheses must be framed conceptually.

While differences in choice of concepts employed are visible and, in a way, obvious, differences in the way the same concepts are used in different theories can be less apparent, though they are no less important. The idea of interest appears in Marxian and non-Marxian theories, but connotations differ in important ways. Because we consider these differences fundamental to understanding the work being done in political economy, we have chosen in this book to focus on alternative approaches.

In order to begin sorting through the methodological and conceptual issues related to alternative approaches, we begin with a discussion of politics and economics in the first chapter. Different approaches to political economy use the terms "politics" and "economics" differently. It matters in thinking about the issues in political economy alluded to whether we treat, for example, authority or the state as the central concept in politics. It also matters whether we think material reproduction, the market, or constrained choice is the central concept in economics. Different notions of economics and politics lead to different political economies.

After considering politics and economics, we survey approaches to political economy. We begin with what we term the classical approach, using the work of the classical economists, especially Adam Smith and David Ricardo, to define a core of issues.

The classical approach argues for the capacity of markets to regulate themselves in a strong sense identified with the policy of laissez-faire. More than this, the classical theorists were the first to treat the economy as a system separable in principle from politics and family life. Their argument for market self-regulation treated the market system as a reality *sui generis,* connected to, but not a subsidiary organ of, the state. This idea was very much an innovation of classical political economy.

The classical innovation, once well established, tended to make the term political economy unsuitable. A main point of the classical theory was that economy is not, or at least need not be, political. The rise of capitalism would, in this view, depoliticize the economy. It is not surprising, then, that in the wake of the classical theories, the term economics came to displace the term political economy.

Today the classical innovation is often treated with skepticism. Over the past twenty years, social scientists have retrieved the term political economy, in part to insist that the economy is unavoidably political. Some invoke the theories of Karl Marx to support this claim. In Chapter 3 we explore a part of Marx's theory with an eye to the way he understands the links between economics and politics. We argue that Marx carried forward the classical project. He did not consider the capitalist economy an inherently political system. Nonetheless, he attempted to show how powerful political forces originate in the dynamics of the capitalist economic process and how that process spawned political struggles of historic dimensions.

To demonstrate the political implications of the workings of capitalist economy, Marx advanced a critique of the classical claims for market self-regulation. He did not do so with an eye to justifying state-regulated capitalism, but with the intent of demonstrating that capitalism was not viable in the long run. We will not attempt to review Marx's arguments concerning the contradictions of capitalist economy. Instead, we consider the way Marx connects political agendas to economic forces. In our view, while continuing the classical idea of the economy as a distinctive arena of society, Marx advanced a distinct conception of the relation between the political and the economic.

The neoclassical theory introduced at the end of the nineteenth century continues to apply the classical innovation, treating the economy as a separable system. It does not, however, carry forward the classical analytical scheme. In its place, the neoclassical theory applies the utilitarian philosophy to the problem of the nature and purpose of market economy.

In Chapter 4 we explore the neoclassical approach. This approach defines the relation of politics to economics on the basis of the idea of market failure, defining market failure with reference to individual preferences and the efficient use of resources. For the neoclassical thinker, "economics" refers to private transactions in pursuit of utility maximization, "politics" to the use of public authority in the same cause.

In the 1930s John Maynard Keynes proposed a critique of the claims for market self-regulation advanced by classical political economy, later by his immediate neoclassical predecessors. Like the neoclassical argument, his emphasizes a kind of market failure. Yet the market failure Keynes studies runs deeper and poses a more basic challenge to the institutions of a private enterprise system. His critique of the market calls into question the role assigned to the public authority by the classical theorists. Changes in that role carry implications for the classical innovation – the depoliticization of the economy.

In Chapter 5 we explore both the Keynesian argument and some of its implications for the shifting relation between politics and economics. As the public authority takes over more and more of the terrain once governed by the market, our way of thinking about economy undergoes subtle but important changes. The effort to shore up the capitalist economic system challenges foundational assumptions of that system concerning the proper limits of the market.

The method introduced by the neoclassical economists provides the basic components of an approach we explore in Chapter 6. This approach applies the economic calculus to politics. It makes individual maximizing behavior and rational choice the substance of political process and political decisions. In so doing, the "economic approach" inspired by the neoclassical method challenges the classical separation of the economic from the political. It does so not, however, by returning to the older idea of public responsibility for economic affairs, nor by enlarging the scope of market failure, but by interpreting politics as one focus of applied economic logic. The economic approach to politics explores the broader implications of neoclassical economics for the way we understand the relation between the economic and the political.

The debate over the self-regulating market inspires those approaches surveyed that respond most directly to the classical argument and are most clearly rooted in the classical project. But contemporary work in political economy includes more than the debate over the market. It also includes contributions from those setting out from somewhat different starting points.

One approach seeks to overthrow the classical idea of the economy as a reality *sui generis*. This approach identifies politics with the use of power and, by finding power in the economy, claims to have established that the economy is political. Here the term political economy strikes a radically new chord. It advances claims about the political nature of the economy, insisting on this political nature whether the market is subject to government regulation or not. In Chapter 7 we explore this way of thinking about economics, politics, and the relation between the two.

In Chapters 8 and 9 we explore two alternative ways of constructing the relation between politics and economics, one centering on the state, one on the concept of justice. Political economy in the classical tradition begins with the economy and the analysis of its operations. The state is generally cast in a responsive role. State-centered approaches shift the balance between market and state by liberating the state to pursue its own agendas in relation to society.

A state-centered approach need not begin with market failure in identifying the role of politics vis-à-vis the economy. If the state has its own ends, and if pursuit of those ends has implications for economic affairs and institutions, the state may seek to control the economy not to correct market failure, but to impose purposes of its own. Political economy begins with the imperatives of political rather than economic affairs. It refers to the imposition of political agendas on the economy.

The last approach we consider focuses on the concept of justice. Approaches centering on justice illuminate key features of the classical innovation. They grapple with the question of the appropriate terrain of the economy not in terms of the market's success or failure in satisfying wants, but in terms of the rights embodied in the market and their limits. A market is, ultimately, a system of property rights. Its boundaries indicate the limits of property rights. The political process can define and alter rights. When it does so, it defines and redefines the limits of the market.

The political process may serve to increase the level of private satisfaction (correcting market failures). It may also respond to the pressure of interest groups. But underlying action motivated by market failure and interest group pressure is a basic understanding of the nature and significance of rights with regard to the economy. Theories of justice address the problem of the limits of the market by exploring the system of rights. In Chapter 9 we briefly consider three justice-centered approaches to see how they conceptualize the relation between politics, economics, and the public authority.

Exploring the ways different approaches frame issues reveals a set of fundamental themes. These themes can be placed in the broader context of the problematic status of the rise of economic (or civil) society. As we show in the chapter on the classical approach, political economy responds to and contributes to a depoliticization of society, so far as the older sense of politics is concerned. In making this theme central, we pursue an idea explored by Sheldon Wolin in his *Politics and Vision* (1960). Most approaches to political economy treat the private sector as the primary arena. It sets agendas and ultimately governs outcomes. The idea of a collective or public reality different in nature from the system of private interests holds little appeal for political economy.

In our view, a main difficulty of political economy, common to different approaches, lies in a tendency to gloss over the separateness of the two spheres of the economic and the political, absorbing one into the other. A main theme of our survey is the importance of understanding and appreciating the categorical distinction between politics and economics, and the dangers of making one or the other dominant in both realms. We develop this theme explicitly in the last chapter, although it informs the discussion throughout.

The image suggested by our survey of approaches to political economy is in some ways unsettling. Because we do not adopt one of the approaches and interpret the others from that vantage point, we see in the state of political economy less that assures us of progress toward resolution of controversial issues, more evidence of continuing debate over long-standing problems. This stems less from any conviction on our part that, in fact, little progress has been made, and more from our sense that the core issues in political economy remain contested, that the contest is far from over, and that fundamental differences of concept and method are not easily resolved.

1

Politics and economics

Politics

It is often assumed that political economy involves an integration of politics and economics. It is less often conceded that the very idea of political economy rests on a prior separation of politics and economics. If politics and economics are conceptually fused, political economy cannot be thought to involve a relation between distinguishable activities. Since this point is often confused by talking about politics and economics as "organically linked" or the boundaries between the two as "blurred," we will comment on what this sense of separation means.

Distinguishing politics from economics does not mean that they are completely separate, isolated from each other, or indifferent to each other. It does not mean that politics and economics do not influence each other or "occur" within the same concrete structures. For example, allocation of goods and services may take place within market or political structures. And concrete organizations, such as banks, firms, interest groups, and unions, may be political or economic according to the activities in which they are engaged and the analytic categories of the investigator (Maier, 1987). So when we say that economics and politics are separate, we mean only that they are analytically distinct.[1]

If economics and politics are distinct, it follows that a book on various theories of political economy must take account of these differences. The challenge is twofold. First, we must identify different conceptions of the economic and political. What are the major ideas associated with these two central concepts? Second, we must identify the theoretical relations between economics and politics. Sometimes, these theoretical relations are more or less in place. Other times, we attempt to build them ourselves. The relations

[1] Some have argued that the separation of economics and politics is itself the result of a protracted historical process. Sartori (1973) points out that the ancient Greeks considered politics a central aspect to man's life and did not differentiate a separate political sphere, as we do today.

between politics and economics are what we mean by political economy. It is a theoretical enterprise.

The remainder of the chapter examines various conceptions of economics and politics. It will become clear that both economics and politics have multiple meanings. It is best to confront this diversity at the outset. The various approaches to political economy discussed in the book will be clearer if these differences are taken into account.

Conceptions of the political

Concepts of politics are not as analytically sharp as those of economics, a fact reflected in the numerous competing conceptions of politics. In Swift's *Gulliver's Travels* the key character laments how, in his discussion with the king, he happened to say "there were several thousand Books among us written upon the Art of Government [and] it gave him (directly contrary to my Intention) a very mean Opinion of our Understandings" (Swift, 1726).

There are many competing ideas of what is political, none of which has gained ascendancy by demonstrating clear theoretical superiority. Politics has meant "who gets what, when, and how" (Lasswell, 1936), "the struggle for power" (Morgenthau, [1948] 1960), "the art and science of government," "the socialization of conflict" (Schattschneider, 1960), "patterns of power, rule, and authority" (Dahl, 1956), "the science of the state," "the authoritative allocation of values" (Easton, [1953] 1981), "pure conflict, as in us against them" (Schmitt, 1976), and "the conciliation of conflicting interests through public policy" (Crick, [1962] 1964). Power, authority, public life, government, the state, conflict, and conflict resolution are all bound up with our understanding of politics.

The preceding discussion points to some of the problems of conceptualizing the political. We will develop here three ideas of the political that make sense, have some coherence, and have potential for connections with economics. Though not the only three ways of talking about politics, these conceptions do represent three important traditions. They are politics as government, as public life, and as the authoritative allocation of values.

Politics as government. One conception of politics makes it essentially equivalent to government. By government, we mean the formal political machinery of the country as a whole, its institutions, laws, public policies, and key actors. Sometimes government and the political are made equal by definition. Politics then refers to the activities, processes, and structures of government. What goes on within the U.S. Senate, the German Bundestag, and the British Parliament is by definition politics. What happens in society – that is, outside the scope of the government proper – is not political. Societal phenomena may have political implications, but they are not political *per se*.

Politics in this sense has a locus, a structural address. The central political institutions reside in the capital of the country. They are the ones that are authoritative in the sense of being able to decide for the country as a whole and being able (that is, having the capacity) to achieve compliance. If something occurs within this arena, it is political; if it doesn't, it is not.

The politics-as-government approach offers a definition of politics in terms of organization, rules, and agency. "Organization" refers to relatively concrete structures (formal organization). These might include courts, legislatures, bureaucracies, and political parties. "Rules" refers to rights and obligations as well as permissible procedures and strategies to be employed in the political process. The basic rules of a government are set down in its constitution, written or unwritten. These rules cover the organization and distribution of political power as well as procedures regarding voting, legislative strategies, and the permissible range of influence behavior. The basic rules for the United States include both a functional and territorial division of powers, the former involving a "separation of powers" among legislative, executive, and judicial branches, the latter a splitting of powers between central and outlying political units (federalism). England's basic rules are quite different. Here executive power is not a formally differentiated "branch" of government. Instead the prime minister's power rests on a majority in the House of Commons. Finally, government includes agents or personnel. These agents, situated in the overall political organization, "act" in the sense that they undertake political initiatives (to retain office, increase power, pass laws, and so on).

The study of government in the United States has been closely tied to an emphasis on law. As Charles Hyneman put it in *The Study of Politics*, "The central point of attention in American political science . . . is that part of the affairs of the state which centers in government, and that kind or part of government which speaks through law" (1959:26–7). Similarly, Harry Eckstein, though careful to put some distance between the state and politics, sees formal-legal studies as integral to the state (1979:2). Eckstein uses the term "formal-legal" because the study of government was closely tied to formal organization and to public law. Carl Friedrich's *Constitutional Government and Democracy* (1937) provides an example of the importance of numerous governmental characteristics, while Douglas Rae's book, *The Political Consequences of Electoral Laws* (1967), demonstrates the importance of differences in electoral rules.

The governmental approach does not rule out nongovernmental phenomena as having political relevance; it places government at the center and evaluates other phenomena as they impinge upon or are affected by government. Thus, the political role of the media, or the influence of interest groups or economic classes, while not directly part of government as defined here, may affect and be affected by governmental policies. The importance of such phenomena is recognized as part of society. They affect governmental politics but are not definitionally a part of the government.

The meaning of government can be clarified by distinguishing it from the state (see Carnoy, 1984, and see *Daedalus*, 1979, for surveys). The term "state" generally refers to a set of phenomena that are more inclusive than government. It is broader than government in that the state includes institutionalized authority, laws, and patterns of domination, including those resting on force, politically manipulated incentives, and reigning ideas. Benjamin and Duvall define the state as "the enduring structure of governance and rules in society" (1985:25). Defined in this way, the state does not "do" anything in the standard sense. The state is not an agent or actor – governments are (Wendt and Duvall, 1989:43). "Government," on the other hand, refers to agents, differentiated organizations, and rules that are embedded in the state, but they do not exhaust our meaning of the state.

What does the state include that is not encompassed by government? The idea of the state is tied to a broader conception of laws and rules than is usually signified by the term government, including informal rules embodied in customs, ideas, and parapublic institutions, what Peter Katzenstein calls "policy networks" (1978:19). Policy networks are combinations of public and private power made up of parts of the state bureaucracy and private associations. Similarly, the Gramscian idea of hegemony reflects a concept of rule that relies on ruling ideas and social forces as well as government more narrowly defined (see Gramsci, 1971).

The attempt to equate politics and government raises two critical questions. Is everything that happens "within government" political or is politics only a portion of government? Are there phenomena outside government that are political? If government defines what is political, we have to address ourselves to the heterogeneity of what is entailed by this term. Much of what goes on in government is private in goal if not in arena or institutional means. It is concerned neither with public goods nor with means that are recognized as part of the public sector. A politician may use public office to advance his or her private career. A temporary appointment to a highly visible governmental position may be coveted to enhance one's income from speeches and book royalties after resigning public office. Our point is not that these examples are nonpolitical but that there is an aspect of them that can be viewed as private (seeking personal wealth) and possibly even economic.

What does the governmental focus leave out that is normally considered political? It omits what, following Easton's concept of the political system (1965), we can call "political inputs" such as the expression of interests and political demands by societal actors, their aggregation into broad programs, the communication of political information by the privately owned media, and the experience of political socialization by parents, schools, and churches. It also omits combinations of private and governmental forces from active consideration since these combinations reach outside the governmental sector. Finally, the governmental notion of politics omits ideas of politics tied to state structures conceived more broadly than government. Cox's notion of a "historic bloc" encompassing governmental institutions, social forces, and ideology is exemplary (Cox, 1986). Clearly the focus on government excludes much that is often considered relevant. The justification for such exclusion is that, if the concept of government is to be useful, it must refer to something definite and precise. Expanding the concept of government causes much of what is otherwise thought of as societal to become part of government (such as schools, churches, families). A valuable distinction is weakened if not lost.

Politics as the public. One way of thinking about economics and politics is to link economics to what is private, politics with the public. Individual ends and activities resolve into two categories: those that are private (in motive and result) and those that imply others. We do not want to minimize the difficulty of making this distinction in practice or to suggest there are some actions that are insulated from the rest of society. Nevertheless, in liberal societies (by definition) there is a realm of the private that is treated as personal. Thus, religious worship, sexual activities within the household, the details of consumption (food and clothing preferences), and most aspects of child-rearing are private matters.

A sharp distinction between private and public is difficult to enforce. Certainly in the empirical world, boundaries shift. "Private" refers to affairs that are substantially limited to individuals or groups directly involved in exchange. The "public" is defined as the arena or activities that involve others in substantial ways. While *no* action is ever without social determinants, meanings, and implications, this does not necessarily make everything public. Neoclassical economists ground the distinction between private and public in what is and is not transmitted by the price system. Benefits and damages resulting from exchange not charged or paid for are external effects (externalities) and invite management by the state. John Dewey (1927) makes the same distinction in terms of the scope and persistence of consequences of transactions among individuals.

The idea of the public is broader than the neoclassical concept of externalities and public goods, yet narrower (in its politically relevant version) than society as a whole. It is broader than externalities and public goods in that it includes collective identities and shared values relevant for political discourse. It is narrower in that there is a public arena not overtly political (public dress codes, appropriate behavior in public places such as waiting rooms and elevators, and so forth). It is more narrow in that not all aspects of politics, at least in some versions, are public. Crick reminds us that "Palace politics is private politics, almost a contradiction in terms. The unique character of political activity lies, quite literally, in its publicity" ([1962] 1964:20). And social spheres such as the family, the church, and private associations are often seen as going outside the public realm.

In *The Politics*, Aristotle defended public life in the *polis* as essential to the expression of man's higher social nature. In ancient Rome, the *res publica* represented "bonds of association and mutual commitment which exist between people who are not joined together by ties of family or intimate association" (Sennett, 1978; original edition 1973:3). In *The Public and Its Problems* (1927), Dewey identifies the public as both the raw material of politics and an essential component of the state. And *In Defense of Politics* ([1962] 1964), Crick sees the public character of actions as a core characteristic of the political.

When we connect politics with the notion of public life, we bring to the forefront a set of questions and problems surrounding what is the central quality that makes activity and human interaction public. In responding to these questions and problems two lines of argument need to be clearly distinguished. Indeed, the notion of the public has been interpreted in two radically different directions.

The first, although historically the more recent, defines public by reference to self-interest. The public encompasses either pursuit of self-interests that coincide (a commonly held interest) or responses to ways in which the individual's pursuit of self-interest impinges on the welfare of others. The connected concepts of public goods and externalities are the key terms within this interpretation of public life. Its main distinguishing feature is rejection of any notion of public that either transcends private self-seeking or responds to human needs irreducible to private ends.

This contemporary notion of the public contrasts sharply with the more traditional notion linked to concepts of public interest and public good. These concepts carry with them the idea that the public has an existence, meaning, and purpose irreducible to the pursuit of individual self-interest and the ordering of private preferences. (For an account of this second notion see Arendt, 1958.) Those who advocate the first of our two notions of the public tend to view the second as metaphysical, if not mystical. It is their belief that the only grounded social reality is the individual and his or her preferences. Those who take our second notion of public more seriously argue that social institutions have their own reality. They do not arise in response to individual wants (although they often concern themselves with such wants). Rather, they encompass private agents and make explicit their underlying social connectedness understood as the grounding for their very existence as individuals. This second view presupposes a social capacity that is prior to the articulation of private ends.

When we consider political economy as involving the study of the relation of public to private (or of a part of that relation), it makes all the difference which notion of public we have in mind. If we focus on the first conception, we are led to examine the ways in which individual interests relate to one another, coincide, or negatively affect one another. If we employ the second of the two, then the study of the relationship between public and private means the study of the ways in which collective life undergirds, informs, animates, and gives meaning to private self-seeking, and of the limits of self-interest.

To illustrate these two different conceptions of the public, we explore the use of this concept by John Dewey and Hannah Arendt. Dewey elaborated his ideas about the public in *The Public and Its Problems* (1927). Arendt developed her arguments in *The Human Condition* (1958).

In *The Public and Its Problems*, John Dewey attempts to link the public with the state and to show how the latter, insofar as it is a liberal, democratic state, is grounded in and limited by the scope of what is public. His first task is to identify the core meaning of public. Dewey begins his search for the public from a particular determining ground, a world of individuals and their transactions. To the extent that their transactions are limited to themselves, that is, to the extent that they do not involve consequences for others, he speaks of their activities as private. The germ of the public is found in those transactions that involve others:

We take then our point of departure from the objective fact that human acts have consequences upon others, that some of these consequences are perceived, and that their perception leads to subsequent effort to control action so as to secure some consequences and avoid others. Following this clew, we are led to remark that the consequences are of two kinds, those which affect the persons directly engaged in a transaction, and those which affect others beyond those immediately concerned. In this distinction we find the germ of the distinction between the private and the public. (1927:12)

Dewey's idea of the public seems closely related to the neoclassical concept of externality. Couldn't we just as easily say that the public refers to the set of people whose preferences are affected (positively or negatively) by the consequences of market exchanges? To be sure, a family resemblance does exist, but so do important differences. Dewey is willing to talk about interests as well as preferences. Thus a public interest may be affected even while public preferences are not. For example, people may be dying because of dirty air or a depletion of ozone in the atmosphere but may be unaware of

the connection. Their interests in clean air and ozone have not become preferences.

A second difference lies in Dewey's readiness to include the sick, insane,
infirm, and young in the public. Dewey asks why people in these groups are
peculiarly "wards of the state" (1927:62). They are because in their transactions with others, "... the relationship is likely to be one-sided, and the
interests of one party [will] suffer" (1927:62). The reasoning here is quite
general. It involves the inequality of status (and, Dewey might have added,
of power and resources) of parties to the transaction. Once this principle is
introduced, numerous so-called private transactions assume a public content:
minimum wages, relations between workers and capitalists, care of the young
and the old, access to health and educational facilities, and so on. Dewey in
fact raises all these issues and makes a case for placing them within the public
domain in a way that is consistent with his general idea of the public. Whether
this effort works is not our concern here. The point is that Dewey's public
is considerably broader than externalities.

Hannah Arendt's interpretation of the public differs sharply from that just
summarized. Her interpretation brings our attention to dimensions of the
problem often lost sight of in more recent discussions that focus on limitations
of private want satisfaction. Her approach is in some ways more traditional
and gives evidence of its classical origins. We think it important to retrieve
the alternative she suggests and to consider it, however briefly, together with
those more in line with contemporary ways of thinking.

The term "public," according to Arendt, refers to two distinct but closely
connected phenomena. The first has to do with the importance of what she
refers to as "appearing in public."

> The presence of others who see what we see and hear what we hear assures us of the
> reality of the world and ourselves, and while the intimacy of a fully developed private
> life, such as had never been known before the rise of the modern age and the con-
> comitant decline of the public realm, will always greatly intensify and enrich the
> whole scale of subjective emotions and private feelings, this intensification will always
> come to pass at the expense of the assurance of the reality of the world and men.
> (1958:50)

The necessity for a public realm stems from the dependence that our "feeling
for reality" has on such a realm. In other words, Arendt's notion of the public
connects to a prior judgment regarding the way in which we experience,
perceive, and construct the reality of our lives individually and collectively.
The dependence of our sense of reality on the public presupposes that our
reality is already intersubjective. Notions of the public considered up to this
point do not carry this presupposition. In neoclassical economics our subjective reality does not depend on our connection to a larger whole. Indeed,

within the neoclassical way of thinking, the world outside is understood as an opportunity set and relates instrumentally to already defined preferences. The idea of "appearing in public" carries a meaning lying outside the instrumental conception of public. On the contrary, Arendt's idea of public has a constitutive connotation. To the extent that we treat personality as, in important part, a social construct, "appearing in public" takes on special importance, as part of our effort to connect with the social whole or to confirm that connection with the whole without which we risk loss of our sense of identity.

This observation leads naturally to Arendt's second dimension of the public, the public as the "common world."

> To live together in the world means essentially that a world of things is between those who stand around it; the world, like every in-between, relates and separates men at the same time.
> The public realm, as the common world, gathers us together and yet prevents our falling over each other, so to speak. (1958:52)

Arendt emphasizes that this common world is a human construct; indeed, it is constructed in order to provide a world of things to instantiate our common life. What is striking about this idea is the notion of a common world that binds us together. The public not only helps to satisfy our private wants, it binds us into a larger whole. In order to do this, it must have its own objectivity, it must be made up of appropriate sorts of things.

Arendt's notion of the public can have different relations with politics. We can, of course, identify the public with the political. This makes politics the appearance in public needed to secure our sense of reality and connectedness. both of which depend on our having a life in common. But public and political need not be synonymous. The need for a public in Arendt's sense can encompass politics and more than politics. Forms of mass communication are public insofar as they provide (some of) us with an opportunity to appear. Yet this appearance may not be a political act (for example, a concert need not be considered a political act although under appropriate circumstances it may be that).

So long, however, as politics takes a part of the space of the public in Arendt's sense, it will have ends not considered within the utilitarian calculus (see Benhabib, 1989). These ends involve our sense of common life, the reality we gain from participating in a common life, and our need to participate in construction of the social artifacts of our life together. If politics includes this dimension, it has a significant constitutive function for the individual lost sight of when we assume that individuals have fully formed preference orderings prior to both politics and public life.

Politics as authoritative allocation of values. According to this conception, politics and economics are similar in that both are methods of allocation. The economic and the political processes are alternative ways of making allocations regarding scarce resources. Politics refers not to the formal structure of government but to a distinctive way of making decisions about producing and distributing resources. Unlike economics, which emphasizes juridically voluntary exchange, the system of political allocation involves authority.

Quite possibly, this difference in mode of allocation may reflect differences in the types of goods being pursued (for instance, excludable versus nonexcludable) as well as the normative criteria governing interaction (such as self-interest versus collective interest, individual gain versus equity). David Easton ([1953] 1981) suggests that the central question of political science is how values are authoritatively allocated for society. He vigorously defends this focus against competing conceptions of politics based on the state, power, and conflict resolution. It is not that the authoritative allocation of values is unrelated to these things but that focusing on these other things hits the core of what is political only by accident, by virtue of their correlation with authority patterns. The state is closely involved in authoritative allocations in the sense that these allocations often take place within the state, through state institutions, and are often activated and executed by state agents. But the congruence is limited: Authority patterns occur outside the state too, and much of what goes on inside the state is not authoritative. For Easton, the strongest argument for this focus is that political science is not interested so much in a particular institution as it is in the activity "that expresses itself through a variety of institutions" (1981:113). Easton's argument implies a decoupling of politics as abstract process from the institutions normally associated with this process (government).

Where does this approach lead? It does not have to lead to the search for authority in every nook and cranny of society – in the factories, schools, family, and armed services. The societal component of the definition keeps our focus on authoritative allocations for society as a whole. In one sense, this leads us back to government, since government is the only societywide political structure. But government does not equal politics. It is a structure within which politics can take place. The activities and institutions of government are not by definition politics. Some governments, as Crick (1964) points out, allow very little politics. Some strive to reduce politics to a minimum – for example, by ruling through coercion or managed consensus.

In addition, there is much outside governmental boundaries that is political. These interactions, to the extent that they are regularized and related to authoritative allocations in particular ways, are included in the concept of "the political system." For example, in pluralist systems the activities of interest groups and political parties would be considered political, in that they are concerned either with the holding of authoritative positions or with the organization and activities of shaping authoritative public policy. Similarly, the acquisition of political images and information (of the nation, the president, the central political institutions), although more remote than the activities of pressure groups and parties, is often considered political.

The focus on authority implies an important normative question that needs to be asked if the scope of the political is not to be indeterminate: What is the proper reach of the authority system? If the boundary between economics and politics is to be determined by the region in which voluntary exchange shades into authoritative relations, we need to know something about those activities best suited for market exchange and those best suited for authority systems. One answer is that authority should be reserved for those activities where voluntary exchange breaks down or where the structure of interests among actors does not spontaneously yield mutually beneficial and self-enforcing results. Another answer is that authority is called for to institute and enforce rights or to achieve goals such as equality, universal health care, and justice, ends that are not assured by the market. A third answer is that the wielding of authority is not a normative issue, not a question of "the proper sphere of government." Instead, it has to do with political enforcement of particular (special) wills against others, such as capitalist against worker, Catholic against Protestant, and so on. Politics deals with situations in which there is simultaneously conflict and pressure for collective decisions. Some will gain and some will lose. Thus, politics cannot be about collective mutual gains and authority cannot be about what everyone approves. The focus on legitimacy is a diversion that distracts us from the cleavages overridden by state policies.

Relations among three approaches to politics

Before attempting to reconcile the three approaches discussed in the preceding section, we should point out that there is a case for viewing them separately. Each approach can be viewed as essentially different and can, when elaborated, take us in a different direction. The politics-as-government approach relies on a particular institution, politics as affairs of the public relies on the specification of a noninstitutional realm outside of private exchange, and the authority focus depends on a certain way of making decisions and of securing compliance. Each conception has its "home domain," its core concepts, its notions of what is centrally political, and its often implicit rules about what is outside the political arena. Yet few would deny that all three approaches say something about politics. What are the relationships among the three approaches? What similarities and points of convergence are suggested?

Let us begin to answer these questions by focusing on the second approach, politics as public. The public refers to either the regulation of unintended consequences of private actions and market failure or to the sense of common interest, mission, identity, or conception of what it means to be a citizen of a community.

While the idea of the public provides an approach to politics, it does not stand alone. In one sense, it identifies the raw material out of which politics takes place. The activities of government are concerned with taking binding decisions for society as a whole. As such, government takes as its point of departure those matters that significantly involve "others." It does not try to legislate individual affairs *ad seriatim*. In this light, the public and government are not two unrelated approaches. Indeed, they need each other to complete their meanings. Without a public to serve as foundation, government is cut adrift. How can it devise policies to settle societal conflicts or to pursue harmonious social goals without a grounding in public society? "Politicking," the struggle for governmental office, and modern equivalents of court intrigue would still occur, but politics pure and simple would not.

Conversely, without a governmental structure the public is only an inarticulate mass of commonly affected interests, more or less privately held. The public in this sense is simply an aggregate, a *set* of persons neither cognizant of shared experience nor alert to its political potential. When these separate circumstances are collectively understood, and when individuals play a role in forging this collective understanding, the situation becomes political. When this occurs, collectively mobilized interests are brought to bear as pressures upon government, working through governmental channels, political parties, the bureaucracy, legislatures, and courts.

At the intersection between government and society, the public is a crucial lever. From the vantage point of government, it is the raw material, the subject matter of politics. From the public's vantage point, government is both the arena for its expression and the instrument to achieve its aims, which may include, significantly, the desire for a particular sphere of society (child care, medical insurance) to be declared public.

The public does not simply use government as an instrument to its own ends. It is also constituted by government. In some countries the government charters and licenses interest groups, thus granting them public status and the acknowledged right to affect public policy. The public becomes politically articulate in part through government action.

In France, part of what is meant by the "strong state tradition" concerns the capacity of the state to constitute (that is, to organize, recognize, control) private associations. In pluralist theory, it is groups and group interests that are the driving forces, "freely combining, dissolving, and recombining in accordance with their interest lines" (Bentley, 1908:359). By contrast, in France all private associations are required to register with the Ministry of Interior; the Ministry grants them legal status, and it may dissolve certain associations if they are deemed a threat to the state (Wilsford, 1989:132). This pattern is characteristic of many countries that fall into what Stepan calls the "organic-statist" tradition (1978:26–45).

How does the focus on authority relate to government and the public? This focus takes us close to what we often mean by politics – commands binding on society as a whole and enforceable by a sovereign (in other words, an institution beyond which there is no legal appeal). However, unless we are to treat authoritative decisions as definitionally identical to politics, we cannot help feeling uncomfortable with authority as the exclusive focus. Its connections to government and public are not clear.

This difficulty is not at all surprising. Indeed, Easton argued for the focus on authoritative allocations of values precisely because of its imperfect correspondence with governmental institutions and activities. These incongruities reach in two directions: Not everything government does is authoritative, and not everything that is authoritative is governmental. As examples of the former, we can think of private gain in public settings, the utilization of public office in the pursuit of private goals, and the maneuvering for private advantage apart from the policy implications of such. Oddly, the term "political" has evolved to become one of the ordinary meanings to describe such activities. We use the word "politicking" to describe those activities, reserving the word "politics" for other activities.

One omission concerns the scope of authoritative actions. Can any issue, activity, or interest be the object of binding decisions for society? By itself, the focus on authoritative decisions tells us nothing about what kinds of activities are within the jurisdiction of the authority system. Perhaps this is as it should be. With the scope of authority open-ended, the substance of the political is unspecified and the distinctive focus of politics shifts to the process level. In one country the production and distribution of food goods are authoritative matters. In another, medical care is provided by a governmental bureaucracy. In a third, the emission of industrial waste is subject to authoritative regulations. In a fourth country, all three may be dealt with by private exchange, or perhaps in the case of industrial wastes, simply neglected.

We need not, however, consider the substantive content of authoritative decisions totally arbitrary. Without specifying which activities qualify for authoritative decision making, we can define some limits in terms of the relationship between society and government. The focus on authority makes most sense when integrated into a scheme where both public and government

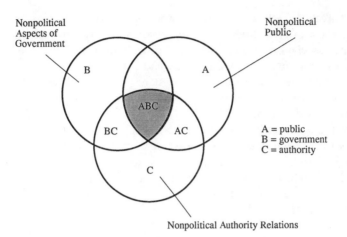

Figure 1. Relationships among conceptions of politics

are present. The public anchors the idea of authority to a particular set of social conditions. It ties nonarbitrary authoritative policies to a certain sphere and by so doing provides some normative constraint on what authority structures can do.

If the scope of authority is limited to what is in some sense public, the institutions through which authoritative decisions take place are governmental. Of course there are informal political organizations too, and these are often involved in making decisions binding on society. But by and large, in the modern system of the nation-state, the institutional locus of politics is government. We suggest this focus as a starting point for political analysis even if some political "locations" are minimized by doing so.

Our summary definition of politics is as follows: Politics refers to the activities and institutions that relate to the making of authoritative public decisions for society as a whole. This definition sees the focal point of politics in the overlapping of three conceptually distinct areas. We represent this overlap in a diagram, Figure 1.

In the figure there are three circles, each representing one of our approaches (or constituents) to politics. There is a public sphere that is not political, such as codes governing dress, speech, and behavior in public places. Much of this is highly informal, enforced through norms and informal understandings. There is a governmental sphere that is neither public nor authoritative, at least in some sense. Part of what occurs in government concerns the motivations, ambitions, and career goals of politicians, even though the pursuit of those goals takes place within a public space. Finally, authority relations may be found in the family, church, factory, and school. Authority by itself need not be political. Often enough, these three spheres overlap. The shaded section (ABC) points to the overlap between government, the public, and authority. Our definition points us toward this overlap.

Economics

In modern usage, the term "economic" has several meanings. These different meanings are not exclusive, yet each is a core idea that anchors a distinct approach to defining the subject matter of economics. Emphasis on one or another of these meanings will lead toward different ways of thinking about what is definitive about the economic dimension of our lives. In this chapter we explore three core notions of the economic. Clearly distinguishing between these notions will help us define different theoretical approaches in economics, and thus also in political economy.

First, the term economic is sometimes used to refer to a way of doing things, as in the word "economically." If we use the term in this way, it carries the connotations of efficiency, minimum effort, and close adaptation of means to ends. Second, the term economic sometimes refers to a kind of activity, usually aimed (as in production) at acquiring things we want or need. The term "provisioning" expresses this sense of what is economic. A third usage of economic ties it to market institutions. These institutions seem to embody most forcefully the achievement of efficiency in the activities aimed at acquiring for us the things we need. Economists often argue that we will be most efficient in satisfying our wants if we organize the process through market institutions. Mancur Olson notes that in nineteenth-century Britain, the very word "economist" was taken to mean an advocate of laissez-faire and "the belief that economic theory is applicable only to goods that fetch a price in the markets of capitalist economies . . . [that] has survived to the present day" (1969: 140–1).

These three meanings of economic do not map neatly onto schools, theories, or approaches. Nonetheless, each theory tends to favor one of the meanings over the others. Because of this, we can learn something important about the differences between theories by exploring the different ways we use the term economic.

Conceptions of economics

Economic calculation. The first meaning of "economic" directs our attention to a way of thinking and an associated orientation of the individual to the world. Sometimes termed the "economic approach," this way of thinking seeks to understand human action as an effort to achieve given ends in the face of external constraints. Such constraints originate in the limited supply of means, or resources. How well we can satisfy our wants depends on the means to which we have access. This depends both on what is available over all, and on the part specifically available to us. The latter depends on the way society defines property rights and allows property to be allocated among its members.

Economic calculation is a way of utilizing what is available, given wants. It is a way of judging institutional arrangements for using available means according to how well they satisfy wants. It is also a way of understanding social action as the outcome of private calculations of the likely impact of action on private want satisfaction.

While currently dominant in economics, this approach has broad expression in the social sciences. In sociology, Max Weber ([1956] 1978) emphasized the link between rational calculation (understood as a relation of means and ends) and economic activity. His work provides a broad perspective on the link between rationality, efficiency, and the definition of the economic advocated by many modern-day economists.

When based on the idea of calculation, economics defines its subject matter in terms such as efficiency and constrained choice. Economics in this mode begins with the activity of a choosing agent, the individual, attempting to do the best he can to satisfy wants to the greatest degree possible in the face of opportunities and constraints. From this starting point, analysis proceeds to consider the implications of want satisfaction in the context of a group of individuals characterized in this way. The better we adapt our means to our ends, the more efficient we are in using our resources. Greater efficiency means that we can satisfy our wants better.

This way of thinking about what is economic has a static quality that follows from the notion of limited resources and given ends. Economizing is a way of adapting to the way things are, not a process of change and development. The central metaphor is *allocation*. We attempt to allocate our means among our ends so as to achieve as much as we can with what we have. "Economizing" carries this connotation of constraint captured in the maxim "There's no such thing as a free lunch." If we are more efficient, we can sometimes get more with what we have, but we cannot have more. If we could, we might orient ourselves toward getting more rather than using efficiently what we have.

Joseph Schumpeter (1942) made the point that an inefficient system might grow more rapidly and in the long run achieve higher levels of productivity. Schumpeter thought that capitalism is such a system because monopoly gains from entrepreneurship stimulate innovation. In his theory, inefficiency implied in monopoly is necessary to economic development. If this is so, the goal of efficiency recedes in importance. Our first notion of the economic rejects this claim and holds that the economic problem is that of doing better with what we have.

The approach to economics centering on the notion of calculation is distinguished by its static orientation, with emphasis placed on constraints and allocation. It is also distinguished by its generality. Unlike the other two ways of thinking about what is economic, this approach makes the term broadly applicable to human affairs. Indeed, it becomes a way of thinking about all of our activities. The approach centering on calculation makes constrained choice virtually synonymous with human action. This attribute is of special importance for political economy, which concerns itself with the boundaries between economics and politics. Identification of economic with a way of calculating implies no restriction of the economic to particular sets of human relations and activities. It allows and encourages us to think of politics also as a sphere of economic calculation. Let us consider this implication somewhat more closely.

Within the means-ends framework, understanding why people do what they do means knowing their ends and the means available for them to achieve those ends. Because we can characterize all human action and motivation in terms of the ends pursued and the means available, the link between the economic and the act of economizing makes all human action potentially economic. This link makes it possible to evaluate instrumental action according to economic criteria: Is it efficient in its use of means to achieve the stated ends?

Weber emphasizes the rise of economic calculation and what he terms "instrumental rationality" as the hallmark of the modern age. Modern man relates to the world outside as means to his ends. Thinking about and understanding the world resolve themselves into making calculations of the way we can best use it for our ends. Rationality is instrumental when it treats things and other persons as means and not ends in themselves. Economists working within this framework assume that individuals adopt an instrumental attitude. They explain human behavior and judge human institutions according to an economic calculation of outcomes. In principle, this approach can be applied to any human behavior and to all human institutions. Economists and other social scientists influenced by this vision have applied it to political processes and personal life (marriage, voting, suicide) as well as to economic affairs more narrowly conceived.[2]

While economists who understand their subject matter in the language of calculation treat the problems of production and circulation of goods as instances of economic activity, they do so not because such activity is in-

---

[2] See Becker (1976) for a discussion of and examples of the extension of the concept of the economic to encompass the broad range of social institutions.

herently economic (as would be implied in our second meaning), but because it can be interpreted on the basis of the notions of choice and efficiency. Yet production and circulation of goods need not be done economically in the sense that those engaged in productive activity need not work efficiently at it and what they do need not be characterized in terms of choice.[3] If we want to think of the activities associated with provisioning needs, whether involving calculation in the above sense or not, as economic, we must leave behind the first usage of the term and consider an alternative.

Material provisioning. The second usage of the term "economic" characterizes earlier thinking about economic activity from Aristotle to Adam Smith and Karl Marx. It also motivates the work of modern economists influenced by the older traditions in economics.[4] These economists also use the term "economic" to refer to a kind of activity. They identify this activity not by its characteristic mode of calculation, however, but by its purpose: the production and reproduction of goods, or the material provisioning of wants. Economists working within this framework do not deny that activities can be done more or less efficiently. They do, however, consider production of the material things needed to sustain life economic whether or not it is done efficiently, and whether or not those engaged in it are conceived as making choices.

This approach tends to equate economic activity with the "material life process of society" (Sahlins, 1972:xii) and with concern for the "material, substantive, things that sustained human beings" (Polanyi, 1957:83). The interpretation of economic life as a process of material reproduction receives its most general and deliberate formulation in the work of Karl Marx. For Marx, "it is quite obvious from the start that there exists a materialistic connection of men with one another, which is determined by their needs and their mode of production, and which is as old as men themselves" (1964:41). Notions such as material life and material connection refer to the processes by which the members of a social order participate in the activities that lead to their collective reproduction.

This emphasis on the "material" merits further consideration. From a modern-day standpoint, identification of wants with material things seems less compelling. Many of the goods economies provide (information or entertainment, for example) are not primarily material. During the period of the classical economists (considered in Chapter 2), however, the material

---

[3] Whether and how it is possible to conceive of production and distribution as being in some sense inefficient depends on our concept of efficiency. The concept itself raises serious difficulties, especially as it is identified with economic rationality. For a discussion and critique, see Godelier (1972:ch. 1).

[4] See, for example, Sraffa (1960) and Dobb (1973).

dimension dominated, and it was not unreasonable to assume that provisioning of needs was a matter of providing things in appropriate material form.

A more general interpretation of the idea would focus our attention not on the physical makeup of goods, but on the use of our human energies in providing them. This provision of goods has two important dimensions: production and circulation. Economic activity either produces the goods that satisfy needs or moves those goods from those who produce them to those who need them. This latter is the circulation of goods most often identified with exchange.

The physical makeup of a good does not determine whether we use human energy to create it or whether it can circulate from owner to owner. Property rights in nonmaterial things (such as ideas) also change hands, and in this sense circulate from one owner to another. Thus, we can employ the provisioning idea whether or not we think that most wants demand material things for their satisfaction.

Yet the spirit of the provisioning approach emphasizes material goods over nonmaterial, often giving the former a special status and larger role in economic affairs. While not inevitable, this emphasis follows naturally from the perspective that sees provisioning as a kind of material circulation of the things necessary to sustain life – to provide nutrition, warmth, and shelter. The provisioning approach focuses our attention on basic needs and the goods that sustain life in its more elemental senses.

The term "material connection" depicts the relation of person to person and of the individual to social institutions in a way different from that of economic calculation. This difference centers on the perception of individual agents and of the constraints in which they operate. It also centers on the way the agents are understood to relate to the social structure and material universe that sustain them. We will briefly consider each of these differences.

When we identity the economic with a way of calculating, we immediately place emphasis on the mental processes of the individual agent who does the calculation. That is, the economic occurs in the mind of the agent, or at least it begins there. Further, the specific calculation centers on subjective ends ultimately known only to the individual. We outside know them only by inference from the actions taken in their pursuit (the choices made by the agent tell us something about his preferences). In the provisioning conception, the economic does not refer us to an attitude or mode of calculation on the part of the individual, but to a systemic process.

In this framework, the starting point is not the individual and his preferences, but the system or structure of reproduction of the society as a whole, or at least of that aspect of society tied to satisfying wants. Here, we imagine a system of interconnected needs determined not by the individual's private, subjective life, but by objective social facts. What we need depends not on our subjective lives, but on our place in a larger structure.

The classical economists discussed in the next chapter provide us with two instances of the structural or objective determination of wants: the placement of the producer in a social division of labor, and the placement of the individual into a social class. Placement of the producer in a social division of labor refers to the way he depends on other producers for inputs needed to produce his specific output – how the carpenter depends on those who provide wood, nails, glue, paint, and other things needed to make a table, chair, or house. The producer's needs do not depend on his subjective preferences, but on what he produces and the technique used to produce it. Knowing what he produces and the technology determine the nature of inputs required. These required inputs are determined objectively, and the need for them is likewise determined objectively. The economist influenced by this way of thinking tends to focus on the objective determination of wants within a system of the reproduction of a social division of labor.

The emphasis on provisioning links motivation to need rather than choice. Through our economic pursuits, we seek to acquire things we must, in some sense, have. These objects are requirements of life. As such, we do not *prefer* to have them, or simply choose the best option among numerous alternatives. Instead, we do what we must to assure provisioning of our needs.[5] Choice and preference fall away, and with them the framework of thinking favored by those seeking to identify economic with a form of calculation.

Even within the provisioning framework, of course, there remain wants not immediately linked to reproduction of a division of labor: the wants of the individual for means of consumption. Economists favoring the calculation approach direct our attention to these wants and interpret them in terms of preference and choice. The classical economists, or those influenced by their method, do not operate this way. They understand consumer wants to be determined socially and objectively rather than individually and subjectively.

To arrive at this social determination, theorists generally refer us to the class position of the individual, especially his position with regard to ownership of the means of production. In Marxian language, your class position depends on whether you own and gain your income from capital or whether your only property is your laboring capacity. If the latter, then you are a worker and your consumption needs are determined by the "subsistence." The subsistence is an important idea in models such as these; we explore it somewhat further in the next chapter. For the moment, we introduce it only to emphasize that the idea of a worker's subsistence allows us to circumvent any reference to the subjective state of mind and preferences of consumers

_____

[5] For a further discussion see Levine (1988:ch. 1).

when we think about the consumption needs of most of the population. What these consumers need is their basic subsistence – food, clothing, shelter – in a form and amount determined by objective social, historical, and cultural factors. Differences among individuals have less importance than social practices in determining what workers eat and wear or where they live.

Reference to class position and to the social division of labor solves problems in the material reproduction approach that are correspondingly solved by notions of subjective preference and choice in the economic calculation approach. It solves those problems in a way that places less emphasis on choice and calculation of how to maximize satisfaction, more emphasis on objective structure, objective needs. The activity of the agent is understood differently in this second conception of the economic.

How we understand constraints also differs here. This difference stems from a shift toward a more dynamic conception of economic affairs, one centering on reproduction and growth rather than allocation.[6] The notion of fixed resources for satisfying wants plays little or no part. How much we have available to satisfy wants depends on how much we invest in production of goods. Without a notion of fixed means, it is difficult to apply the economist's notion of efficient allocation. Inputs are themselves products of past production, rather than given resources. This shift alters many of the basics of the analysis in important ways.

Piero Sraffa suggests this shift in the title of his short essay toward a critique of economic theory, *Production of Commodities by Means of Commodities* (1960). Sraffa's framework is one in which needed inputs to production are themselves produced. The emphasis is on reproduction rather than allocation. What constrains the system is not limited resources, but the history of the economic process. In particular, the historical constraint has to do with the size and utilization of the economic surplus.[7]

The term "surplus" refers to the difference between output and the necessary costs of its production. If we take the total product in a given period, the surplus is that part not needed as inputs for the reproduction of the same product in the next period. The surplus enters into the constraints of the system because its magnitude and use determine whether the economy grows or remains the same.

With a positive surplus, the opportunity exists for investment in additional inputs that will make the level of output increase in the future. The surplus is a fund for investment and economic growth. It represents the potential to break the constraints on want satisfaction built into the existing level of economic activity. The economic problem is not primarily that of using

---

[6] See E. Nell (1967).
[7] For a discussion in more general terms, see Baran (1957) and Walsh and Gram (1980).

existing available inputs efficiently (this is more of a technical or engineering problem), but of assuring the investment of the surplus so that the quantity of inputs available will increase. Thus, constraints have an historical quality about them: how much has been invested in the past, and how much is currently being invested.

Identification of the economic with reproduction of a system of provisioning of wants takes us in a different direction than does the idea of economic calculation. Both see the economic as a kind of activity, but the nature of the activity varies in significant ways. Our third way of thinking about what is economic does not identify it simply with an activity, and thus takes us in a distinct direction.

The economy. The separation of society into an "economy" and a "polity" does not flow directly or inevitably out of either of the two approaches considered so far (although it probably fits more easily into the approach that identifies economic with provisioning rather than calculation). The idea of the economy as a socially and historically specific institution is, nonetheless, an important one. When we speak of *the* economy, we already assume the existence of a separable entity: a place (perhaps the market if we can consider that a place), a sphere (as Marx would have it), a moment of the whole in the Hegelian sense, a distinct set of relations between persons not in essence political or familial.

This usage parallels the historical emergence of the economy as a separate institution. Karl Polanyi, more than any other contemporary thinker, has drawn our attention to this aspect of modern social organization.

A self-regulating market demands nothing less than the institutional separation of society into an economic and political sphere. (1944:71)

As is shown in the next chapter's discussion of the classical approach, the argument for the self-regulating market is an argument for the separateness of the economy as an institution.

References to the separateness of the economy immediately invoke objection and doubt from those convinced that the modern project of political economy is to rethink that separation and explore the interpenetration and integration of economic and political processes. Because of this, the third sense of the economic, since it insists on separability, raises most clearly the central theme of this book. It will prove helpful, therefore, to explore it more closely to assure that we are clear on what separateness connotes.[8]

Separateness of the economy does not mean its independence of the other aspects of social life. It does not mean that the economy can, in fact, stand

[8] See Levine (1989).

alone. Even those economists most committed to the idea of market self-regulation maintain that the market depends on the state for a set, albeit a limited set, of requirements for its own survival. Adam Smith insists that the state not only maintain internal order and security from foreign invasion, but also engage in substantial public works where the private sector lacks the means needed given the scale of the project. Separateness does not, then, mean either autonomy or the absence of significant state involvement in economic life.

In order to understand what it does mean, it may prove helpful to suggest an analogy. When we speak of the separateness of persons, of their autonomy or independence, we do not mean that they could survive by themselves, that they are not in important ways socially formed and determined, or that they relate to others with indifference, unaware of the ways in which, together with those others, they form a single larger whole. We mean instead that each is recognizably distinct, related to others yet different from them. Separateness allows us to speak intelligibly about the individual.

The same holds for the separateness of the economy. It means that the economy is distinct, different from, and not equivalent to polity or family. When engaged in our economic affairs, we are not directly engaged in family life or politics. This holds true when the economy is indeed separate, even though our economic affairs presuppose a political and legal framework. Considering it separate allows us to talk intelligibly about the economy.

The reality of an economy as a distinct system of relations is not contingent on individual preferences and choices. Economic institutions endure; individuals find their way in and through them. Individuals may not form them as means to satisfy their wants, although economic institutions have a purpose bound up with want satisfaction.

When we refer to "the economy," then, we move away from the more individualist methodology favored by those who identify economics with a mode of calculating. The notion of an economy understands it as an enduring social reality of its own kind capable of influencing, forming, and even determining motivations and ways of thinking. The economy has its own social purpose irreducible to those we associate with politics and family life. This purpose is not contingent on the preferences of agents or the universal demands of material reproduction. We can think of preferences and of material reproduction without thinking about the economy. When we think about the economy, we must have in mind something more than, and something different from, the central concepts of economic calculation and material reproduction. What is this something more and different?

The answer refers us to the institutions of private property and contract. These institutions involve us in a distinct set of relationships with others and in a specific orientation to our private ends. The economy is a sphere of pursuit of self-interest, a place that validates preoccupation with our private concerns. The relations we enter into are normally understood to be instrumental to those private concerns. This makes the economy at least potentially a set of relations between persons distinct from the social relations that connect persons politically or personally.

For this reason, Polanyi links the separateness of the economy to the prevalence of the institution of contract. The economy connects independent property owners pursuing private interest through the use and exchange of their private property. So long as family and polity are not formed by links of exchange and pursuit of self-interest, they are not part of the economy. Neither, then, is the economy part of family or polity.

Thus, so long as we think the buying and selling of votes is antithetical to the political process, voting is not part of the economy. We can impose other demands on the election process than those associated, in the economy, with self-interest. Similarly, so long as we consider it inappropriate to treat the family as a sphere in which members pursue their respective self-interests and contract one with the other, we do not consider family a part of economy. If we treat family members as ends in themselves, such relations are not instrumental and not subject to economic calculation. When we recognize the obligation, in certain spheres of social interaction, to treat others as ends, we narrow the domain of economy, separating it off as a distinct sphere.

If we understand the economy as an enduring reality, we can begin to think about institutional imperatives built into its structure. Such institutional imperatives do not derive from the preferences of individuals. We can derive the goals of social structures from individual ends only if we make the structure contingent on those ends. This would violate the notion of the structure as an enduring social reality. The structure precedes the participant. If the actions of the participant are to be intelligible, that intelligibility must stem from attributes of the social structure that envelop him. One way to put this is to note that this approach implies that the economy understood as a structure *sui generis* moves the individual according to its own structural imperatives and that economics needs to consider what those imperatives are. We will pursue this possibility further in the next chapter. In anticipation of that discussion, we mention here some salient features of the problem.

The end or goal most closely associated with the institutional reality of markets has traditionally been that of capital accumulation and economic development. Adam Smith considered accumulation of wealth the main justification for free-standing markets. Within such institutional arrangements, individual self-interest works for the goal of the maximization of the national revenue. Karl Marx continues this theme of the revolutionizing impact of market economy in his famous discussion of the progressive mission of capitalism in *The Communist Manifesto* (Marx and Engels, [1848] 1955). And, in the twentieth century, Joseph Schumpeter developed his argument for capitalism as a system of change and development whose *raison d'être* was the transformation of the methods of production, the means of consumption, and the forms of organization of economic institutions.

These classic contributions to economics all treat economy as an organization that drives us in a particular direction, and economics as primarily the study of the logic of that organization and the ends likely to be achieved by it. This is the logic of the self-regulating market, the sphere of voluntary contractual relations between property owners including owners of labor and means of production. The institutional reality of the (market) economy becomes the subject matter of economics.

Economics and political economy

The three different meanings of economic bear on how we think about the relation of economics to politics. It is not simply a matter of how we relate economics to politics, but of what we mean by the terms. How they are related follows from how we define and use them.

When we use "economic" in the sense of economic calculation, then politics becomes one place to apply such calculation. Economics is a way of acting, politics a place to act. In politics, we can exhibit economic behavior or not. If we do not, however, this poses a problem for those who identify economic with a form of calculation. For them, the intelligibility of our action depends on the connection between means and ends. The action becomes intelligible when we can show how it follows from a means-ends calculus. If action does not make sense in this way, it does not make sense. Thus, if it is not ultimately economic, it does not make sense. Those favoring this approach tend to assume that economic refers us to a basic perspective on human motivation and behavior so that it is necessary to assume economic calculation in both if we are to think coherently about politics or markets.

One result of placing emphasis on economic calculation is that economics tends to dominate. The economic approach explains what we do and why we do it. Politics simply describes the context. If we wish to explain politics, we need to think in terms of economics. This dominance of economics expresses an important and enduring theme of political economy as we suggest in the Introduction. Political economy has been less about the interrelation between economics and politics understood as separate endeavors, more about the subordination of the political to the economic.

This dominance clearly has to do with the necessity, given the identification of the economic with a mode of calculating, that we start out with the interests of the individual agent when we attempt to explain both individual and group activity. Emphasis on calculation leads to emphasis on subjective preference, individual motivation, and self-interest. The approach centering on calculation necessarily involves us in a method that starts from and refers back to individual states of mind and calculations.

The use of economic in the sense of calculation works against the idea of the separation of the economic from the political. It tends to expand the terrain of application of economics well beyond its traditional boundaries either in market relations or in the material provisioning of wants.

The idea of material provisioning does tend to limit the economic and thus allow for a meaningful separation of economic activity from political. It does not, however, require such a separation. In some systems, material provisioning takes place within a political system and in some it takes place through familial relations. Indeed, in its original meaning, the term economic referred to household management. The reference was not to an economy, but to one of the dimensions of family life. Economic relations were also familial relations. This statement makes sense within the provisioning definition of the economy.

The generality of this approach allows it to consider economies separate from or integrated into the political system. At the same time, the approach exhibits some difficulty in conceiving of the economy as a system of social relations. Thinkers following the logic of the notion of provisioning tend to attempt to do so in technical-material language – for example, depicting economic activity in the framework of an input-output system. This makes the social world of the economy an external context within which economic activity takes place. The term economic tends, then, to refer us to nonsocial relations that follow nonsocial laws.

The third approach, as we have already seen, emphasizes the separateness of the economy. It focuses our attention directly on the social relations that define economic affairs and not on pre- or extrasocial processes variously integrated into the economy or left separate. This approach gives up the generality of the first two in exchange for a deeper social rooting of the economy. Here, the economy is one social sphere, rather than material activity or private calculation situated in relation to the genuine social realities of life outside of economy.

We can refer to this approach as a kind of benchmark precisely because it does emphasize the separateness of economy rather than its merger into the other social realms. It allows us to focus attention on the implications of (1) the modern penchant for diminishing the separateness of the spheres of social life, and (2) the associated tendency to make one or the other (often the economic, as we have seen) dominant.

2

The classical approach

Political economy in the classical tradition

In this chapter we explore the classical approach to political economy. The classical economists of the eighteenth and nineteenth centuries were the first to use the term "political economy."[1] The period covered by classical political economy cannot be stated exactly. A restricted definition would extend from Adam Smith's *Wealth of Nations* in 1776 to John S. Mill's *Principles of Political Economy* in 1848. A more encompassing periodization would stretch from the work of the Physiocrats in the middle of the eighteenth century to the death in 1883 of Karl Marx, whom many saw as the last important classical political economist. Marx himself is credited with coining the term "classical political economy" (Dasgupta, 1985:12), dating it from the time of William Petty.

We will divide our consideration of classical political economy into two parts: the argument for market self-regulation and the theory of value and distribution. The first part concerns the nature of the market system and its relation to the state. The second concerns production and use of the economic surplus. The second part draws on more recent contributions within the classical tradition. Although using elements of the classical analytical framework, these recent theories suggest an approach to political economy in some ways at variance with that of the classical economists themselves.

The classical approach frames the central themes of political economy in a distinctive way. Most fundamentally, the classical economists played a major role in introducing and elaborating two core ideas: the separability of the economy and the primacy of the economic sphere. The first part of this chapter emphasizes this side of the classical theory, which has special importance for the themes of this book.

Modern theorists working in the classical tradition (see Walsh and Gram,

[1] For historical discussion of the term "classical economics" or "classical political economy" see Roll (1953:ch. 4) and Walsh and Gram (1980:chs. 2–4).

33

1980) tend not to frame issues of political economy in this way, however. In the second part of this chapter, we consider the implications of the theory of value and distribution for the central concerns of political economy as we define them in this book.

The founders of political economy perceive a change in the relationship between political life and the nonpolitical activities loosely termed the satisfaction of private wants. This perception leads to a redefinition and realignment of terms used to talk about social order, terms such as political society and civil society; private and public; economy and state. This realignment involves a shift of emphasis toward the idea that society organizes itself and develops according to its own laws, processes, and imperatives. The vitally important social institutions do not develop according to plans articulated and instituted by political decisions, but according to underlying and unintended imperatives of group life. If this is true, then history becomes less an account of political processes, conflicts, or deliberations, more an account of the unintended consequences of private activities. Adam Ferguson's *Essay on the History of Civil Society*, published in 1773, marks an important moment in this shift of perspective. Ferguson expresses our idea in the following words:

If Cromwell said, [t]hat man never mounts higher, than when he knows not wither he is going; it may with more reason be affirmed of communities, that they admit of the greatest revolutions where no change is intended, and that the most refined politicians do not always know wither they are leading the state by their projects. (p. 205)

Political economy gave considerable impetus to the shift of focus away from politics in understanding the forces that account for the large historical movements that mold the social world. Adam Smith saw the rise of civilized society as the result of profit-seeking behavior rather than of any plan known to and instituted by a political process or public authority. The transition from the "savage state of man" to civilized society was, for Smith, the historical work of capitalism. Yet, it was the unintended consequence of a multitude of actions taken for purely private purposes.

Marx took this idea much further. He described the process by which epochal changes were brought about in methods of production, social relations, and ways of life, all as the unintended consequences of the pursuit of private gain. Marx's materialist conception of history expresses with special force the subordination of politics and of the decisions of a public authority to the immanent and inexorable forces set loose and operating within society.

The emergence of political economy helped to mark the demotion of politics and the elevation of the nonpolitical part of civil life. Indeed, it contributes to the redefinition of civil life away from politics and in the modern direction of private affairs pursued outside of the household, in the world of business. The rise of political economy means the rise of civil society in contradistinction to politics.

The demotion of politics could hardly be better expressed than by the invisible hand metaphor of Adam Smith. Although Smith's view is in some ways extreme, it very clearly articulates a new relationship between political and civil society (or politics and economics). This new relationship arises, in part, out of a rethinking of the possible and reasonable purpose of the state. To see this clearly, consider the following description of government provided by Steuart, and more in line with older ways of thinking:

The great art of government is to divest oneself of prejudices and attachments to particular opinions, particular classes, and above all to particular persons; to consult the spirit of the people, to give way to it in appearance, and in so doing to give it a turn capable of inspiring those sentiments which may induce them to relish change, which an alteration of circumstances has rendered necessary. ([1767] 1966:26)

Steuart attempts to combine two important ideas. First, he expresses the notion (which we have emphasized) that change arises out of forces and processes immanent in society and not decided by the state. Second, at the same time, he sees a crucial role for the state in recognizing the necessity of those changes and leading society through them. Changes in what Steuart terms the "spirit of the people" are gradual and immanent rather than planned. Because these changes are gradual and immanent, they may escape the perception of the people. This failure may lead individuals to misjudge their own and society's interest. The state must take a leading role in educating individuals to their genuine interest, both private and public.

Smith and Steuart, while writing at approximately the same time, judge the possible and desirable functions of government quite differently. Steuart does not directly participate in the devaluing of politics, although his acceptance of the necessity of the laws of political economy points him in that direction. Smith travels the whole route and is driven that much faster to do so by his judgment of politicians, whom he considered "insidious and crafty animals" ([1776] 1937:435). This difference is important in understanding the meaning of political economy and the significance of its emergence in the late eighteenth century.

Smith's judgment depends on his now well-known solution to the problem of economic order. The solution comes in two parts. First, nonpolitical group life (civil society) must organize and perpetuate itself more or less independently of political decision making. The unit that incorporates the work of satisfying private wants is a political unit, but within that unit the production and distribution of things needed to perpetuate private life is nonpolitical. Second, as we have seen Steuart arguing, the laws and imperatives of civil society must dominate politics. Economic laws constrain the statesman or politician. In the limit, these laws reduce the statesman to a caretaker role (for example, to the administration of justice centering on the protection of property rights).

In the classical approach the term political economy refers to a system of private want satisfaction made up of independent private agents. During the period of classical political economy, several distinct but related terms are used to refer to this system of want satisfaction: civil society, market economy, bourgeois society, capitalism, and others. Each term describes the way in which society becomes predominantly an economic rather than political system. As it grows in strength, this system tends to displace politics even though it initially appears under a political designation. It sets up an ordering principle for society which, since it is nonpolitical, challenges the idea of society as a political system. In the next section, we explore in greater detail the classical idea of a system of economic relations.

Civil society

In societies where the production of subsistence takes place within the family (or kinship group) and on the basis of the division of labor in the family, it must be subordinate to the goals and relations that make up family life. These goals and relations may include biological reproduction, paternal authority, child rearing and personality growth, nurturance, and so on. Provisioning of subsistence needs occurs, but in tempo with the noneconomic purposes of the family. These purposes also limit economic activity: The scale and composition of output are limited by the needs of the family, by the labor available within it, and by the division of labor appropriate to it. Thus we cannot reasonably envision a family organizing its productive activity along the lines of a factory, partly for reasons of scale and partly for reasons of social organization. Families large enough to provide the labor adequate to factory production are much too large to be proper families – that is, to continue to satisfy the social purposes of family life. Similarly, families whose social organization parallels that of a factory must treat their members (as wage-workers) in ways inconsistent with the rationale underlying family life (having to do with child rearing and nurturance, for example).

The embedding of the economic in noneconomic institutions (see Polanyi, 1957:71) means that the elements of material reproduction (the activities that form the division of labor) are united by noneconomic links. If the division of labor is restricted to the family, this means that the tasks will be allocated to family members appropriate to their status within the family (as male or female, child or adult, for example). This division also allows for the products of their labors to be brought together directly through personal contact. No contract intermediates. The problems of division and reunification are resolved directly and on the basis of the structure and logic of family life.

If, now, we consider the separation of economic activities from the family, as from all social institutions, we must have a method for accomplishing this division and reunification. This method must occur within, and be appropriate to, a new institution, the economy. Since the activities that constitute social reproduction do not take place within the family, nor are they assured by rules of direct political authority, they must be connected by a social bond that links otherwise independent producers. This bond is the exchange contract. As Karl Polanyi asserts, "it is not surprising . . . that a society based on *contractus* should possess an institutionally separate and motivationally distinct economic sphere of exchange, namely, that of the market" (1957:70). When contract replaces kinship, marriage, authority, religious associations, and other social institutions as the social link connecting the different parts of the reproduction process, the result is the emergence of the economy as a distinct institution. Now social production falls into the hands of legally independent, private producers, the social stock becomes so much private property, and labor becomes a commodity owned by the laborer until sold in exchange for money to the owner of capital. As a result of these developments an idea emerges that is of central importance to political economy: the idea of a pure private property system within which all persons are property owners and relations between persons consist of contractual relations for the exchange of property.

When the economy is embedded in noneconomic institutions, individuals pursue their economic activities on the basis of motivations carried over from (originating in) those institutions. Family members engage in productive activity as part of their participation in the family. Their motivation stems from the familial bond: recognition of and subordination to paternal (or maternal) authority, desire to nurture, and so on. The disembedding of economic from noneconomic requires that individuals engage in economic activity on the basis of motivations peculiar to the economy itself. These motivations have been termed "self-seeking," "self-aggrandizing," and the like.

It is certainly plausible that motives of this sort will dominate persons set free from all connections to their fellows other than those associated with contract. Under these conditions, individuals fall back on themselves. They come to see themselves as separate, independent, and autonomous. Separated from institutional loyalties, they find their only remaining loyalty is to themselves. The term "civil society" refers not only to a system of private want satisfaction regulated neither by the family nor the state, but to a system motivated by self-interest, within which "each member is his own end, every-thing else is nothing to him" (Hegel, [1821] 1952:267).[2] Shlomo Avineri summarizes this idea as follows:

> Civil society is the sphere of universal egoism, where I treat everybody as a means to my own ends. Its most acute and typical expression is economic life, where I sell and buy not in order to satisfy the needs of the other, his hunger or his need for shelter, but where I use the felt need of the other as a means to satisfy my own ends. My aims are mediated through the needs of others: the more other people are de-pendent upon a need which I can supply, the better my own position becomes. This is the sphere where everyone acts according to what he perceives as his enlightened self-interest. (1972:134)

Whether this accurately depicts the motivations of actors in the economy (and surely in important ways it does), it will be very familiar to anyone who has studied economic theory. Over the past two hundred years and more the development of economic analysis has been synonymous with the investi-gation of the logical implications of the assumption that individuals act on the basis of their self-interest (variously defined as profit seeking, utility maximization, and with other similar terms). Much of the agenda of economic theory has consisted of investigating the logical properties of a system of independent and autonomous property owners, each pursuing his self-interest and each constrained only by the requirement that he respect the property rights of others (including their right to property in their own persons). Such an agenda focuses on the validity of important propositions about the market economy. The most important proposition is that the market must succeed in assuring a reasonably stable process of the reproduction and distribution of things capable of satisfying the wants of those dependent on it. We will examine this proposition in the next section.

The self-regulating market

Because of their utilitarian leanings, many economists tend to assume that if the market succeeds in satisfying the private ends of participants, given those ends and given the means available to satisfy them, then it has *ipso facto* accomplished its human and social purpose. To achieve private ends is the same as to achieve the public good. The question about the market, then, is the following: Will a system of private persons pursuing their self-interest without overall regulation lead to a set of voluntary transactions (exchanges) that satisfy the wants of those persons to the greatest extent possible given the productivity of the capital stock and the original distribution of property?

---

[2] For discussion of the concept of civil society, see the articles collected in *The State and Civil Society* (Pelczynski, 1984) and Avineri (1972:141–54).

By now a vast literature exists addressing this question from various per-spectives.[3] The following summary should give an intuitive sense of the issues at stake.

The market works well when individuals act both as buyers and as sellers. In selling commodities, the seller acquires the money needed to purchase the things that satisfy his needs. Those, for example, who sell their labor for a wage thereby acquire the money they need to purchase their means of con-sumption. Similarly, those who sell commodities they have produced thereby acquire the money (proceeds from the sale) needed to replace (and possibly expand) their means of production. In both cases, the sale of commodities leads to the purchase of other commodities. Indeed, the anticipated purchase of those commodities motivates the sale of products and of labor.

When each participant acts both as buyer and seller, money and com-modities "circulate" through the market. The market simply facilitates a rearrangement of property according to the wants of property owners. It is a social mechanism to assure satisfaction of private wants. It is also a passive mechanism because it does not affect the property or the wants satisfied by it. By working for himself (buying and selling), each person works for others. Each provides goods to others and money with which others can buy goods. When this circuit functions smoothly, the sale of commodities leads to the purchase of other commodities. At the same time, no guarantee exists that any particular commodity will find a buyer. Thus an individual seller who finds no demand for his goods will be unable to acquire the things he needs. This holds also for workers. No assurance exists that any individual worker or group of workers will find employment. Buyers may not exist for the kind of labor they have to sell. If they have only that kind of labor and nothing else, they will be unable to acquire the wages needed to purchase their means of consumption.

With nothing but the market to appeal to for income, individual hardship is inevitable. The classical economists do not count this against the market. Without this hardship the market could not create incentives that drive individuals to adapt their skills and means of production to the needs of others.

The classical economists claim that only individual hardship can result from the market. That is, the income and welfare of a seller may suffer due to lack of demand for his product; but the income and welfare of the set of sellers as a whole cannot suffer in this way. The classical economists also argue that individual hardship will be temporary, lasting only so long as is required for the individual to adapt his skills and capital to producing goods in demand. David Ricardo, one of the major figures in political economy

---

[3] See, for example, Weintraub (1979) and Sowell (1972).

during the first half of the nineteenth century, summarizes what we have said so far about the market:

No man produces, but with a view to consume or sell, and he never sells, but with an intention to purchase some other commodity, which may be immediately useful to him, or which may contribute to future production. By producing, then, he necessarily becomes either the consumer of his own goods, or the purchaser and consumer of the goods of some other person. It is not to be supposed that he should, for any length of time, be ill-informed of the commodities which he can most advantageously produce, to attain the object he has in view, namely, the possession of other goods; and therefore it is not probable that he will continually produce a commodity for which there is no demand. ([1821] 1951:290)

This argument provides important support for the classical idea that while individuals may fail to find buyers for their goods, the market as a whole will not fail:

Too much of a particular commodity may be produced, of which there may be such a glut in the market, as not to repay the capital expended on it; but this cannot be the case with respect to all commodities; the demand for corn is limited by the mouths which are to eat it, for shoes and coats by the persons who are to wear them; but though a community, or a part of a community, may have as much corn, and as many hats and shoes, as it is able or may wish to consume, the same cannot be said of every commodity produced by nature or by art. (Ricardo, [1821] 1951:292)

The idea of a general failure of the market has a meaning significantly different from that of an individual failure. It means that the aggregate of goods that people need are available and yet cannot be bought and sold because the market mechanism that circulates money into the hands of those who need the goods has broken down. The very idea struck the classical economists as paradoxical. The French economist J. B. Say went so far (with the subsequent approval of Ricardo) as to assert the logical impossibility of overall market failure (a notion now referred to as Say's law). Particular failure results from individual miscalculation or misfortune; systemic failure means that the market mechanism is inherently flawed. Systemic failure means that the market frustrates individuals even if they have made the "right" decisions regarding what goods to bring to market.

During the depression (as, for example, experienced in the world economy during the 1930s), productive capacity exists to produce the goods people want, but it is not used. Workers are available to set that productive capacity in motion, but they are not employed. Capital and labor stand idle because money is not in the hands of those who need their products. Had the workers been employed, they would have received incomes enabling them to purchase the products they needed but were not producing. Producers would then have made revenues, including profit that would justify the employment of labor. Otherwise, productive capacity remains idle because of inadequate demand, but demand is inadequate because of idle productive capacity. Thus workers are unemployed and lack purchasing power adequate to justify use of the idle productive capacity. This represents an instance of market failure if it results from the workings of the market taken by itself and not from efforts by government to regulate the market. The continuing debate in economics centers on whether the cause of market failure is in the market or outside. The classical economists tended to favor the second interpretation. They did so for the following reason.

So long as those who sell commodities use their money revenues to purchase commodities, effective demand (need tied to money) never leaves the market. The classical economists thought it would be irrational for sellers to hold money which, in their view, satisfies no need, when they could have commodities. Workers must certainly (and rapidly) use up their wages in acquiring consumption goods. Producers, motivated by the desire to expand their capital and wealth, must use their money revenues to buy productive inputs capable of yielding profit (which, in general, money does not). Assuming that this is correct, and that agents act rationally, money will continue to circulate and aggregate demand will not falter.

The key, then, to the classical argument was the assumption that no reasonable motive could lead a seller to hold money rather than one of the goods money could buy. By purchasing such goods with his money revenue, the individuals as a group, though not in every case, will find buyers for their goods and will be able to acquire the things they want in proportion to the amount and value of what they have to sell.

An important problem in the argument summarized above for market self-regulation is that even were the market self-regulating, the satisfaction that the individual takes out of the market depends on the property he brings with him into the market. It is not his need that determines what he consumes, but his ability to satisfy the needs of others.

In some ways this characteristic of the free market can be thought of as a virtue. The market disciplines self-interest to work for the interest of others. In another sense, this characteristic of the free market sounds like a vice. It means that well-being depends on circumstances that it may be outside the power of the individual to affect. Self-interest may not provide the individual with the ability to satisfy the wants of others even if it provides him with the motive to do so. What we bring to the market can depend as much on accidents of birth and circumstances as it does on incentives and self-interest. The market then confirms these accidents and enables us to satisfy our wants only so far as those accidents allow.

The German philosopher G. W. F. Hegel was quick to underscore this limit of the self-regulating market and to see in it an argument for government intervention.

Not only caprice, however, but also contingencies, physical conditions, and factors grounded in external circumstances may reduce men to poverty. The poor still have the needs common to civil society, and yet since society has withdrawn from them the natural means of acquisition and broken the bond of the family ... their poverty leaves them more or less deprived of all the advantages of society, of the opportunity to acquiring skill of education of any kind, as well as of the administration of justice ... and so forth. The public authority takes the place of the family where the poor are concerned in respect not only to their immediate want but also of laziness of disposition, malignity, and the other vices which arise out of their plight and their sense of wrong. ([1821] 1952:148–9)

Private interest and public good

The argument summarized in the previous section has important implications for the relation between the public agent (state) and the system of private relations (economy). We now turn to those implications.

Adam Smith's now classic formulation of the link between private interest and public good in a market economy depends heavily on the argument that markets, if allowed to, will regulate themselves. Smith develops his argument as part of a critique of the policy of placing "Restraints upon the Importation from Foreign Countries of such Goods as Can be Produced at Home." Smith begins by noting that the "monopoly of the home market" resulting from restraints on imports encourages certain domestic industries and increases the share of labor and capital devoted to those industries ([1776] 1937:420). But he questions whether this serves the public good. Serving the public good means increasing the "general industry of society" or channeling that industry in "the most advantageous direction."

The linchpin in Smith's argument is the assumption that society's capital stock is always fully utilized and that the problem of market failure outlined in the preceding section does not arise. Assuming full utilization of capital stock, the effect of policies that restrain trade (in this case imports) can only be on those lines of industry in which the capital stock is invested. The importance of the composition of investment (its distribution across industries) is for two interconnected concerns: (1) the ability of the capital stock to satisfy needs and (2) the profitability of the capital. If our policies direct investment into the wrong industries, this will reduce profitability and less adequately satisfy private needs. Smith summarizes these ideas as follows:

No regulation of commerce can increase the quantity of industry in any society beyond what its capital can maintain. It can only divert a part of it into a direction into which it might not otherwise have gone; and it is by no means certain that this artificial direction is likely to be more advantageous to society than that into which it would have gone of its accord.

Every individual is continually exerting himself to find out the most advantageous employment for whatever capital he can command. It is his own advantage, indeed, and not that of society which he has in view. But the study of his advantage naturally or rather necessarily leads him to prefer that employment which is most advantageous to the society. ([1776] 1937:421)

For Smith, profit measures the advantage to the individual of alternative employments of his capital:

But it is only for the sake of profit that any man employs a capital in the support of industry; and he will always, therefore, endeavor to employ it in the support of that industry of which the produce is likely to be the greatest quantity either of money or of other goods. (p. 423)

By leaving the decision on the direction of the flow of labor and capital in the hands of the individual (capitalist), we allow profit to determine the development of industry. The capitalist is the agent, and not the directing force. Indeed, no individual or group takes responsibility for directing economic development. The concern for profit channels investment in the most socially advantageous way. It assures that revenue and industry will increase as rapidly as possible.

The individual intends only his own gain, and he is in this, as in many other cases, led by an invisible hand to promote an end which was no part of his intention. (p. 423)

Summarizing the classical approach to the relation between private interest and public good: Under its normal workings, and in the absence of regulation from outside, the market will assure the full utilization of society's capital stock. Given the overall amount of capital and labor available to society, the proportions devoted to different industries should depend on profitability because profitability measures the contribution each industry can make to the size of the social revenue and to the growth of social wealth. The only way to assure that profit directs investment is to place that investment into private hands and subject it to decisions based on self-interest. This works because self-interest is best served by the pursuit of profit. Given that profit seeking is a private rather than public motive, this approach argues against public guidance of investment. Public regulation means, for the classical economists, that something other than profitability will determine investment. The unregulated but self-ordering market will encourage the growth of society's capital stock and achieve the public good.

This definition of the public good supports a strong argument in favor of the free market, one that economists otherwise as opposed as Smith and Marx both recognize. Smith and Marx both argue that the free market has as its historical purpose the development of society's material technical productive foundation, its capital stock. The "invisible hand" organizes the pursuit of private gain into the historically significant project of developing social wealth. Smith sees this as a transition from the "savage state of man" where men are "miserably poor" to "civilized society" in which "all are abundantly supplied" ([1776] 1937:lviii). Marx argues that capitalism has as its "historical mission" to develop the "material forces of production" and to create an "appropriate world market" ([1894] 1967b, Vol. III:250). In this view, the economy disembedded from other social institutions has a *raison d'être*. This *raison d'être* is (1) an unintended consequence of self-seeking, so that it can be treated as a hidden, or implicit, social purpose and (2) accomplished through the accumulation of capital on the part of independent wealth holders.

Classical economics assumes the existence of a public good connected to, but distinct from, private ends: the growth of society's capital stock. But, the classical approach contends that the public good so defined will best be accomplished without the intervention of a public agent. This judgment, if correct, resolves the problem of economic order raised earlier in this chapter. The self-regulating market displaces the decisions of a political agent. Indeed, were the state to make well-conceived decisions in accordance with the laws of political economy it would guide society to just those ends best achieved when the state does not act. It can do no more. Very likely, however, it will do considerably less. Given uncertainty regarding the wisdom of political decisions, better to make the development of society an unintended consequence of private acts and decisions, to allow and encourage the displacement of political society by civil society.

The state and society

Within classical economics, then, what remains for the state to do, especially with reference to the world of private affairs? We refer again to Adam Smith:

According to the system of natural liberty, the sovereign has only three duties to attend to; three duties of great importance, indeed, but plain and intelligible to common understanding: first, the duty of protecting the society from the violence and invasion of other independent societies; secondly, the duty of protecting, as far as possible, every member of the society from the injustice or oppression of every other member of it, or the duty of establishing an exact administration of justice; and, thirdly, the duty of erecting and maintaining certain public works and certain public institutions, which it can never be for the interest of any individual, or small number of individuals, to erect and maintain; because the profit could never repay the expence to any individual or small number of individuals, though it may frequently do much more than repay it to a great society. ([1776] 1937:651)

Under the last heading, of public works and public institutions, Smith has in mind primarily those aimed at facilitating commerce (roads, bridges, canals), and "promoting instruction of the people" (p. 681).

Imagine a state concerned exclusively with national defense, the administration of justice, public works, and education. Given a narrow enough definition of justice, and assuming that definition well established and well accepted, political deliberation would concern itself at most with a limited range of issues involving the extent of these activities. Indeed, such a state would finance and maintain a standing army, some schools, the courts, and the highways. It would not deliberate on the appropriate ways of life in a well-ordered society; it would not concern itself with collective judgments on the nature of the public good; it would not take responsibility for the welfare of those whose private activities fail adequately to sustain them. Just as civil society displaces political society, administration replaces politics.

And yet the classical economists, including Smith, do not go quite so far as to deny the existence of a public good irreducible to (for example the sum of) private ends. Smith identifies this public good with the magnitude (and rate of growth) of the national product. Clearly a large and growing product will generally benefit individuals as well as the state. Still, the benefit of a large national product is both for the individuals and for the state as a whole. Were we to consider more than just the size of the product, then the equation of public with private ends would become less self-evident. Even given such a split, it can still be argued, for certain definitions of the public good, that a private market economy best achieves that good (if unintentionally). This is the argument we think of as distinctly classical.

The classical argument has more recently given way to one (associated with the neoclassical approach) that defines the public good so as to equate it with a sum (or other aggregate) of private interests. We should not, however, move too quickly to an interpretation of the classical approach to political economy that equates it with this more recent method. To do so loses sight of an important tension in the classical approach absent in the modern. This tension exists in the effort to retain an older notion of the public good while denying the necessity of a public agent who takes responsibility for assuring that private affairs contribute to the public agenda. Smith would like to see public ends accomplished without (or with a minimum of) public life. This hope is an important part of classical thinking. It sets up a problem for subsequent theories, one that leads in different directions.

Recall the contrast drawn earlier in this chapter between Smith and Steuart. The former favors the demotion of politics while the latter tries to retain the idea that politics and the state have an important role beyond public administration and national defense. For Steuart, the state takes a leading role in the private sphere: molding private interests, limiting self-seeking, educating persons to a "higher" viewpoint (the public interest). As we will see in the following chapters, none of the modern approaches to political economy is entirely comfortable with this idea. Several reject it entirely, and this is typical of political economy. Others leave it only a very limited role to play. In this, political economy is very much a part of the modern temperament, which, following Smith, doubts both the necessity that the state take a leading role and its competence to do so. Political economy comes more and more to view the state as an agent acting for private interests rather than an agent entrusted with responsibility for a public good irreducible to private interest. How could the state, acting as the agent of private interest, take responsibility for raising individuals to a higher standpoint? Clearly, we can hardly expect it to do so.

Value and distribution

The division of labor and exchange

The theory of market self-regulation is arguably the central achievement of the classical approach to political economy and the key to understanding how a classically influenced economist might understand the interrelation of the economic and the political. Modern theorists working in the classical tradition have not, however, all taken this viewpoint. Recent contributions have built on a different element of the classical analysis of market economy, one concerned more with the price system as it relates to the determination of wages and profits, less with its implications for market self-regulation. We now turn to this other dimension of the classical theory. This dimension begins with consideration of the relation between the social division of labor and commodity exchange.

The division of labor has a very close association with exchange. In the absence of a market for the product, it makes very little sense for an otherwise isolated individual to specialize in the way demanded by the division of labor. At the same time, participation in the division of labor requires the individual producer to exchange in order to acquire those elements of subsistence he or she does not produce. Adam Smith places this two-sided relationship between the market and the division of labor at the center of his analysis. With the division of labor every man "becomes in some measure a merchant" (1937:22). Our participation in a division of labor forces us to exchange. The type of mutual dependence associated with division of labor gives rise to the system of exchange. At the same time "the division of labor is limited by the extent of the market" (1937:17). The market also plays a part in stimulating the development of the division of labor.

The division of labor occupies a position in the classical treatment of exchange analogous to that played by utility maximization in neoclassical theory. It accounts for the participation of the individual in a larger social reality. And, just as the rates of exchange between individual utility maximizers depend on their preferences and endowments, the rates of exchange that emerge from a social division of labor depend on attributes of the production structure as a whole. The embedding of prices in a production structure within the classical approach has been given two related but distinct interpretations: the labor theory of value and the theory of production prices.

Smith, Ricardo, and Marx cut a direct path between the division of labor and price by arguing that prices depend on the relative quantities of social labor used in the production of commodities.[4] The reproduction of the goods that make up the social product is thought of as a set of "labor processes" (Marx 1967a:ch. 7) linked by inputs and outputs. The sum of the labors of individuals provides society with its productive resource. The sum of labors must be allocated to the various processes that produce the goods needed as inputs into social reproduction. This classical framework encourages us to visualize a single pool of social labor divided among particular tasks and reunited by exchange. The proportions defined by the needs of social reproduction taken as a whole determine the appropriate rates of exchange. These rates assure that each producer will receive in the sale of his output a value adequate to renew his means of production.

This idea has a simple and direct interpretation if we assume that the price of a commodity measured in terms of another commodity equals the ratio of the amounts of labor used in their respective production. Thus, if it takes twenty hours of labor to produce a chair and ten hours to produce a jacket, then the jacket price of chairs (the number of jackets required to purchase a chair) must equal two. In this case, the exchange of jackets for chairs brings about an exchange of jacket-producing labor for chair-producing labor.

The labor theory of value provides a direct link between the division of a pool of social labor and the exchange of commodities. The theory runs into a number of analytical difficulties, however, which have convinced modern economists working in the classical tradition to build a materialist basis for exchange by employing a distinct starting point also present in the classical theories: price of production. These authors, rather than rooting price in the division of a pool of social labor, root it in the technical specification of a production structure.[5]

Consider the set of commodities that make up the social product during a given period. The production of each commodity requires the use of a subset of the remaining commodities as productive inputs. We can characterize the method or technique of production for a given commodity as an equation relating the number of each required input to the product. The

---

[4] For a more comprehensive discussion of the labor theory of value, see Meek (1973).
[5] Sraffa (1960) analyzes the relation between price and the technical structure of production; see also Walsh and Gram (1980).

technique is, in effect, a kind of recipe for producing a particular commodity. The set of such recipes constitutes a summary of the overall technology for reproduction of the set of products. It depicts the production structure within which material reproduction takes place. The production structure relates inputs to outputs quantitatively. Commodities appear both as the output of their own production process (captured in the appropriate equation) and as inputs into the production processes of other commodities.

For reproduction to take place, the set of outputs produced must be appropriate in form and sufficient in magnitude to provide the inputs needed for their own production. If the output set is just appropriate in this sense to replace inputs used for its production, the economy may be said to produce a surplus equal to the excess of the set of products over the inputs needed for reproduction.

When an individual producer specializes in production of a single component of the social product, the market value of his output determines his ability or inability to acquire needed inputs given their market prices. If his output also enters as an input into the production of other goods, the system of interdependence in production must establish limits on relative prices. Each price must be consistent with the conditions that it (1) be adequate to cover costs of production and (2) be consistent with the price of products that employ that output as a productive input. The term "price of production" refers to a price consistent with the location of the particular commodity in the reproduction system in this sense. It is the price that allows the commodity to act both as input and output. The production structure, or material-technical specification of the requirements of reproduction of the system of commodities, is the first and primary determinant of the price system.

The classical method effectively eliminates individual choice and decision making from playing a part in determining economic affairs (Nell, 1967). Individuals may make decisions, but ultimately the material-technical rules of reproduction govern the outcome. The method attempts to replace choosing agents with objective rules.

One area in which the classical method contrasts most sharply with the neoclassical is in its treatment of consumption, especially workers' consumption. Application of the classical model to wage determination has led to the treatment of labor on the basis of the idea that its price is determined in relation to costs of production. Otherwise the prices of products employing labor as an input cannot be uniquely determined by technical rules for transforming inputs into outputs. In order to solve this problem, the classical method determines the composition and magnitude of workers' consumption on the basis of rules independent of the desires and choices of individual workers. The term "subsistence" designates consumption needs determined in this way.

The simplest approach to subsistence appeals to costs of reproducing workers. As Piero Sraffa puts it, the notion of subsistence places workers' consumption "on the same footing as the fuel of the engines or the feed of the cattle" (1960:9). This approach, which has its roots in the work of Ricardo and Marx, applies the cost of production idea directly to the labor input. Consumption of the subsistence produces labor, which produces output, including subsistence. Reproduction now requires that (1) the wage equal the sum of the prices of the subsistence goods (given the amounts of each required) and (2) the output of subsistence goods be at least adequate to reproduce the labor needed for its production.

More recently, the notion of subsistence has moved away from the narrow idea of costs of production.[6] Contemporary classical models treat workers' consumption as a given for the market. Subsistence means that the needs the market must satisfy do not depend on the market, and in particular, do not vary with the prices of commodities. Consumers have needs, and they have recourse to the market to acquire the means to satisfy those needs. However those needs may be determined (and the theories do not address this issue), they do not involve trade-offs and do not vary with prices (at least in the short run). By contrast, consumers making decisions on the basis of preferences will vary the composition of their consumption with variations in relative prices of its elements.

The following example may help to illuminate the link between production structure and price (see Sraffa 1960). Consider a simple economy whose reproduction entails the use of only three inputs: iron, wheat, and labor. We may think of iron as representing inputs of means of production and wheat as representing inputs of materials and means of subsistence. This simple economy may be depicted as a set of production relations that together constitute a production structure (t = tons, bu = bushels, hr = hours):

10 t iron + 250 bu wheat + 100 hr labor → 700 bu wheat
15 t iron   + 50 hr labor →   25 t iron
           450 bu wheat   → 150 hr labor

Each line represents the relation between the inputs (on the left-hand side) and a component of the social product (on the right). The production structure is circular in the sense that each input is also a component of the social product (set of outputs). The production structure as depicted is just viable in the sense that when we use the outputs as productive inputs they are just adequate for their own reproduction. There is no surplus.

The simplest classical theories treat labor as a produced commodity that has a cost of production like all other produced commodities. The third

[6] Garegnani (1984) reinterprets the classical notion of subsistence in this direction.

production relation expresses this idea. The consumption of a given amount of wheat (presumably in the form of bread) renews the worker's capacity to labor for a given period of time. In effect, then, when labor enters as an input, it is really so much wheat, which went to produce the labor, and enters as input through its product, the laboring capacity of the worker. By making this explicit, we can simplify our depiction of the production structure into only two production relations:

10 t iron + 550 bu wheat → 700 bu wheat
15 t iron + 150 bu wheat → 25 t iron

In the case assumed, of an economy that is just viable and produces no surplus, there is one rate of exchange that allows (1) for the wheat producer to acquire the iron needed to produce wheat while retaining sufficient wheat to feed his workers and use as raw material and (2) for the iron producer to acquire the wheat that he needs while retaining the iron needed for the production of iron. As can be seen from the production relations, 150 bushels of wheat must exchange for 10 tons of iron. The wheat price of iron must be 15. This example makes vivid the manner in which the production structure and the needs of reproduction determine relative price.

Consider now production with a surplus. We can depict this case with the following modifications of the production relations:

10 t iron + 250 bu wheat + 100 hr labor → 800 bu wheat
15 t iron   + 50 hr labor → 35 t iron
           450 bu wheat   → 150 hr labor

We now have production of a surplus consisting of 100 bu wheat and 10 t iron. Simplifying again to eliminate the explicit statement of the third relationship (production of labor by wheat):

10 t iron + 550 bu wheat → 800 bu wheat
15 t iron + 150 bu wheat → 35 t iron

In the case of production with a surplus, we can no longer determine price directly from the production structure. Indeed the wheat price of iron may settle at any point between 7.5 and 25 bushels of wheat and still allow reproduction to take place. Although differences in price within this range do not affect the ability of the economy to reproduce itself, they do affect the way in which the surplus is distributed between the wheat producer and the iron producer. If the wheat price of iron is 7.5 bushels of wheat, all the surplus accrues to the wheat producer. In other words, at that price, the wheat producer can (1) retain the 550 bushels of wheat needed as productive input for the next period, (2) retain an additional 100 bushels of wheat, and (3) have 150 bushels of wheat left, which at a price of 7.5 bushels allows the wheat producer to purchase 20 tons of iron. The entire surplus consisting of 100 bushels of wheat and 10 tons of iron ends up in the hands of the wheat producer. It can be easily verified that with a wheat price of iron of 25 bushels, the entire surplus will end up in the hands of the iron producer. Thus, in the case of production with a surplus, price must be determined (1) within the range consistent with reproduction and (2) on the basis of a rule for allocating the surplus.

As we have seen, in the classical framework, the possibility exists that the subsistence needs of workers will fall short of the amount of subsistence those same workers (together with the needed inputs) can produce in a given period. More generally, the possibility exists technically that the use of the current output as inputs into production will generate an amount of output in excess of that needed for continuing production at the current level. Society then faces the problem of what to do with this surplus. This means that society must allocate the surplus to particular activities (consumption and production) according to some rule. For different societies, the use of the surplus will vary and thus its material form and magnitude will also vary. Indeed, according to Marx:

The specific economic form, in which unpaid surplus-labor is pumped out of direct producers, determines the relationship of rulers to ruled, as it grows directly out of production itself and, in turn, reacts upon it as a determining element. Upon this, however, is founded the entire formation of the economic community which grows up out of the production relations themselves, thereby simultaneously its specific political form. (1967, Vol. III:791)

In a capitalist society,[7] the surplus primarily adopts the form of profit – the difference between the value of output and its costs of production. This profit accrues to the owners of the capital stock as their private incomes.

As we have seen, when society produces a surplus, the costs of production (including the subsistence wage) cannot fully determine prices. The margin between price and cost is the surplus measured in value and allocated to the producer as his profit or income. Put the other way around, the prices of commodities depend both on their costs (employment of other commodities as inputs) and on the profit that accrues to their producer, normally in relationship to those costs. The price of a commodity equals the sum of its cost of production and of the surplus that accrues to the producer as his profit.

This conclusion has a striking interpretation. Market prices, connected to the social institutions of property and contract, express a deeper reality shared with nonmarket forms of allocation and distribution. According to the classical view, all societies must reproduce themselves by reproducing the sub-

---

[7] Dobb (1936:ch. 1) discusses the idea of capitalism.

sistence of their workers, and they must also distribute their surplus in accordance with the requirements of their particular social institutions. What varies across societies is the form that these processes adopt. The market is one among a number of social mechanisms for meeting a material necessity of life. This means that the economic (in the sense of material provisioning) exists whether or not the market exists, and therefore whether or not our economic activities take place together in a separate sphere we might call an economy.

Income distribution

The version of the classical theory of value briefly outlined in the preceding paragraphs maintains the classical assumption that the level of wages depends on the specification of a subsistence bundle. Under this assumption, the magnitude of the surplus depends on the technology as it determines the productivity of labor, and on the amount of the subsistence. The surplus is a kind of residual, the amount left over once the costs of production are fully accounted for. This surplus is, then, the fund out of which profit and investment arise.

The idea that wages are subject to determination in this way has lost plausibility in the period since the publication of the great texts of the classical economists in the eighteenth and early nineteenth centuries. Modern theorists have, therefore, modified this element of the theory, and in so doing arrived at a striking conclusion.

If we treat the wage as a variable rather than a fixed magnitude, this means that the market system contains an element of indeterminacy. Variability of the wage means variability of the surplus and thus of profit for a given production structure. Thus, given the productivity of labor and the social division of labor, the distribution of the product between labor and the owners of capital remains to be determined.

It might be possible, then, to consider the distribution of income the outcome of a struggle between competing claimants rather than something built into the structure of reproduction itself as the classical model originally would have had it. That structure sets limits on distribution marked on one end by the level of profit or surplus were the wage zero and on the other by the level of the real wage were surplus equal to zero. But between these levels, the conditions of reproduction do not fix income distribution.

The next step is to identify the claimants as social classes defined by their relation to the means of production. Doing so is well within the spirit of the classical approach. Then, the distribution of income becomes a matter of a struggle between social classes over the product of labor.

Focusing on this struggle moves political economy onto a different terrain than that emphasized in the first section of this chapter. That depiction of political economy in the classical vein was the study of the capacity of the economy to sustain itself. The economic refers us to an institutional reality, the market; the political refers us to the state, also an institutional reality. Political economy concerns the logic of the relation between these two institutions. The issue of separability is central.

When we move to the terrain of struggle between social classes over the distribution of income, the idea of what is political economy shifts. Here the economic is not first a sphere, the economy; it is the process of the material reproduction of goods and provisioning of needs. The political refers us first not to the state but to the configuration of social classes and class relations. Maurice Dobb (1936) placed special emphasis on this interpretation of the political in classical political economy.

Of course, a question can be raised concerning the sense in which the interrelation of classes can be the political dimension. Indeed, in the more recent contributions by those influenced by the classical method, the explicitly political element rarely appears in any systematic form. The issue is left hanging.

In many cases, the identification of the political with class relations is more an allusion to an argument than an argument itself. In Chapter 3, on the Marxian approach, we will see how this argument might develop. Indeed, the problem posed here cannot but point us toward the Marxian theory as heir to the classical. For the moment, we will only lay out the issue and identify its classical roots: the sense in which it depends on the classical theory and the point at which it moves beyond that theory.

It is striking that those economists closest to the classical school in analytical framework use that framework to support an approach to political economy very different from that of the classical economists. This was Marx's own method. He took over the analytical framework of classical political economy and employed it to arrive at radical conclusions, arguably implicit in that framework, but surely very far removed from the intent and spirit of the classical economists themselves.

For us, one dimension of the shift has special significance. The classical economists used their framework to argue for the separability of the economy. Modern economists influenced by their analytical framework use it as often to undermine that separation as to support it. In their work, the political dimension identified with class distribution of income enters into the workings of the market system itself.

As we have seen, the magnitude and distribution of the surplus bear on the determination of commodity prices. When that magnitude and distribution depend on a struggle between social groups, the economy is not logically separate from the political system. Thus, much is at stake in the claim that income distribution depends on class conflict and that the struggle between classes is a political rather than economic process.

Modern thinking, then, tends to reverse the direction of movement associated with that of the classical economists. Where the classical economists raised the economic to a level of primacy, some modern economists have used the classical framework to erode the separateness of the economy and to elevate the political struggle to prominence in the economic arena.

It should be mentioned that this is only true of one group of modern classical economists. Others use the classical approach to value and distribution without treating the problem of distribution as one involving the struggle, latently or overtly political, between classes (see Robinson, 1962). The classical approach has also been melded with Keynesian insights to yield a modern theory with a classical flavor not aimed at politicizing the economy.

Many roads lead from classical political economy. The main ones we explore in the following are the Marxian, neoclassical, and Keynesian. Each treats the problems of separability of the economy in a distinct way. Each deploys different notions of the economic and of the political, combining them in ways leading to different approaches to political economy.

3

Marxian political economy

With Marxism, there are many possible vantage points from which one can discuss political economy. Marxists have seen the political in the very separation of civil society from the public arena (limiting rights and equality to the latter), the class process by which surplus value is "appropriated" under capitalism, the role of the state in managing the interests and affairs of capital, political (that is, state-backed) guarantees of property rights, revolutionary activity to alter the political institutions of capitalism, and the bargaining between labor and capital for control of the economic surplus.

Although these vantage points may supply political content to Marxian economics, the senses in which they do so are not obvious. Even the concept of class, certainly a mainstay of Marxian theory, is not obviously political. Classes can exist even in a society where individuals are disconnected, unaware of common interests, and politically unorganized. Nevertheless, owners of capital may exist and hire those who sell their labor power. Further, production of value and surplus value can occur. In this kind of economy, politics would not be evident in the daily operation of class processes (though the state would have to underwrite private property rights). There would be no struggle for the surplus, no power bargaining between labor and capital, and no state intervention to control labor.

The use of the term "political economy" in Marxian theory does not directly refer us to studies of the relation between economics and politics. Instead, it connotes a way of thinking about the economy rooted in the method and theories of the classical economists, especially Adam Smith and David Ricardo. This method emphasizes the idea that a market economy operates according to laws rooted in the ongoing reproduction and expansion of a system of material interdependence between persons – a social division of labor (see Chapter 2). This process follows laws that the classical economists thought were independent of the wills and desires of persons. To be sure, individuals within a market economy act independently and according to their desires. The matrix of individual wants directly determines what happens in the market. Yet behind these private wants stands an objective structure of reproduction whose requirements dominate the individual in the formation of his private interests. This domination justifies the theory in focusing on the (presumably) objective process of reproduction rather than on the subjective process of ranking opportunities or making choices.

The method briefly described here requires us to think about individual interests in a distinctive way. In the neoclassical theories, individuals have an interest in maximizing their well-being defined by their preference orderings. The economy not only works to facilitate this process but, at least ideally, originates in order to facilitate it. Causation runs from individual interest, presumed given subjectively, to economic structure. For Marx, causation runs in the other direction. This makes individual interests a more complex subject. On one side, they refer to the individual. No one tells individuals what they want or what to do to achieve their ends. Initiative lies with the individual agent. In this respect, an economic order results from the unplanned and uncontrolled acts of individuals. Yet control must ultimately reside outside the individual (in the objective economic structure) if the structure is to dominate individual interest.

Thus the Marxian method poses a problem involving how we connect individual interest to social order. For our purposes, the solution to this problem has special importance since it will also be the basis for answering the following question: What is the relationship between individual material (or economic) interest, politics, and the agenda of the state?

In this chapter we attempt to draw out the links between politics and economics in Marxian theory. While recognizing that political economy can be conceived in different ways, we have chosen to focus on three strands of Marxian theory: revolutionary politics (the route suggested by Marx and Lenin); the politics of class compromise (Kautsky's, and later the social democratic route); and Marxist state theory. While these strands differ in important ways, they are unified by the theme of the transformation of interests from private-objective interests to subjective-shared interests that motivate class organization. This transition is complex and covers a lot of ground, but it is necessary to make the journey before material (class) interest can become political. The following subsections analyze this transition in detail. We deal in turn with the relation between material interest and class; with the conflict implicit in class relations; and with how these economic interests become conscious and shared. Finally we examine briefly three strands of political economy: revolutionary theory, social democratic theory, and state theory.

Material interests and economic class

The concept of class is central to Marxian theory. However, politically organized classes do not emerge spontaneously under capitalism. At first, individuals within the economy see themselves narrowly as isolated agents pursuing interests uniquely their own. Such interests may have nothing to do with the interests of others and may even set individuals in opposition one to another. Such interests are not, however, isolated and independent. Capitalist economy works in such a way as to set up a commonality of interest within certain classes of persons. The more individuals become aware of their common condition and purpose, the more they see their narrow material interest in a broader light. This process marks a transition from individual to class interest and ultimately, from material-economic to political interest. Such a transition (1) is implicit in the separate private interests of persons and (2) provides us with the fundamental link between economics and politics. The Marxian interpretation of the relationship between economics and politics centers on the idea of economic interests and the part they play in defining political agendas.

However, the distance covered between pure economic interest and political action is considerable. Before economic interests can play a role in politics directly, individuals must be aware of their shared interests, organize on the basis of them, and overcome collective action problems. We will, therefore, begin with the way Marxists think about interests.

Marxists advance the following claims about interests:

1. Interests arise within the structure of production. The wants of the individual depend upon his place in the process of social reproduction. The individual has "economic" or "material" interests in satisfying his private wants. Within (civil) society, the position of the individual in the social division of labor determines his wants, which determine his interests.
2. Private (or self) interest can best be understood if we first understand the class to which the individual belongs. That is, the divisions within civil society primarily responsible for determining wants divide individuals into classes. Thus, the interests arising within civil society are implicitly class interests.
3. These interests of classes stand opposed. The degree to which one class achieves its material interest measures the degree to which the other fails.
4. Class interests arising within production become political interests involved in the struggle over state power.

While these four points identify important aspects of the transition from material interest to political action, we caution against a mechanical interpretation. There is no one-for-one correspondence between economic location and politics. Indeed, some of the most significant political debates (such as that between Leninist and Kautskyist positions) have taken place over how this transition should be made.

First, how do class interests and classes themselves arise within the economy? Marx's economic theories provide a detailed answer to this question.

As Charles Bettelheim points out, within his economic studies Marx seems to "inscribe the division of society into classes entirely within the *relations of production*" (1985:19, italics in original). In the following, we briefly summarize Marx's argument.

According to Marx, a capitalist economy appears, on first glance, to consist of a vast accumulation of commodities, a set of individuals who own those commodities, and a set of (exchange) relations connecting those individuals. These individuals do not see themselves as members of a class, nor do they see their interests as class interests. In order to get from a world of individual and independent property owners to classes we need to know how the structure and dynamics of the capitalist economy lead to the grouping of persons and of wants, not only on the basis of their personal affinities or unique circumstances, but on the basis of their position within an objective structure of production.

The key element of Marx's argument for the emergence of classes starts by questioning the classical theory's understanding of the purpose of the market. Here Marxian theory argues that the market economy is not so much a mechanism for maximizing the private welfare of individuals generally as it is a means of facilitating the capitalist's appropriation of surplus-value and accumulation of capital. The market makes sense as a social institution because it makes possible self-aggrandizement and private accumulations of wealth in the form of capital. We can use one of Marx's better known formulations to clarify this idea.

Let the letter M represent a sum of money, and letter C a collection of particular commodities (which Marx terms "use-values" following Adam Smith – so many chairs, shirts, loaves of bread, and so on). In a neoclassical world, individuals hold money only in order to use it to purchase some commodity that yields utility to them. In order to acquire the money they need for the purchase of the commodities they want, individuals sell some commodity (or commodities) they own. Some examples: An individual owns his laboring capacity but wants to buy housing, food, and clothing; he or she sells labor (power) for a wage (money) and buys the things needed with it. Marx would depict this sort of activity as follows:

C (laboring capacity) $\rightarrow$ M (wages) $\rightarrow$ C (means of consumption).

Another example would involve the sale of an old car and use of the proceeds to purchase a personal computer:

C (used car) $\rightarrow$ M (proceeds from sale) $\rightarrow$ C (computer).

Marx terms this the simple circulation of commodities and argues that it characterizes noncapitalist market systems and that it also exists explicitly and implicitly within capitalist economies.

Marx distinguishes capitalism by the fact that in addition to and in a sense dominating over this simple circulation, capitalism institutes another circuit that reverses the terms of commodity circulation as previously understood. This reversal characterizes the circuit of capital:

$$M \rightarrow C \rightarrow M'.$$

Unlike the circulation of commodities, the circuit of capital has money rather than useful things as its objective. The capitalist advances money (M) in the hope and expectation that his investment (capital) will return to him with a profit ($M'-M$), which Marx terms the "surplus-value." For Marx, then, the market has two purposes to serve in a capitalist setting. It provides a mechanism for circulating commodities so that those commodities can find their way into the hands of those who need them (C–M–C) and it provides a mechanism for using money to make money or accumulating capital (M–C–M').

What determines whether a particular property owner aims to satisfy needs or to accumulate capital, and why should this distinction in intention (1) ultimately depend upon objective, structural conditions rather than on preferences or psychological disposition, and (2) arise out of a distinction between classes rather than individuals? It must be admitted that Marx's own answers to these questions do not seem terribly well developed, and that while Marxists since Marx have come some way in clarifying the issue, their method has focused attention in other directions. Still, some important elements of an answer emerge clearly enough.

First, which objective an individual adopts must surely depend on which he finds available. Assuming that only some persons have capital to advance for purposes of accumulation, only those will be able to adopt the objective Marx identifies with the capitalist class. Those without capital have nothing to sell but their labor. In Marx's famous formulation the laborer must be

free in the double sense, that as a free man he can dispose of his labour-power as his own commodity, and that on the other hand he has no other commodity for sale, is short of everything necessary for the realization of his labour power. ([*Capital*, Vol. I, 1867], 1967a:169)

Marx develops an argument to demonstrate that this difference between capitalists and workers will reinforce itself over time, making capitalists progressively richer and increasing the size of the barriers to workers becoming capitalists. Second, given the first consideration, those who can and do act as capitalists will find themselves in a decidedly different social condition compared to those who cannot and do not act as capitalists. Their different social positions mean different relationships to the means of production and to the production process as well as to the other classes. Thus, what Marxists call the social condition of the two types of persons will differ and in systematic ways.

This difference in social condition precedes individual interest and individual consciousness. In this sense, the economy itself defines the social positions in which individuals find themselves. The simple scheme outlined above defines only two social positions and it defines them according to the condition of owning or not owning capital. If we use the term "social class" in this purely economic context, it refers to no more than this difference in social condition. This is the most primitive, and problematic, interpretation of class. Membership in a class does not, in this context, impose itself on the mind of the individual who continues to act as an individual, not as part of a class, and need not even be aware of his class identity. Classes in this sense (objective classes, classes in themselves) are politically inert. To see how they become active politically, we pursue three issues below: conflict among classes, class consciousness, and class actors in the political arena.

Material interests, class conflict, and capitalism

Focus on material interests as they arise within the economy raises the following questions:

1. Are those material interests best served, or under certain circumstances served at all, under capitalism?
2. Are the material interests of workers and capitalists in conflict under capitalism, or will both groups benefit and lose together?
3. Do the material interests of individuals within the classes of workers and capitalists converge or conflict; do they reinforce or undermine the perception of a common class interest?
4. Does the conflict that arises over material interests lead to a challenge to the social order of capitalism, or merely involve a shifting of power and benefit within capitalism?

The first two questions direct our attention primarily to the implications of capitalist economic organization for profits, wages, and employment. Marx's own views on these subjects are somewhat complex (Levine, 1988b). At considerable risk of oversimplification we advance the following summary.

Marx sets out from the idea of the "subsistence" wage. This subsistence wage, or "value of labor-power" depends on the "value of the means of subsistence necessary for the maintenance of the laborer" (1967a:171). While this subsistence may depend upon "historical" and "moral" factors, it does not vary with profits, employment, or accumulation. In Marx's view, capitalism does not enhance the subsistence (though for a period it may allow the worker to demand and receive more than his subsistence). In other words, the fact that the worker acquires his subsistence by first selling his labor-power in the market and then using the money received (his money wage) to purchase his means of subsistence does not affect the amount or composition of that subsistence. This makes the wage contract a purely formal condition so far as the worker is concerned. It assures that while capitalism may satisfy a material interest of the worker, it does not provide him with any special material benefit beyond subsistence.

Given the subsistence, what remains makes up surplus-value, the most important part of which goes to the capitalist as his profit. The greater the cost of subsistence, the less the surplus-value remaining to fund profit for the capitalist. In this simple scheme, profits and wages are inversely related: When one side gains, the other loses.

Marx argues that the profit motive drives capitalists to seek ways of increasing their share of output given the subsistence wage. They are able to do so either by increasing the value of output given the value of the subsistence or by reducing the value of the subsistence given the material needs of the workers and value of the output. He terms these respectively production of "absolute" and "relative" surplus-value (1967a:parts III and IV). Marx argues that capitalists attempt to find ways to make workers work harder, longer, and more efficiently without altering their subsistence. As a result, profit increases, the *real* wage (subsistence) remains the same, the worker works harder and longer while his share of the product declines. If true, this means that capitalism advances the material interests of capitalists, leaves unaffected or even harms the material interests of workers, and sets the interests of the two in opposition.

Marx believes that class interests are opposed under capitalism. He also believes that there is a causal link – though a mediated one – between material condition (class interest) on the one side and politics on the other. The validity of this claim depends upon the validity of two kinds of arguments: (1) the argument that establishes how capitalism affects the material condition of workers, and (2) the argument that material conditions determine class consciousness. In the remainder of this section we deal with the first argument. In the next section we deal with class consciousness.

The first of these two arguments has been the subject of extensive debate since Marx (for summaries see Sweezy, 1942). Marx clearly recognizes the crucial difficulty, although he does not deal with the way it undermines a core element of his political economy. This difficulty is the following: The economic growth process under capitalism takes place through the competition of capitals. In Marx's theory, competition operates on the price system. Capitalists seek to expand their markets at the expense of their competitors by reducing prices. This process tends to offset the tendency for profits to rise with increases in productivity. Under these circumstances, we can hardly avoid the conclusion that competition among capitalists, through its effect on prices, tends to assure that workers benefit from gains in productivity in the form of rising real wages.

Furthermore, rapid economic growth can assure maintenance of employment in the face of technical innovation. This follows from the fact that the primary determinant of employment is the rate of investment. Marx did not adequately take into account the way that expansion of capital and growth in the scale of production offset the effect of technical change on the demand for labor (see Levine, 1988b).

Sympathetic critics of Marx have investigated the relationship between investment, employment, and wages (see Steindl, 1952); they do not find compelling support for the conclusions Marx presents under his "General Law of Capitalist Accumulation" ([*Capital*, Vol. I, 1867], 1967a). Problems arise not only for those conclusions involving wages and employment, but also for the central argument concerning "leveling" of the working class. Historical studies of labor market segmentation (Edwards, Reich, and Gordon, 1973) and theoretical studies of uneven growth (Levine, 1986) suggest that capitalism differentiates the circumstances of workers as much as it tends to homogenize those circumstances. Forces work in both directions.

Clearly, the more the worker gains from the accumulation of capital, the less does the appropriation of profit by capitalists conflict with the interest of workers *so long as those profits are invested rather than consumed*. This last issue is precisely the one raised by Keynesians who argue that capitalist economic organization works in the general interest (understood here as the material interests of both workers and capitalists) so long as capitalists maintain a high level of investment.

Marxists have responded to the challenge to Marx's framework for political economy in three ways. Some Marxists attempt to sustain or ressurect Marx's argument, denying the facts and arguments just cited. Other Marxists have sought to recast Marx's argument in a way that takes seriously its weaknesses and yet allows for certain of its important claims to be supported. A third approach redefines the unit of analysis as the global system. This third approach focuses on the ways in which important groups of workers have been excluded from the benefits of capital accumulation. Here, we restrict ourselves to a brief summary of the second approach.

As we observed, capitalism benefits the workers so long as capitalists maintain a high level of investment. It follows that should they fail to invest adequately, they undermine the interest of workers in supporting a social order dedicated to private profit making. Economists working in the Marxian tradition have argued that as capitalist economies mature, the incentives for capitalists to act in a way that sustains growth of the system diminish (Steindl,

1952; Kalecki, 1965; Baran and Sweezy, 1966). It turns out that this is due to a weakening of competitive forces. As Marx himself points out, competition tends to be self-limiting when its effect is to drive the weaker producers out of business. As competition weakens, the process that translates productivity gains into rising wages also weakens. But this means that effective demand does not expand at a pace adequate to maintain investment. Put somewhat loosely, a failure to stimulate market growth results from a failure to enhance real wages. With stagnant markets, investment falls off. The result is economic stagnation. Under these circumstances, capitalist economic organization serves nobody's interests.

When the economy stagnates, capitalists make little profit and accumulate little capital. Productivity stagnates. Wages do not improve and workers suffer from high levels of unemployment. This situation characterizes an economic crisis of the system. Since Marx, reference to economic crisis has provided the linchpin in arguments by Marxists for the development of a political challenge to capitalism. This approach conforms to Marx's method, which connects political consciousness to economic conditions. But, how exactly does this connection operate? The discovery of a compelling answer to this question provides Marxian political economy with one of its great challenges. With regard to this link between politics and economics, the distinguished French Marxist Charles Bettelheim observes:

[T]his – it must be acknowledged – *is not really developed*. In effect, even if what Marx writes on this really corresponds to the laws of capital's movement, nothing proves that the operation of these laws will ideologically and politically strengthen the proletariat, pushing this class in a "necessary fashion" to rise up against the bourgeoisie, to impose itself as the dominant class, and to make use of its dictatorship to establish a classless society. Marx's "economic" arguments are incapable of providing the demonstration of such an historical tendency of class struggle. (1985:17, italics in original)

This "historical tendency of class struggle" presumes that individuals and classes articulate, commit themselves to, and pursue a broader (class or political) interest. It also presumes that this broader interest, while rooted in economic relations, rises above material interest to counterpose conceptions of the common good or well-ordered society only one of which (that of the capitalist class) is consistent with capitalist economic organization.

While these broader interests may have material roots in the narrower interests discussed previously, they must not be equated with them. Since these broader interests are inherently political in nature and since they derive from the circumstances of classes within the system of economic relations of capitalism, they constitute a vital part of Marxian political economy. We will therefore consider them in somewhat greater detail.

Economic interest and class consciousness

In Marxian theory, classes refer to categories of persons who have similar positions in the production process. As such, classes have an objective (observable, verifiable) existence apart from the subjective awareness of the agents involved. But classes in this sense have little political significance. If workers or capitalists are not aware that they share certain interests that are opposed to others, they can hardly translate these interests into a political agenda. This is not to say that class is unimportant until it is recognized. The economic consequences of class processes may be significant. Direct producers may produce their own subsistence and surplus value. That value may be appropriated and used for investment or capitalist consumption, and so on. Nevertheless, the political significance of class awaits shared awareness and organization.

In this section, we consider the awareness of class interests within capitalism under three headings: (a) the nature of class consciousness and its relationship to economic interest, (b) the nature of class consciousness as it applies to workers, and (c) the nature of the political interest of capitalists.

Class consciousness

In order to arrive at a notion of class consciousness appropriate to the development of a political agenda, the Marxian approach requires the fulfillment of two conditions. First, the individual must come to see his private and particular circumstances in a broader light, understanding their connection to the circumstances of other members of his class. Second, the class thus constituted must translate its narrow economic interest into a political agenda, and this means that the interests of the class must take on the characteristics of an interest appropriate to society as a whole.

The first step toward class consciousness is the one linking a typical position in the relations of production to an individual's thought concerning that position. Thus, class consciousness is an ideal and thus abstract construct deduced from an objective condition. In a sense, the definition of class consciousness requires us to undertake analytical or theoretical work. This theoretical work links political with economic life. Out of the analysis of the objective reality and meaning of the material life of a class emerges its political consciousness. But how is this analysis itself undertaken? What forces bring about the needed abstraction as an historical event? How do individuals develop class consciousness to complement their private interests?

In answering these questions, the Marxian theory proceeds along two dimensions. First, it uncovers those characteristics of the (objective) economic condition of the class that provide the content of its political consciousness.

Second, it specifies a political agent for articulating the implied (or imputed) consciousness. This political agent translates and transforms material conditions into a political agenda. For the workers, the appropriate agent is argued to be the party, for the capitalists the state.

The working class

Two characteristics of the economic condition of workers are essential in providing the basis for the development of class consciousness: deprivation and collectivization. We consider each briefly.

In a subsequent section we outline the dynamics of the capitalist economy as Marx conceived them and indicate how he deduces a tendency toward the leveling of workers toward the standard of living defined by their subsistence. This economic analysis substantiated for Marx an insight at which he had arrived prior to his work in economics. The insight is not, in fact, original to Marx but can be found in one form or another in works of Adam Smith and G. W. F. Hegel with which he was certainly familiar. Shlomo Avineri summarizes Marx's contention regarding the implication of deprivation for class consciousness (1969:59–61). Avineri's quotations from Marx's early works provide a flavor of and the elements of Marx's argument:

A class must be formed which has *radical chains*, a class in civil society which is not of civil society, a class which is the dissolution of all classes, a sphere of society which has a universal character because its sufferings are universal, and which does not claim a *particular redress* because the wrong which is done to it is not a *particular wrong* but *wrong in general*. (p. 59, italics in Avineri's quotation)

For Marx, the working class is, indeed, "in civil society but not of civil society." Civil society creates, recreates, and extends the scale of the working class but never allows the working class access to its benefits. This "wrong" to the working class is its deprivation not simply of material goods but of the kind and level of civilization represented by those goods, which Marx also considers the products of the worker's labor. "Wrong in general" thus refers to exclusion from the civil life that your own work makes possible. This deprivation of the working class endows it, according to Marx, with the attributes of a "universal class," whose "suffering and dehumanization" are, according to Marx, "a paradigm for the human condition at large" (Avineri, 1969:52).

Whether correct or incorrect, the argument that attempts to root political consciousness in deprivation suffers from a crucial limitation. Deprivation is essentially negative. We may oppose something from which we are excluded (though this is not inevitable), but, for political consciousness, it is not enough simply to oppose civil society, it is also necessary to counterpose something to it. The universality of the working class has a positive side as expressed implicitly by Marx in the following statement:

For each new class which puts itself in the place of one ruling before it, is compelled, merely in order to carry through its aims, to represent its interest as the common interest of all the members of society, that is, expressed in ideal form: it has to give its ideas the form of universality. . . . The class making a revolution appears from the very start . . . not as a class but as the representative of the whole society. (From the *German Ideology*, quoted in Avineri, 1969:58–9)

The universal class must have real, positive interests, and this positive side, as much as the negative, must have its roots in the material (economic) conditions of the class. Workers must see in the circumstances of their exclusion from civil society the germ of a social order different from the one (capitalism) that creates them. This social order must not only overcome the circumstances of their exclusion, it must do so in a positive and universal way. What concerning the objective condition of workers under capitalism nurtures in them receptivity to a broader understanding of their interests?

Marx's answer to this centers on the collective nature of labor under capitalism (1967a:ch. 12). Capitalism brings about the development of

the cooperative form of the labour-process, the conscious technical application of science, the methodical cultivation of the soil, the transformation of the instruments of labour into instruments of labour only usable in common, the economising of all means of production by their use of the means of production of combined, socialised labour, the entanglement of all peoples in the net of the world market, and with this, the international character of the capitalist regime. (From *Capital*, Vol. I, quoted in Avineri, 1969:172)

Statements such as this suggest that economic development affects more than workers' income and employment. Of greatest importance, Marx contrasts the isolated and specialized character of what he calls handicraft labor with the collective, rationalized, and universal character of labor under capitalism (for a more detailed discussion, see Levine, 1978:ch. 7). Not only do workers work together but the nature of their work creates a bond between workers in different industries. Workers lose those specialized skills that set up qualitative barriers between those working in different crafts. Now all workers *labor* no matter what their product. In this sense, capitalist development makes the objective condition of the worker universal and places him into a collective rather than individualized work process and environment. All that remains is for the worker to recognize the implication of his own conditions.

The capitalist class

The economic condition of capitalists is one of opposed private interest and individualized circumstances. Within the economy, the interests of capitalists in amassing private wealth set them into competition with one another. What, within these circumstances, could define a political consciousness appropriate to a class? The Marxian answer has to do with the destructive implications of individual self-seeking for social order.

In some respects the Marxian argument parallels the neoclassical argument for economic policy based on the idea of externalities (see Chapter 4 of this book). Private decisions often (perhaps always) have consequences beyond those taken into account by the parties directly involved. Sometimes those consequences can, in the large, be destructive for social order and individual well-being. In some cases those consequences may threaten the social order of a market economy and therefore the ability of individual capitalists to pursue private accumulations of capital.

In the previous section of this chapter, we encountered an example. When individual capitalists (or firms) decide that prospects for profit making are not satisfactory, they refrain from investing in new capacity. This means that they reduce their demand for labor and for capital, and this leads to a fall in wages and revenues for the producers of capital equipment. Falling wages mean falling demand for consumption goods, which, together with declining demand for capital goods, imply falling aggregate demand. This means a deterioration in the profit of firms producing those goods, which further discourages investment. In cases such as this, the pursuit of private interest by capitalists becomes self-defeating; it threatens the viability of the economic system as a whole.

A second, and related, example has to do with the condition of the working class. The individual capitalist benefits by lower wages because he experiences wages as a cost. Yet, as we have seen, by working against wage increases, the capitalist deprives the worker of purchasing power in the capitalist system. Furthermore, for the class of capitalists, wages are a primary source of demand for their products, and this means that capitalists as a class may benefit from higher wages (since this provides workers with a stake in capitalism and maintains aggregate demand) even though the individual capitalist taking a purely private view does not see things that way.

Each capitalist has two kinds of interest: an interest in his wealth position (and in the prospects for enhancing it) and an interest in the security of the social system that allows pursuit of private accumulations of wealth. The first implies the second, but it may also work against the second. The first interest is purely private; capitalists do not share it, they compete over it. The second interest is held in common. It secures the basis upon which capitalists can articulate a political interest.

Clearly, and by definition, the capitalist class has a stake in the preservation of capitalism as the only system within which it can exist. The capitalist economy is, after all, designed with the capitalists in mind. Claims for universality of the broader interests of the capitalist class arise not out of the commonality of situation of each capitalist with every other member of the class but on the universality of its aspirations.

Many have argued that the pursuit of private accumulations of wealth constitutes a universal aspiration of men and that since capitalism frees this aspiration (and nurtures it) it is the only truly universal system and its universality is best represented by the capitalists. The inevitability of conflict between the pursuit of private interest and the securing of the aggregate conditions needed for pursuit of private interest casts the problem of the relation between narrow material interests and the broader class interests of capitalists in a different light. It suggests that narrow material interests do not directly and smoothly translate into broader political agendas. Indeed, this translation now seems both complex and problematic. Marxian analysis of the state speaks to this issue. Particularly important is the Marxian analysis of the autonomy of the state in relation to what we have termed the narrower material interests of the capitalists.

Summary

The issues raised by the Marxian approach to class consciousness and political interest refer us to basic features of Marx's method. This method directs our attention to the circumstances of persons in (civil) society and finds in those circumstances both the logical and the historical origin for their political agendas. In one respect this method differs little from the utilitarian since both root politics in civil society. Unlike the utilitarians, however, Marxists retain the idea of universal interest and make claims regarding the universality or lack thereof of the interests emerging within the private sphere. Because of this, Marxism confronts issues not well defined within the utilitarian theories.

Marxism concerns itself with the ways in which the circumstances of persons within the private sphere form and determine their consciousness, and how the development of society determines the private circumstances and their associated ways of life and ways of thinking. As theory, Marxism concerns itself with the clash between differing conceptions of the well-ordered society. It sees the struggle between capital and labor as a struggle between fundamentally opposed judgments concerning what is, indeed, universal to the aspirations of persons. Does capitalism express the fundamental human aspiration to individual self-aggrandizement and pursuit of wealth? In this sense does capitalism accord with the general interests of society as well as the narrow interests of capitalists? Or, does the material situation of workers imbue them with a communal and egalitarian ethic more in line with the universal interests of persons?

Bear in mind, as we pursue the Marxian approach, the underlying methodological judgment concerning where we look for the source of universal interests – in civil society and not in politics or in the state. As one Marxist expresses it, civil society is the "real home, the theatre of history" (Bobbio, 1979:31). Politics provides a space for the confrontation of concerns emerging elsewhere. This raises a problem: How can interests emergent within an explicitly private sphere (the economy), a sphere within which individuals are encouraged and required to focus on and act on their private interests, become universal? Clearly, a tension exists between the fractioning of interest demanded within the economy – where workers oppose not only capitalists but also one another, and the constitution of the interested parties as persons sharing a goal.

One way in which Marx resolves this tension is by recourse to his argument concerning polarization. If this argument holds, then the tendency of capitalism is to relegate larger and larger proportions of the population to a common circumstance within civil society – the circumstance of those with nothing to sell but their labor power. If, as Marx also argues, the development of capitalism reduces and eliminates differences (of skill and so on) among workers, making them into a more and more homogeneous mass, then differences that tend to particularize workers and oppose their private conditions and private interests become less and less important. The working class becomes universal in two senses. First the working class becomes the class of the vast bulk of the population. Second, the circumstances within the working class become progressively more homogeneous.

Within the Marxian method, politics makes the implicit universality of private circumstances explicit. Economics takes the active role. This theorem underpins the Marxian theory of the state and also defines the important challenges to that theory. The state does not take an active role in forming society and determining the social structure that creates private interest. It incorporates a process for making the universal aspect of private interest explicit.

Economic interest and politics

Up to this point, we have focused on the formation of conscious classes, classes aware of their position in an objective structure of production. The existence of classes that are aware of their collective condition is seen as a prerequisite to political action, thus to political economy.

In this section we consider three ways in which political economy can be discussed in the Marxian tradition: revolutionary politics, the politics of class compromise, or social democratic politics, and Marxian state theory. Each of these foci identifies a distinctive way in which politics and economics come together in Marxian theory.

Marxism and revolutionary politics

Marxian theory is well known for its theory of revolutionary politics. The theoretical basis for this work is set out by Marx and Friedrich Engels in *The Communist Manifesto* (1848) and by Marx in *Capital* (1867). In these texts, Marx identified the conditions immanent in capitalism that would lead to a revolutionary consciousness among workers and lay the foundation for revolutionary actions that entail seizing and destroying state power.

In developing his theory, Marx attempted to explain revolution by reference to the laws of motion of capitalism *per se*, independently of the particular histories, class situations, and political institutions of different countries. Starting from the same point – the analysis of market capitalism – Marx differed profoundly from the classical economists in his assessment of the durability and self-organizing character of capitalism. Not only were capitalist markets not self-organizing, they contained the very forces that would eventually bring about their demise. These forces were identified and developed in "The General Law of Capitalist Accumulation" ([*Capital*, Vol. I, 1867], 1967a). The same forces that propelled capitalist development also prepared the way for labor's revolutionary potential.

According to Marx, capitalist development involves the production of commodities (goods exchanged on markets) whose value is enough to reproduce labor and capital in their original state (simple reproduction) and then some. The additional amount is surplus, which can be used in a number of ways, including additional investment in productive capital, that is, accumulation. In addition to the expansion of capital, absolutely and relative to labor, capital also becomes more concentrated; that is, it resides in fewer and fewer economic units of a larger size. Marx summarizes the process this way:

> The cheapness of commodities depends, *ceteris paribus*, on the productiveness of labor, and this again on the scale of production. Therefore, the larger capitals beat the smaller. It will further be remembered that, with the development of the capitalist mode of production, there is an increase in the minimum amount of individual capital necessary to carry on a business under normal conditions. The smaller capitals, therefore, crowd into spheres of production which modern industry has only sporadically or incompletely got hold of. . . . It always ends in the ruin of many small capitalists, whose capitals partly pass into the hands of their conquerors, partly vanish. (Marx, [1867], reprinted in Beer, 1955:76–7)

If the long-term tendency is for capital to increase, the consequences for labor are important. As capital advances, it displaces more and more workers, creating an "industrial reserve army" of labor. This reserve army continually bids down the wages of workers, since there are many willing to work for less wages than those employed. And, as capital becomes more concentrated, workers are drawn closer together in large factories and urban areas. This leads to a better collective understanding of their class situation and makes it easier to organize politically. We explore these points below.

According to Marx, the capitalist's effort to increase his profit has additional and significant harmful effects on the ability of workers to satisfy their material interests. In order to raise profit, capitalists work to raise the productivity of labor. But, in order to do so they introduce more mechanized methods of production, which replace workers with machinery. According to Marx (1967a:394–446), the introduction of machinery intensifies the worker's labor, adversely affects his working conditions, and increases unemployment. As Marx puts it, "it is capitalistic accumulation itself that constantly produces, and produces in the direct ratio of its own energy and extent, a relatively redundant population of laborers" (p. 630). This leads Marx to conclude that capitalist development implies the "immiseration" of the worker and the polarization of the material conditions of the two classes:

The greater the social wealth, the functioning capital, the extent and energy of its growth, and, therefore, also the absolute mass of the proletariat and the productiveness of its labor, the greater is the industrial reserve army. The same causes which develop the expansive power of capital, develop also the labour-power at its disposal. The relative mass of the industrial reserve army increases therefore with the potential energy of wealth. But the greater this reserve army in proportion to the active labour-army, the greater is the mass of a consolidated surplus-population, whose misery is in inverse ratio to its torment of labour. The more extensive, finally, the lazarus-layers of the working class, and the industrial reserve army, the greater is official pauperism. *This is the absolute general law of capitalist accumulation.* (p. 644, italics in the original)

Marx goes on to claim that this "law" "establishes an accumulation of misery, corresponding with accumulation of capital. Accumulation of wealth at one pole is, therefore, at the same time accumulation of misery, agony of toil, slavery, ignorance, brutality, mental degradation, at the opposite pole" (p. 645).

The accumulation of capital also affects the differences among workers. Capitalist development tends to have a "leveling" effect (Bettelheim, 1985:25) on the working class, throwing them more and more into a common material-economic condition. The less differentiated the material conditions of workers, the less hope individual workers have of bettering their *particular* conditions, the less opposed the material interests of workers one to another. The polarization of labor and capital means that the level toward which this more and more uniform condition gravitates implies that workers, individually and as a group, have no stake in capitalism. The development of the material conditions of individuals under capitalism implies a political response:

Along with the constantly diminishing number of the magnates of capital, who usurp and monopolize all advantages of this process of transformation, grows the mass of misery, oppression, slavery, degradation, exploitation; but with this too grows the revolt of the working-class, a class always increasing in numbers, and disciplined, united, organized by the very mechanism of the process of capitalist production itself. (Marx, 1967a:763)

To summarize, Marx's theory of revolutionary politics provides an account based on capitalism's internal laws – that is, laws that flow from the nature of capitalist economy itself. This account includes an explanation of why capital expands, how it concentrates in certain industries and firms, and how it displaces workers. On labor's side, Marx explains unemployment, low wages, the doing away with differences among particular labors, and the coming together in cities and factories and the development of revolutionary consciousness.

Marxian economic theory provides at least an explanation of the revolutionary situation, if not the specific politics of revolutionary activity. Some "analytic Marxists" (or rational choice Marxists) see a collective action problem in the revolutionary situation. They do not necessarily disagree with Marx's explanation of why capitalism (that is, workers in the capitalist economy) is ripe for revolt. They simply argue that this is not enough to explain why some revolutions occur and others don't.

It is better for an individual worker not to participate in revolutionary activity while others do. The individual then free rides on the collective benefit, presuming there is one. It is true that revolutions are not spontaneous and that situations characterized by widespread grievances do not necessarily erupt into revolutionary violence. The debate over which model of revolutionary behavior to apply includes both individual rational choice models and models that rely on group identification and solidarity (see Booth, 1978; Roemer, 1978; Taylor, 1988). Marx's main contribution is not in the area of the proximal causes of revolution, or the immediate factors facilitating (or obstructing) political organization. Instead, Marx tried to show how the conditions for revolution – polarized classes, concentration of capital, unemployed and low-paid workers – were endogenous to capitalist development.

Marxism and social democratic politics

To many who subscribe to Marx's analysis of the laws of motion of capitalist economy, violent revolution is the inevitable outcome. Classes are irreconcilably opposed to one another and capitalist development "merely" accents these differences and renders them visible. To others, even some who subscribe to Marx's theory of capitalist development, revolution is not the only possible outcome. Improvement of the workers' lot could take place through social democratic methods. This strategy involves worker participation in interest groups, parties, and electoral-legislative processes. The goal is to alter the position of labor and capital from within, by using established institutions and practices of political democracy.

Social democracy differs from revolutionary politics in that it attempts to achieve its goals by peaceful rather than violent means and from within (in established "bourgeois" institutions) rather than without. The social democratic route does not provide an unequivocal answer to the issue of whether private property is to be supplanted by socialism through democratic means or whether the purpose of participation is simply to reform the system, to "use" it to extract a larger share of the benefits capitalism creates.

It is noteworthy that during the latter half of the nineteenth century and first part of the twentieth, many socialists believed their advent to power followed logically from the development of capitalism: The growth of capital and its technical sophistication assured that more workers would be thrown out of work than would be hired to tend new machinery. In other words, proletarianization was proceeding apace. As Przeworski puts it:

Those who led socialist parties into electoral battles believed that dominant classes can be "beaten at their own game." Socialists were deeply persuaded that they would obtain for socialism the support of an overwhelming numerical majority. They put all of their hopes and their efforts into electoral competition because they were certain that electoral victory was within reach. Their strength was in numbers, and elections are an expression of electoral strength. Hence, universal suffrage seemed to guarantee socialist victory, if not immediately, then certainly within the near future. (1985a:16– 17)

While many socialists continued to believe in the inevitability of revolutionary change, others experimented with a different brand of social democracy, one where workers permanently accepted capitalism as the framework for economic action and confined their struggles to improvements within this system. The emphasis in this reformist strand of social democracy is on class action – in the workplace and electoral arenas – to garner a larger share of the product consistent with a large economic pie. Benefits pursued could include higher wages, job security, pensions, control of work, and so on.

In sum, social democracy avoids many difficult questions associated with violent revolutionary change, such as what happens *après la révolution*. It also avoids problems inherent in radical redistributionist strategies, particularly the accumulation (investment) crises that such uses of the surplus foster (Weisskopf, Bowles, and Gordon, 1985). Workers may gain in the short run only to see the size of the economic pie dwindle in the long run. And one can question whether such strategies are available to labor in an increasingly open and competitive world economy, where, if workers in one country take a larger share, they will lose out to more abstemious rivals.

The main idea of the reformist social democratic approach is to foster the material interest of workers within the framework of capitalism and liberal democracy. Its attempt is to "tame" capitalism, to make it beneficial for more people, not just a narrow capitalist class. The core belief is that the welfare of citizens (workers and capitalists) can be advanced "by gradually rationalizing the economy [so that] the state can turn capitalists into private functionaries of the public without altering the judicial status of private property" (Przeworski 1985a:40).

Marxian state theory

The third type of political economy we discuss centers on Marxian theories of the state. How does the state, considered as government or authority system, relate to the economy under capitalism? The Marxian interpretation of the state consists of a series of variations on a central theme: the necessity that social order (and cohesion) be maintained where the social conditions of persons set them into fundamental opposition. Classic statements of this theme appear in Friedrich Engels's *The Origin of the Family, Private Property and the State* ([n.d.] 1984) and in V. I. Lenin's *State and Revolution* (1932). Lenin sets out from the following formulation of Engels:

The state is . . . by no means a power imposed on society from the outside. . . . Rather, it is a product of society at a certain stage of development; it is the admission that this society has become entangled in an insoluble contradiction with itself, that it is cleft into irreconcilable contradictions which it is powerless to dispel. But in order that these antagonisms, classes with conflicting economic interests, may not consume themselves and society in sterile struggle, a power apparently standing above society becomes necessary, whose purpose is to moderate the conflict and keep it within the bounds of "order"; and this power arising out of society, but placing itself above it, and increasingly separating itself from it, is the state. (Quoted in Lenin, 1932:8)

We must bear in mind that the "order" that the state preserves, protects and corresponds to the interests of one class and thus denies and leaves vulnerable the interests of the other. By protecting a particular kind of order the state works for one class and against the other.

According to Marx, the state is an organ of class *domination*, an organ of *oppression* of one class by another; its aim is the creation of "order" which legalizes and perpetuates this oppression by moderating the collisions between classes. (Lenin, 1932:9)

To summarize:

1. Irreconcilable conflict exists between the economic interests of classes. This conflict arises within society and is based upon its defined social positions.
2. This irreconcilable conflict threatens social order.
3. Social order means a social organization designed (so to speak) to work to satisfy the economic interests of one class and not the other.

4. Given irreconcilable conflict and the oppressive character of the social order, preservation of order is maintained against the interest of one class. Thus, the social order must oppress one of the two classes that compose it.
5. The state, or organ that maintains order, is an organ of class oppression.

A theory of the state that arrives at a conclusion such as this seems radically different from other theories of the state. Close examination indicates, however, that the key difference has less to do with the way in which the state acts and much more to do with a different understanding of society. The pluralist theory would clearly break down in the face of a polarization of interest groups such as that suggested in the Marxian theory. Indeed, the idea of a repressive state can hardly be avoided once we grant that society consists of groups whose fundamental interests cannot be reconciled. In the Marxian theory, a world in which pluralism applies needs no state, "the state could neither arise nor maintain itself if a reconciliation of classes were possible" (Lenin, 1932:9).

The Marxian formulation leads in the following direction. Objective divisions in society define the agenda for, and the reason for the existence of, the state. The state is an organ that acts forcefully against a part of society; it is not equivalent to "government"; it does not calculate, aggregate, or transmit preferences. But, while the state works in the interest of part of society (one social class), it does not do so directly, as would be implied for example by the idea of the state as an "instrument" of class rule. Instead, the state works to maintain a defined social order that favors one class over another (see Poulantzas, 1973:50–4). Within that order, satisfying their interests is something the members of the favored class do on their own (at least under normal conditions). In principle (though not necessarily in all cases) one class does not *use* the state to oppress the other even though the state is an organ of class oppression. This may seem unnecessarily convoluted, but it is important to understand the way in which the state goes about its business and the specific sense of class oppression the Marxian theory connects to it. As one Marxist puts it:

A given kind of relations of production may be reproduced without the exploiting (dominant) class defined by them being in "control" of the government in any usual and reasonable sense of the word, even though the interventions of the state further and/or allow these relations of production to be reproduced. And yet the fact that a specific form of exploitation and domination is being reproduced, *is* an example of class rule and is an important aspect of power in society. (Therborn [1970] 1982:233, italics in original)

If we follow this interpretation, we cannot treat the state as an instrument of class rule for a striking reason. The capitalist class, partly for reasons discussed in the previous section, lacks an adequate sense of its unified interest to act as a single agent capable of using an instrumentalized state. As Therborn puts it, the capitalist class "is not a unified power subject" (p. 244). The inability of the capitalist class to find its unified interest means that a state, autonomous from the standpoint of individual capitalists or groups of capitalists, must act for a class that cannot act for itself:

> The bourgeoisie's incapacity to raise itself to the strictly political level stems from its inability to achieve its own internal unity: it sinks into fractional struggles and is unable to realize its political unity on the basis of a politically conceived common interest. . . .
> What then is the role of the capitalist class state in this context? It can be stated as follows: it takes charge, as it were, of the bourgeoisie's political interests and realizes the function of political hegemony which the bourgeoisie is unable to achieve. But, *in order* to do this, the capitalist state assumes a relative autonomy with regard to the bourgeoisie. (Poulantzas, 1973:284–5)

While the capitalists exist, as we have seen, implicitly as a class within society – their social condition defines a common purpose – they do not succeed in coalescing into a unified political force. In a sense, the capitalist class exists as a politically conscious agent only in the form of the capitalist state, which, however, is relatively autonomous with regard to that class. This can make it difficult for us to find the capitalist class as such and raises questions about the sense in which the capitalist class can be said to exist. If the capitalist class cannot define its agenda and establish itself as an agent outside the state, the state cannot be its instrument and cannot act according to the dictates of its private interest. The capitalist class does not tell the state how to define its agenda, how to define the "order" that the state protects. This means that the state must define and ensure this order. And this means that the state defines the political interests of the capitalist class whose interests determine state action and policy.

The Marxian approach to political economy, as we have characterized it, attempts to deal creatively with the relationship between the state and the economy. On the one side, it insists that the ends of the state have their roots in class (and thus private) interests. This insistence sustains the idea that the state works to perpetuate a social order based upon the exploitation of one class by another and in this sense works in the interests of a particular class. This makes the economy dominant. At the same time, the Marxian approach maintains that the interest protected by the state is not that of any one capitalist (for example, in enhancing the profitability of his own enterprise), but that of the capitalist class, that this interest might not be recognized by the capitalists involved, and that its defense might even adversely affect the profitability of some individual capitalists. What the state does to defend the interest of the capitalist class might even affect adversely the material condition of capitalists and benefit workers. As Poulantzas puts it:

[The] state, by its very structure, gives to the economic interests of certain dominated classes guarantees which may even be contrary to the short-term economic interests of the dominant classes, but which are compatible with their political interests and their hegemonic domination. . . . this simply shows that the state is not a class in-strument, but rather the state of a society divided into classes. (1973:190–1; see also pp. 283, 301)

Understood in this way the class interest defended by the state is not, at least in the first instance, a material (or narrowly economic) interest. This means that when the state acts as agent of a class in this sense it represents the political rather than material interests of that class. We can, then, understand Marxian political economy in the following terms. The political institution or agent (in this case the state) defines and protects the political interests of a class and it does so on its own initiative, not as an "instrument." This means, more concretely, that the state defines and defends a social order including a set of "rules of the game" for the pursuit of private interest. Within these rules, the interests of the dominant class (for example, in private wealth accumulation) are protected in principle, though not necessarily in every case. Conversely, the system of private relations (the economy) per-petuates a definite set of objective social positions (classes), certain of which are favored by the prevailing rules of the game. The implicit interest of those in such positions is to perpetuate the rules of the game and, in this sense, the political interest defined and defended by the state can also be said to originate in society.

The relation between economy and state becomes complicated in this way for the following reason. It is in the nature of a privatized economy to focus the attention of agents on their private circumstances and to impede their development of an interest beyond the narrowly material. Thus, the economic life of the agent tends to deny him an adequate understanding of his own political interest (even though that political interest has economic roots). If this is the case, economic and political interests tend to repel each other, and social order will require a force working against this repulsion. Antonio Gramsci identifies this force in the "educative and formative role of the state" (1971:242).

According to Gramsci, the aim of the state is always that of creating new and higher types of civilization; of adapting the "civilization" and the morality of the broadest popular masses to the necessities of the continuous devel-opment of the economic apparatus of production, hence of evolving even physically new types of humanity (1971:242: see also pp. 246–7). And, fur-ther on:

In my opinion, the most reasonable and concrete thing that can be said about the ethical State is this: every State is ethical in as much as one of its most important functions is to raise the great mass of the population to a particular cultural and moral level, a level (or type) which corresponds to the needs of the productive forces for development, and hence to the interests of the ruling class. (pp. 258–9)

According to Marx, the state is part of the superstructure, the political shell of capitalism that is ultimately responsive to economic forces. Contemporary Marxian theory, particularly structural Marxism (see Carnoy, 1984:ch. 4), makes the relation between the state and the capitalist class a more complicated matter. A key idea of structural Marxism is that the state may act "on behalf of" the capitalist class even if not necessarily "at its behest." By so doing, structural Marxism severs the tie between an agent-oriented view (at least one based on acting out preferences) and the interests of capitalists, or more broadly, capitalism.

Still, how one accounts for the existence of politicians motivated to preserve and enhance capitalism while (many) capitalists are not is a troubling issue. Nevertheless, we argue that this paradox can tell us something. Perhaps part of the paradox emerges as a result of a conflict between the short-term and long-term interests of capital, between individual capitalists and capitalists as a class, or between proximal interests of capitalists (profits, market shares) and systemic interests (property rights, competitive environment). Structural and analytical Marxists are working on these issues, if in very different ways.

4

Neoclassical political economy

The time since the publication of Adam Smith's *Inquiry into the Nature and Causes of the Wealth of Nations* in 1776 to the present day spans over two hundred years. Although there are important elements of continuity from Smith to the present world, neoclassical economics is not just a modern, updated version of classical political economy. The beginnings of the neoclassical system are placed in the 1870s with the rise of marginalist economics. Before the 1870s economics as a system of thought was dominated by the classical agenda: growth, distribution, and the labor theory of value. After the 1870s, this agenda changed in important ways, although it did not change overnight.

To simplify a complex chapter in this history of economic thought, the marginalist revolution succeeded in doing two things. First, it advanced a theory of value grounded in the intensity of subjective feelings (subjective utility theory). And second, it developed the marginal calculus as a powerful conceptual and methodological tool. The upshot of these two developments was that, over the span of the next three to four decades, the emerging neoclassical consensus succeeded in replacing the labor theory of value with one grounded in subjective utility and placed the ideas of "marginal product" and "final demand" at the center while elbowing into the wings the concepts of total product and total demand. With these new ideas gathering momentum as they spread during the last quarter of the nineteenth century, the economy came to be thought of less in terms of material production and reproduction and more as a logic of human action.

The structure of the neoclassical theory

Central to neoclassical thinking is the notion of "constrained choice." In this perspective, the individual is understood as a choosing agent, someone who decides among alternative courses of action according to how he imagines those actions will affect him. Economists educated in the neoclassical tradition assume that we are all motivated to seek the highest level of satisfaction of our wants, thus the highest degree of happiness we can achieve given the resources available to us.

The idea of human motivation translates into a definite theory of human action. Individuals judge what to do according to how it will affect their levels of satisfaction. How to spend one's time, what to buy in the store, whom to marry, and so on, all depend on a judgment regarding the likely impact of choices on levels of satisfaction.

In order to choose we must compare the satisfaction of various alternatives. This comparison results in a ranking of the options according to the level of satisfaction or happiness each might provide. This ranking is termed a "preference ordering." We place each option in rank order according to our preferences and attempt to attain that option highest in the ranking of our preferences or desires.

The term "rational choice" refers to decision making based on an internally consistent ordering. A preference ordering is consistent if a preference for any item A over another item B joined to preference for B over C implies preference for A over C. Rational choice seeks the highest feasible level of subjective satisfaction for the individual. By making rational choices that follow our preferences, we *ipso facto* maximize our welfare. Rational choice means maximizing behavior.

A complication arises when we look more closely at the underlying necessity of choice. What about their circumstances requires agents to choose? Choice between options may mean deciding which among a set of mutually exclusive options we want and which we do not. Such a choice faces an individual when he or she decides, for example, which school to attend or which candidate to vote for. Alternatively, choice between options may mean deciding which among a set of desired options we want more (or most) when we would like to consume the entire set but, for some reason, cannot. Such a choice faces us, for example, when we would like to have a video recorder and a microwave oven but have money enough for only one. In the latter case, our welfare would be maximized if we make the "right" choice. The difference between the two cases has to do first with the presence (in the second case) and absence (in the first case) of mutually exclusive alternatives, and second with the presence and relevance of an additional condition: scarcity.

The significance of the concept of rational choice depends on the ability of competing goods to satisfy (if to different degrees) the same desire. In order to assure that this condition holds, the neoclassical theories assume that acts of consumption of different goods all provide a common result: the satisfaction or utility of the consumer. Rational choice, interpreted in this way, requires a foundation in the utilitarian image of persons as agents seeking a single end – subjective satisfaction, utility, or happiness – through alternative means. While the measure of this satisfaction remains unique to each individual, so that we cannot compare or sum satisfactions experienced by different people, within each person the consumption of different goods yields a single result measured by a common unit (usually termed "utility").

Given the possibility of comparing the degree of satisfaction (for a particular agent) from different goods, choice also presupposes scarcity. When the naturally available means are inadequate to satisfy desires fully, they are considered scarce. Scarcity depends both on subjective conditions (desire) and natural (or objective) conditions (availability of resources).

Although scarcity is a necessary condition for choice, it is not sufficient. It may simply mean that even in consuming his entire endowment, the individual will remain unsatisfied. Scarcity forces the individual to choose when his endowment includes items with alternative uses. If, for example, the individual's labor can be used to acquire different means of consumption but is not sufficient to acquire all that the agent desires, the agent must allocate labor among tasks according to a decision-making principle. Within this context, scarcity requires choice among competing ends.

Thus far, we have treated choice on the basis of competing goods. But the ideas of choice and maximization can apply more broadly. Whenever we act in ways that affect our level of subjective satisfaction, we are choosing on the basis of maximization in the face of scarcity. In this sense we can interpret nearly all of life as the application of economic calculation, as economizing behavior. This result works against any effort, based on the neoclassical approach, to identify a distinctively economic subset of our lives and our social relations. It erases the distinction between the economy and the other spheres of social interaction.

The neoclassical approach begins with the idea of the maximization of individual satisfaction. The next step is to use this idea to define conditions for maximization of the welfare of an interconnected system of individuals. Welfare for the group must be defined differently from (although on the basis of) the welfare of the individual alone. Maximum group welfare results from maximization of welfare on the part of each member separately only when the welfare of each is entirely independent. Group welfare takes on meaning when either of two conditions is met. First, acts of consumption affect individuals other than those who have chosen to engage in them. Second, other persons provide opportunities for mutual enhancement of welfare through exchange.

The first condition requires that the activity by which an individual experiences utility (consumption) affects other individuals either positively (that is, when my act of consumption yields an unintended benefit to someone else) or negatively (when my well-being is enhanced by an experience that harms others). Neoclassical theory terms these effects on others "externalities." When such externalities (or social consequences of private want satisfaction) exist, the welfare of the group cannot equal the sum of the welfare achieved by each individual on the assumption that satisfaction-yielding experiences are separable.

Even where externalities do not exist, the problem of defining group welfare arises when each member can (potentially) improve his or her level of satisfaction by acquiring goods owned by others. In this case, we need a definition of group welfare that takes into account the possibility that voluntary transactions between members can enhance their well-being. What constitutes the maximum welfare of the group subject to the condition that each pursues his private ends and that interaction takes the form of voluntary transactions?

Consider the case of a group composed of two individuals. Each has his own preference ordering and endowment of goods for satisfying his desires. Consumption of his endowment will yield a given level of satisfaction. Assume, however, that if we treat the endowments as a single pool of goods, there exists a distribution of those goods different from the one represented by the initial allocation that would improve the well-being of each and can be thought to maximize the joint or group welfare of the two taken together.

The implied notion of group welfare carries the same meaning as the notion of voluntary transaction based on individual rational choice. Such transactions must be welfare-improving or they would not take place. Given appropriate information, the desire to maximize their individual satisfaction will drive the parties to exchange elements of their endowments. In this sense, and under these conditions, the institution of voluntary transaction based on respect for property right (exchange) leads to an improvement in the welfare of the contractors taken as a group.

Since the conditions specified determine an appropriate exchange of goods between property owners, they must fix the prices at which goods exchange. If a redistribution of x units of good A held by the first individual for y units of good B held by the second improves the welfare of both, a price of good B equal to x/y of good A allows for a welfare-improving transaction.[1]

In a "perfect" market characterized by a very large number of participants there will, under appropriate conditions, be a unique price for each good

---

[1] This may not be the only price that improves the welfare of both parties. In general, two-party, two-good exchange does not yield a unique price in this sense. Increasing the number of parties will reduce the range of indeterminacy.

that allows all welfare-improving transactions to take place. Such a price arises out of independent and voluntary actions of the individuals pursuing maximization of private satisfaction. If prices are flexible in the sense that parties are free to pursue transactions at whatever rates they deem mutually beneficial, they will, under appropriate assumptions, tend to settle at levels that allow for all welfare-improving transactions. Under these assumptions, free market processes yield an optimum of social welfare.[2] Economists term this type of group welfare the Pareto optimum after its discoverer, Vilfredo Pareto.

Clearly, criteria other than Pareto optimality could be used in the effort to evaluate alternative allocations of the wealth held by the members of a group. The attractiveness of the Pareto criterion stems from its loyalty to the preferences of individuals *taken by themselves*. That is, it does not require us to impose any preferences on the group as a whole other than those already given in the orderings of its members, no one of which is given precedence over the others. Thus, the attractiveness of the Pareto condition depends on the attractiveness of the premise that social outcomes should derive from the subjective preferences of individuals.

Acceptance of the Pareto criterion has significant implications for the judgments we make concerning when to use markets to determine patterns of group consumption. Because of the link between free markets and optimization, acceptance of the Pareto criterion for determining the allocation of resources appropriate to a group of persons constitutes a powerful argument for the use of markets to determine production and distribution. The strength of this argument depends both on the validity of the theorem linking markets to welfare[3] and on our acceptance or rejection of its assumptions. The following assumptions are especially important: (1) that markets are, or can be, perfectly competitive, (2) that social welfare should be defined on the basis of individual preferences, and (3) that the idea of given initial endowments provides a satisfactory basis for making welfare judgments.

On a practical level, the neoclassical approach links welfare with choice. The greater the range of choice, the greater the feasible level of social welfare, all other things equal. Markets increase choice; nonmarket allocations inhibit choice. Consider a favorite example of the application of economic reasoning to economic policy:[4] gasoline rationing. The example involves resource allocation in the face of a shortfall in supply of gasoline relative to existing and

---

[2] The theorem linking competitive markets with optimality is a centerpiece of General Equilibrium Theory; see Koopmans (1957:ch. 10).
[3] For a more comprehensive discussion of these assumptions see Koopmans (1957:ch. 10).
[4] This example is taken from Schelling (1984).

recent levels of consumption. In such cases, we can bring demand into line with supply simply by allowing price to rise until demand falls to the point at which it equals supply (assuming, of course, that demand and price are inversely related, which they may not be, especially in the short run). Alternatively, the government can bring demand into line with supply by fixing the price level and rationing consumption. The government can, for example, distribute rationing cards equal to supply and require that purchase of gasoline at its regulated price be limited by available rationing cards. The argument against rationing follows the contours of the argument linking choice to welfare, optimality to free markets.

Assume that the government fixes the price of gasoline at a level that stimulates more demand than can be met with the available supply. It does so, for example, in order to prevent hardship for low-income consumers resulting from a substantial increase in the price of a basic consumption good. In order to limit demand, the government distributes rationing cards according to some principle deemed equitable (that is, the same number of cards to all individuals owning cars, perhaps adjusted in various ways to particular circumstances).

Application of the kind of reasoning outlined immediately suggests that under these conditions welfare gains will result if individuals can buy and sell the rationing cards allocated to them. The existence of a market in rationing cards allows those who would prefer to consume less gasoline, if by so doing they will be able to consume more of other goods, to do so. Since each person remains free to hold his rationing cards and consume gasoline, the presence of a market brings together individuals in voluntary transactions aimed at improving the welfare of each without adversely affecting the well-being of others. The market provides a choice where none existed previously, without removing preexisting opportunities. Taken by itself, the result should be a higher level of satisfaction for those who exercise this choice without any necessary adverse effects on others.

The market for rationing cards sets a price for cards that in effect constitutes a part of the price of gasoline (equal to the sum of its regulated price and the market price of the rationing card). By allowing for a market in rationing cards, we have, in effect, facilitated establishment of a market price for gasoline. The sole remaining function for rationing cards is to redistribute income from the producers of gasoline (or alternatively from those who are taxed to subsidize gasoline producers).

Gasoline rationing combined with a market for rationing cards is now an indirect method of income redistribution. We can also apply the neoclassical method of reasoning to the determination of the price of labor (wage) so that a market determination of incomes also yields maximum choice and a welfare optimum.[5] Even if we refrain from taking this step, and deny the optimality of market outcomes for income distribution, correcting inequities through distribution of rationing cards must seem inefficient and even inappropriate given the more direct methods of redistribution available, for example, through the tax system.

The conclusion, with regard to product markets (if not labor markets also) is that the connection between markets and choice argues against government intervention. The issue of the limits of the market becomes that of the limits within which choice enhances well-being. To specify such limits, we need to consider principles (such as individual rights)[6] that take precedence over choice. We return to this issue in Chapter 9.

To sum up, neoclassical economics sees the market as the institution allowing maximum scope for free exchange and hence efficiency. The market allows one to reshuffle (use in alternative ways) resources and commodities so as to achieve their most desirable use. Viewed from the consumer's standpoint, there is a large number of bundles of consumer goods from which to choose. From the producer's position there is the possibility of combining productive factors in many different ways. Land, labor, and capital – all of which have important subcategories – can be mixed in different proportions to produce goods for sale on markets. This process of substitution will go on until societal resources have yielded maximum product for producers and maximum utility for consumers (Dasgupta, 1985:78–9).

Given the preceding description, it should be clear that, once the values of the exogenous variables (endowments, preferences, technology, and rules) are given, the results on the part of choosing agents can be known with precision. This prompts us to ask if neoclassical economics is an abstract logic of choice or a behavioral science that makes contingent (hence refutable) predictions about the activities of economic man in different situations. To the extent that rationality and maximizing behavior are axiomatic and preferences are derived *ex post* from the explained behavior, actions of economic agents are assumed to reflect just what these preferences are as well as the constraints that must have existed to prevent them from achieving more. To the extent that rationality is treated as a hypothesis about economic agents, an independent specification of preferences and a full account of constraints (the information available to agents, limits on calculating ability) is needed *ex ante*. If information on these factors is present, it is possible to treat

---

[5] The neoclassical theory of distribution applied to the labor market can be interpreted to imply that the price of labor (wage) set by supply and demand reflects choices and achieves a socially desirable outcome; see Friedman ([1962] 1982:ch. 10).

[6] For a discussion see Singer (1978).

outcomes as tests of refutable hypotheses about rationality, self-interest, and maximizing behavior.

Political economy in the neoclassical approach

How is the relation between economics and politics conceived in the neo-classical framework? Economics is the process by which we seek to maximize the satisfaction of our wants given the means available (and usually their distribution among us). This process underlies the workings both of markets and of political institutions. Whether we engage in private contract or collective action, our objective is to satisfy wants to the greatest degree possible. Thus, the ends of political and market action do not differ. Economizing underlies both.

In the first instance, the market consists of a system of voluntary transactions between independent property owners pursuing their self-interest. To the neoclassical thinker, these transactions take place when they are deemed welfare-improving for both parties. When contracts are in fact voluntary, when no impediments exist to welfare-improving transactions, and when the consequences of those transactions affect only the contracting parties, market interaction should allow individuals to exploit fully opportunities to increase their level of satisfaction.

This observation regarding the neoclassical way of setting up the problem leads naturally to two sets of political agendas. The first involves securing the system of property rights so that transactions are in fact voluntary. This means establishing and enforcing a set of property rights designed to support the stated objectives of the neoclassical ideal of individual well-being. The second involves circumstances in which parties other than those contracting are affected by transactions or in which potentially welfare-improving transactions cannot be undertaken for reasons other than limitations on property rights.

Neoclassical political economy applies the basic economic logic of constrained choice to circumstances in which private transactions fail to maximize welfare. The term economic is used here in two of our senses. Most fundamentally, economic means economizing or constrained choice; it applies to politics and markets. Second, economic refers to markets as one method for achieving an improvement in individual want satisfaction. Politics is another. Thus political economy sometimes refers us to the study of the limits of the market as an institution for want satisfaction and sometimes to an economic theory of politics. In this chapter, we explore the first sense of political economy.

This idea of political economy is, for reasons suggested above, synonymous with that of market failure. It points us toward circumstances in which the market falls short of enabling individuals to achieve the highest level of want satisfaction available given their endowments. In the remaining sections of this chapter we focus first on the idea of property rights as the framework for private want satisfaction, a framework for the market but not created by it. Politics can play an important role as the process for setting up the framework of property rights and contract. We then go on to explore three important classes for market failure: externalities, public goods, and monopolies.

Property rights

A system of self-interested exchange requires some prior understanding of rights of ownership and use of property. Yet neoclassical economics has tended to omit discussion of rights from its analysis. The position generally taken is that rules specifying rights may be important but that they are outside the structure of economic models. They are not only exogenous in the sense that the distribution of endowments is exogenous, they are also outside the model in the sense that they are assumed not to vary in the short run, hence they do not affect allocative behavior in the short run. As Field points out, neoclassical economists have made "a categorical distinction . . . between the modeling of short-term self-interested behavior within rules and the rules themselves" (Field, 1979:53).

In recent years neoclassical economists have started to address property rights. They have treated these rights not only as part of the framework of economic activity, but also as part of a system of rules that itself results from economic processes, that is, rational maximizing behavior. This section offers a definition of property rights and provides some examples of the different forms taken by these rights and their significance for political economy. Property rights are rights of ownership, use, sale, and access to wealth. Property includes physical property (consumer objects, land, capital equipment) and intangible property (such as ideas, poems, chemical formulas, and investment algorithms for the stock market). Perhaps the most important forms of property for economic theory are labor and the means of production. A well-defined system of property rights would limit permissible uses of owned capital, that is, the ways in which it could be invested, joined to labor and other productive factors, and who has what claims to the output. It could also limit the range of external effects. During certain periods of history there have been prohibitions on lending capital beyond certain rates of interest, hiring labor below a certain wage, reaping profits beyond a certain level and so on. However, a private property rights system gives broad scope over disposal of property by its owner. With respect to financial capital, one can invest it, hide it, use it for consumption, transform it into physical assets, use it to hire wage labor, or purchase unproductive holdings such as art, antiques, jewelry, and so on.

Similarly, one could specify alternative property rights for labor. Under capitalism, everyone's labor is self-owned. It cannot legally be coerced or pressed into service. One may feel the compulsion to work, but this comes from the need to have an income to purchase the essential consumption goods. Thus, under capitalism, one sells his or her labor in return for a wage. By the same token, workers do not have entitlement to a job. Unemployment may be a structural part of the economy and may not be the result of people's unwillingness to work. But productive capital is privately owned and owners are not forced to make this capital available for the employment of the labor of others. Denial of access is an important property right of capitalists.

The specification of rights and limits to property is crucial for the productive inputs – land, labor, and capital. Some of these rights are so elementary that violation of them is immediately recognized as criminal. Theft – acquiring the property of others through coercion or stealth – comes readily to mind. Other examples are more subtle; they include selling "insider information" on the stock market or establishing a consulting firm on the basis of knowledge acquired by serving in a governing administration for a brief period. But the principle is the same, the extent of rights to property (intellectual property in the case of the stock market and consulting examples). Finally, even governmental policies, though of shorter time horizon than more elementary rights, have important property rights implications. Tax policy defines how much of output goes to the state; minimum wage legislation sets a floor to the price at which labor may be hired, and unemployment insurance establishes rights to income (usually temporary) when people are out of work.

How do issues surrounding property rights bear on political economy? The political process institutes property rights and, in so doing, sets their limits. Over time, these limits change and develop as society's conception of rights and property themselves change and develop. In some ways this process of development occurs outside of politics. But eventually it expresses itself within the political arena in the form of contention over rights. In this sense, the issue of property rights has an important political dimension.

The presence of such a dimension may or may not justify us in characterizing rights as inherently political, however. Two different theories of rights express different responses to the notion that rights are political. The positivist school argues that rights are created by the political system. Our rights are whatever that system designates as such and are limited to what can be enforced in courts of law. Rights are historically and empirically determined. The natural rights school argues that we have innate rights (sometimes referred to as inalienable rights). We can claim such rights against the state. In other words, even if law does not recognize our right to freedom of speech (for example) we still have such a right due to its close association with the universal claims of human dignity. Thus, the positivist school identifies rights with law, while the natural rights school tries to ground rights outside of existing laws.

For the positivist school, it would seem appropriate to consider rights political in that they are the output of a political process. They may be contested in the same way all outcomes are contested. But the winners can make no special claim for their position beyond that of its (perhaps temporary) political dominance. The existence of such rights is a political fact (which is not to deny, as suggested previously, that the political struggle has links to broader social conflicts). For the natural rights school, it would not be appropriate to treat rights as essentially political. The claims rights have over us stem not from their success in a political debate, but from their significance to our sense of what is demanded of a society organized to respect and protect the dignity of its members. Such rights may be politically instituted, but they are not in essence political.

Second, property rights are not static. They do not refer only to an original condition that must exist for exchange relations to emerge and deepen. The nature and extent of property rights are open to change. Legislation can create or eliminate property rights by establishing which classes of goods can or cannot be privately appropriated (for example, handguns, gold, or slaves), or it can alter the degree and limits of rights over classes of goods. Modern capitalist societies are concerned with the "best tax rate" (to encourage individual motivation and the provision of social services), the "optimal tariff," the control of externalities, and the stimulation of technical innovations. A property rights structure in which individuals do not gain from wealth-producing activities may lead to low levels of output. The current concern in the United States about our "litigious society," "paper entrepreneurialism" (Reich, 1983), and rent-seeking (Krueger, 1974; Bhagwati and Srinivasam, 1980), attests to the significance of property rights in our contemporary setting.

Externalities

The voluntary transaction is the *sine qua non* of the neoclassical conception of human interaction. It is the archetype of all forms of human relatedness. This is so for reasons suggested earlier in this chapter. Indeed, the elevation of the exchange contract to this special status follows from the idea that human life is ultimately about maximizing private satisfaction in the context of resource constraints. The voluntary character of exchange, together with the assumption that each person knows best what he or she wants, leads naturally to the theorem stating the optimality of free markets.

But free markets are not always optimal by neoclassical standards. The first reason for this is that the theorem that links free markets to welfare maximization assumes that no one is affected by a transaction who is not party to it. That is, no one has his level of want satisfaction affected by a contract he does not voluntarily enter into. The term "externalities" refers us to a set of effects of transactions on persons not party to those transactions. If transactions have such effects, they are not necessarily welfare-improving. If they are not, the market has failed to achieve its purpose, and other than market methods must be introduced to fulfill the end of maximization of private want satisfaction. These nonmarket methods include those instituted by political processes and political institutions.

What exactly are externalities? Externalities refer to "effects on third parties that are not transmitted through the price system and that arise as an incidental by-product of another person's or firm's activity" (Rhoads, 1985:113). In ideally functioning markets, all transactions are either private, or, to the extent that third parties are involved, they are compensated or charged. Under such conditions, the cost to producers equals society's costs and benefits to society equal producer benefits. If these conditions obtain, the market sends the correct signals to the producers and neither "too much" nor "too little" of the good in question will be produced. But in certain cases this equation of private and social costs and benefits does not hold. In practice, there are often uncompensated external effects of production (and consumption).

Let us emphasize a point that is important for understanding the theoretical linkages between externalities and the state. It is best illustrated by starting with several questions: Why is it undesirable for externalities to exist?

What special problems do they create in neoclassical theory? One could argue from the standpoint of social justice that, with externalities, people are required to pay for or benefit from certain states of affairs they had no part in bringing about. They are rewarded or punished on grounds irrelevant to their own performance. While this argument has some appeal, the neoclassical economist reasons on a different basis: that of efficient operation of the economy. Mansfield argues that the pattern of resource allocation is distorted when externalities exist.

If a man takes an action that contributes to society's welfare but which results in no payment to him, he is certainly likely to take this action less frequently than would be socially optimal. The same holds true for firms. Thus, if the production of a certain good, say beryllium, is responsible for external economies, less than the socially optimal amount of beryllium is likely to be produced under perfect competition, since the producers are unlikely to increase output simply because it reduces the costs of other companies. By the same token if a man takes an action that results in costs he is not forced to pay, he is likely to take this action more frequently than is socially desirable. The same holds true for firms. (1982:453–4)

Consider a negative externality produced by a firm, such as pollution that imposes a cost on agents outside of the firm in the form of ill health and medical expenses. The cost is imposed on agents independently of their will. In a sense these agents are victims of an imposed exchange (in which they receive ill health in exchange for no payment) and as such is not to the agent's benefit. By the Pareto criterion, the outcome cannot be optimal. We can also see this by considering the firm's calculation of the profit-maximizing level of production.

Assuming that the firm aims to maximize profit, neoclassical theory tells us that it will increase its level of production until the cost of additional output, the marginal cost, equals the price at which it sells that output. If the marginal cost exceeds the price, the sale of the additional output costs more than the revenue generated, which implies a loss to the producer. If the marginal cost falls short of the price, additional profit can be made by producing more. So long as the price (therefore the revenue) exceeds the additional cost, the firm should continue increasing its level of production. Only when the additional cost is just offset by the additional revenue (that is, marginal revenue equals price) will no incentive exist for the firm to change its level of production.

If we take the price to be given and assume diminishing returns, we can easily see how externalities will lead to inefficient levels of production. Diminishing returns means that higher levels of production impose higher unit costs (marginal cost rises as output rises). The profit-maximizing output, given price, depends on the level at which marginal cost equals price. The higher the level at which marginal cost equals price, the more output produced. But the higher the level of marginal cost at each level of output, the lower the level of output at which it equals the price. As the firm increases its level of production, its marginal cost rises, so it continues to increase that level until the marginal cost rises to the price.

Now, consider two situations. In one, part of the cost of production (that part borne by those suffering the negative externality) is *not* calculated into the firm's marginal cost; in the other, it is (for example, by a tax on the producer). When the cost to the agent suffering the externality is not calculated into the firm's costs, the profit-maximizing level of production must be higher than it would be were that cost included. This is for the following reason. When we force the firm to include in its own calculation of its cost this additional cost imposed on others, its marginal cost is higher at each level of output so that given the price, the profit-maximizing level of output is lower. Thus, the market, left to its own devices, since it is incapable of imposing the cost of the externality on the producer, induces that producer to produce too much (that is, more than the efficient amount) of the good involving a negative externality. By a similar logic it is easy to show that a positive externality leads to lower than optimal levels of output.

For the neoclassical thinker, the idea of a set of activities in which economic agents engage others involuntarily opens the door to politics, in the sense of state action (see Baumol, [1952] 1965; Whynes and Bowles, 1981; Mansfield, 1982). First, the political process can be used to correct market deficiencies by bringing private costs and revenues into line with social costs and benefits. There are different policy instruments that could be used to equate private and social cost. One of them is fines; another is subsidies. Fines are imposed on the producer of the externality. If a firm is polluting, government can impose a fine. How large a fine should be imposed? The fine should be just large enough to cover the gap between private and social cost. By imposing a fine of this magnitude the government forces the firm to take account of (to internalize) the full costs of production. And by facing squarely the true social costs of their actions, firms will produce (and pollute) the optimal amount. Subsidies work differently. Here the government pays the firm a subsidy for pollution abatement. The reduction of pollution becomes part of the process (and cost) of production. The objective of both of these policies is the same: reduction of externalities. However, the approach is different and the costs of these reductions are distributed differently.

The second major approach to controlling externalities is government regulation. In contrast to fines and subsidies, which attempt to limit externalities through the price system, regulation seeks control through establishing rule-like standards that can be legally enforced. In other words, regulations involve authoritative prohibitions and demands. Regulations may concern permissible pricing behavior for monopolies, bidding standards for the weapons industry, safety standards for airlines, legal limits of pollution for polluting firms, and rules for the disposal of toxic waste.

The third governmental response to externalities is provided by the judicial system. Instead of a governmental regulation, fine, or subsidy, injured parties might file a suit and take the accused party to court. While this approach has some advantages, its drawbacks are notable. As Stiglitz (1988:233) points out, for this approach to work, property rights must be well defined. Judicial action would not work if the resources being used were held in common. In addition, transaction costs for those mobilizing to bring legal action (the injured parties) could be extremely high and subject to the same collective action problems as exist for public goods. Just the information costs associated with determining who was injured, and how much, might be prohibitive. And the costs of legal action for one person may be prohibitively high in relation to the benefit, while for a group the costs may be far outweighed by the benefits.

Public goods

The third entry point for political economy within the neoclassical paradigm has to do with public goods, or collective consumption goods as they are sometimes called. Neoclassical economists have written about education, roads, and research and development, as well as property rights as public goods, while political scientists, influenced by this way of thinking, have contributed to the literature on leadership, regimes, and the institutional framework for economic action. The importance of public goods spans many levels of government activity: sanitation and traffic rules at the local level, defense policies at the international level.

As with externalities, neoclassical theorists treat public goods as examples of market failure. With an externality, an activity has a consequence that confers a (nonpriced) cost or benefit on a nonparticipant. Where public goods are concerned, the problem is that these goods often will not be produced by the market. The reason for this underproduction of public goods is that the market will produce only those goods for which the producers who bear the costs can also capture the benefits. Such goods are in some sense "own-able," fungible, and transferable.

Many goods do not fit these criteria. These goods, by virtue of their indivisibility and diffuseness, are difficult to own. Once produced, they enter the public realm. Indeed, one definition of a public good is a good that, once produced for any member of a group, automatically is available for any other member of that group. This definition highlights the importance of nonex-cludability for public goods. The beneficial effect of a technical improvement on economic growth, the existence of a well-tended public park, the public educational system, national disease control, and an effective deterrence system are all examples of the nondiscriminating quality of public goods.

The general properties of public goods are their nonexcludability and non-rivalness. Goods exhibit nonexcludability when there is no practical way to channel their benefits exclusively to those who have paid for them – or, to put it the other way, those who have not purchased the good cannot be excluded from consuming it. They become "free riders," enjoying all the benefits without any of the costs. The property of nonrivalness means that as one person consumes the good, no less will be available to someone else. These two properties are practical categories rather than logical absolutes. They depend on the goods in question or, more importantly, on the speci-fication of property rights. Additional cars on our highways can create rivalness due to congestion. Defense can be selectively used to protect certain parts of a population, and deterrence, which is often treated as the closest thing to a "pure public good," can even be invoked selectively. European critics of the United States' policy of graduated deterrence certainly believed this.

How do public goods bear on the concerns of political economy? Within the neoclassical world, public goods are of interest because they suggest limits to the self-seeking, perfectly functioning market model. If we go back to our self-seeking individual and join our knowledge of him to the knowledge that markets underproduce public goods, we immediately see the problem. Our maximizer would not be able to achieve all he would like within a market setting. Public goods like clean air, disease control, an educated citizenry, safe roads, and defense – all in his utility schedule – would be largely unsatisfied by the market.

Let us turn to some of the reasons why goods such as those mentioned in the preceding paragraph are not produced by the market; and after that, we will show how this defect of the market encourages recourse to politics. The major problem of public goods production at the microeconomic level is that there is little incentive to invest energy and resources into their production because those who invest such energies cannot capture all the benefits. Of course the producer will enjoy the benefits of the good in the same way that everyone else in a particular jurisdiction does, but no more so. He enjoys the same fraction of the benefits as everyone else. At a macroeconomic level the difficulty is that private costs and benefits cannot be linked to social costs and benefits. As with externalities, this distorts resource allocation and leads to an undersupply of public goods.

The often cited case of the lighthouse illustrates the basic principle well. A single operator of a ship, or owner of a fleet of ships, may find it advantageous to build a lighthouse and may do so if the costs are less than the benefits received. However, it is more likely that the costs for any one shipowner will be larger than the benefits received. Yet the costs for a lighthouse are constant, whereas the benefits can expand depending on the number of ships that can use it. However, since these ships cannot be excluded from the benefits once the lighthouse is in existence, they have no incentive to pay. They have an incentive to free ride, in the language of public goods theory.

It follows that even where total benefits exceed total costs, lighthouses may not be built. As Stiglitz points out, this underproduction of public goods involves an inefficiency and provides a rationale for government intervention (Stiglitz, 1988:75). Of course, the fact that markets cannot produce goods of a public nature does not mean that the government can. Neoclassical economists like to point out that governments fail too. However, some classes of public goods seem so important that they are provided, with varying degrees of success, by nearly all countries. We can think of education, defense, a legal system, police, sanitation, and health (particularly control of contagious diseases) as goods typically provided by government. Of course, a particular good is often not exclusively provided by the market or the state. We have private education, personal bodyguards, private lawyers, and a health-care system that relies on private doctors and health-care providers as well as their public counterparts. In addition, in some countries there is an increasing tendency to introduce market principles into government policymaking.

Since the market works through voluntary exchange, many persons who are not public-spirited would not pay their share of the cost of public goods provision but would still enjoy the benefits. In addition, public goods involve teamwork. There are collective action problems involved. The state can more easily overcome these problems. It has coercive powers to force individuals to do what is in their interest (that is, to pay for the benefits enjoyed). And the fact that government is inherently more centralized than the market helps it overcome the coordination problems associated with decentralized decision making.

Monopoly and oligopoly

A central theme of neoclassical economics is that there is a link between perfectly competitive markets and efficiency, defined in terms of the maximization of private want satisfaction. Yet three previous sections (property rights, externalities, public goods) suggest that even with perfectly competitive conditions, there are market failures. In this section we briefly consider the case of what happens when markets cease to be perfectly competitive. To make the contrast strong, we compare perfectly competitive markets to oligopoly and monopoly.

In a perfectly competitive market, there are a large number of buyers and sellers. Each producer and consumer is so small in relation to the rest of the market that he or she cannot affect aggregate market properties, especially prices. In fact, under perfectly competitive conditions, individual firms have very little power at all. Their choices are limited to which products to produce and how much. For firms to be restricted in this fashion is simply to say that markets are functioning as they should.

Some scholars (e.g., Lindblom, 1977) have objected that modern industrial economies do not fit the description of perfectly competitive markets. While departures from perfectly competitive markets include numerous analytic distinctions, we frame our discussion in terms of the most extreme deviations, monopolies and oligopolies.

Oligopolies occur when several firms control a large share of the market (or assets) in a particular sector. In these circumstances, firms may affect key market parameters such as prices. Indeed, firms might set prices well above the level allowed in a perfectly competitive market. The difference between the price and the costs of production may be reaped as an excess profit, called a rent. Along with raising prices, firms may limit output, satisfying themselves with selling fewer units at a higher price.

From the standpoint of efficiency, the above scenario is troubling. Firms produce "too little" and charge "too much" in comparison with the baseline of pure competition. Individuals and firms who could have purchased goods at lower prices are excluded. Utility satisfaction is lowered. Under these circumstances prices will not reflect real costs and scarcities and, as a result, will not be efficiently allocated.

In the case of externalities and public goods, markets fail even under ideal circumstances – that is, even if they are perfectly competitive. With oligopoly, there are also inefficiencies, but they result from the erosion of the competitive nature of markets themselves. Nevertheless, the rationale for government intervention remains the same. The economy is impaired in its function of efficiently allocating resources. The government can intervene to break up large firms, to prevent collusion (cooperation among firms and price fixing), and to discourage or prevent mergers that would restrict competition.[7]

Conclusion

Neoclassical economics is a theory of voluntary exchange and efficient allocation of resources. Its analytical starting point is the self-interested individual, operating in an environment where many potential objects of satisfaction are in commodity form, and where, in Macpherson's words, the aim of action is "the competitive maximization of utilities" (1973:5). In this kind of world, individuals will freely contract to do the best they can, subject to endowments, technology, and existing rules.

Clearly, market exchange and efficient allocation are central to neoclassical economics. Once this view of the world is in place, it invites a particular way of thinking about political economy. It highlights the contractual arrangements that individuals and firms make to improve their lots. For the con-

---

[7] For some scholars, there is a second theoretical link between oligopoly and politics. This link is supplied by the idea of "market power," a term that under the conditions of perfect competition is an oxymoron. Under conditions of perfect competition, strategic interaction cannot exist. Each actor must behave as if the environment is given. By contrast, when oligopoly exists, the maximizing individual, far from confronting an anonymous environment, faces a set of rivals implying a quite different set of calculations. Instead of calculating how much of X to produce, a firm may devise a strategy that intends to increase market shares or one that defeats a rival firm (Diesing, 1982:40).

sumer, the relevant question is how to dispose of resources so as to maximize utility. For the producer, the question is how to utilize endowments so as to maximize output and profit. Thus economics, as Schelling puts it, has become the science of superior trades, the "something better" approach (1984:15).

The neoclassical idea of political economy is subsidiary to the central focus of efficient exchange within markets. Once individual welfare is at the center, and this welfare is equated with fulfillment of preferences, politics becomes an alternative instrument to achieve what cannot be efficiently achieved by the market. This makes market failure the master idea of neoclassical political economy. Markets may fail in the ways we have discussed. They do not define and institute property rights; they cannot put into place their own preconditions. They may involve significant externalities, problems of public good production and loss of competition through industrial concentration.

We have explored the idea of linking political economy to market failure. When we focus on market failure, we leave out of account one important feature of neoclassical thinking. The welfare improvement stemming from voluntary contracts (in the absence of public goods and externalities) is relative to the initial distribution of endowments. It is the best we can do accepting who owns what at the outset.

"Voluntary," in this context, means absence of coercion by another person. It does not require that any specific set of options actually be available to the individual. The less wealth we own at the outset, the fewer the options the market affords, the less well off we are likely to be as the result of exchange. The market does not redistribute property in the interests of equality of life chances or of removing goods from those that have a surfeit and giving them to those having little.

Thus, it is important to bear in mind that neoclassical propositions regarding the virtues of the free market are all limited in this way. Such a limitation does not in itself make those propositions uninteresting or irrelevant. It does, however, better identify their meaning and significance. In certain contexts (of poverty, acute inequalities, severe limitation of life chances), the neoclassical propositions carry less weight and capture our attention less than they might in others.

If neoclassical political economy is based on the idea of market failure, it is appropriate to evaluate this conception. Our comments center on the special competence of markets and conceptions of the political that are different from the neoclassical idea.

Some theories of political economy concern the way we draw the line between outcomes left to the market and those determined by state action. At issue is a general method or approach rather than specific outcomes (employment, pollution, military expenditures, and others). Neoclassical political economy attacks the question of how to draw a line via the notion of market failure. The line is drawn by reference to a specific conception of the competence of markets – what the market does when it functions well – and the circumstances under which that competence breaks down. When the market fails, it is the function of the political process to carry out the mission of the market by other means.

The notion of (Pareto) optimality best expresses the neoclassical vision of the special competence of markets and their overall mission. So, the success or failure of the market can be judged by the optimality of its outcomes. These, in turn, are not evaluated first in empirical terms, but in relation to a theoretical claim: that perfectly competitive markets will be Pareto optimal and that restrictions on competition will lead to nonoptimal outcomes. Externalities and public goods imply market failure by this criterion.

However interesting and important the notion of optimal allocation, it is only one of several visions of the special competence of markets. Its limitations were vividly depicted by Schumpeter in a well-known comment:

A system – any system, economic or other – that at *every* point of time fully utilizes its possibilities to the best advantage may yet in the long run be inferior to a system that does so at *no* given point of time, because the latter's failure to do so may be a condition for the level or speed of long run performance. (1942:83 italics in original)

Schumpeter echoes the classical idea that markets are about dynamics of accumulation, innovation, and economic development rather than about the static problem of resource allocation and optimization. From the standpoint of this distinct judgment about the social purpose of the market (see Levine, 1981:ch. 7), the question of when the market succeeds and when it fails must appear quite differently. With this difference must follow differences in judgment of the limits of the market and the line separating market outcomes from those determined by state action.

A second limitation of the neoclassical approach is that it understands the state primarily as an instrument to correct market failures. In doing so, this understanding furthers the idea of efficiency. If the market fails to respond efficiently, the state steps in. State actions can be judged by the same yardstick as market activities.

Empirically, the state may be involved in more than market failures and justifications, for state action may extend beyond efficiency. Justice and rights are in the state sphere not because they can be performed more efficiently there, but because the state rather than the market can best enforce equal protection and treatment. Justice can be a slow, cumbersome, and inefficient process.

If justice highlights the normative aspect of state activity, conceptions of power based on winners and losers highlight an empirical aspect of states not captured by market failure. Much of politics concerns the ways in which the political process and the state are used to enforce the desires of some over others. We have seen how the focus on voluntary exchange and Pareto optimality removes this avenue for neoclassical political economy. Situations in which the improvement of some worsens the position of others are difficult for the neoclassical method to grasp. Markets imply voluntary choice and choice implies freedom to leave, to "exit." One may be dissatisfied within markets, but one should never be worse off because of the choices of others. The state as agent of some over others differs from the state as an instrument of mutual improvement. The neoclassical state empowers agents to achieve goods otherwise unobtainable. But the state is also an agent that empowers some to achieve goods at the expense of others.

5

Keynesian political economy

The Keynesian approach advances a critique of claims for market self-regulation common among classical and neoclassical thinkers. The Keynesian critique questions the claim that an unregulated market system will fully exploit society's productive potential.

At its core, the argument for market self-regulation contends that the market system will bring together wants and means in such a way as to satisfy those wants so far as is possible given the means available. This is a claim about prices and demand. The prices of goods will adjust so as to assure the market will clear; what producers bring to the market will find buyers. The price mechanism assures adequate demand. It also directs capital investment into those lines, indicated by higher profitability, where more is needed.

In this argument, individual producers may fail to sell all they produce, or can produce, because what they have to sell is not wanted by those with the purchasing power to buy it. They have miscalculated in their decisions regarding the line of investment for their capital and produced the wrong goods. The low profit and income of these producers is the fate that befalls those who do not provide what consumers want. This can happen to the individual, but not to the aggregate of sellers.

The Keynesian critique argues that failure to find buyers can be a systemic problem having nothing to do with a bad fit between what has been produced and what is needed. It can result from the failure of the market mechanism to assure adequate purchasing power. It can thus fail to bring together wants and means, underutilizing society's existing productive capacity. This failure of aggregate demand differs fundamentally from the failure of particular demand. If the market tends systematically to generate failure of aggregate demand, this will affect how we judge its use as a mechanism for satisfying wants. This judgment bears on how we think of the relation of the world of private affairs to public authority, and therefore of the separability of the economy and its dominance over public life.

The Keynesian critique encourages us to reconsider the relation of politics

100

to markets. Yet many Keynesian economists have drawn the conclusion that aggregate demand failure need not and should not be treated as a political problem. They argue instead that stability and adequate market functioning can be assured by the introduction of automatic mechanisms, and thus by administrative rather than political means.

This claim is, of course, debatable. But, the debate shifts the core issues of political economy onto a different plane. New questions arise, including: In what way does state management of the economy entail a political agenda rather than a purely administrative function? What is that agenda and what sorts of social conflict might it involve? How does state management affect collective judgment of the limits of the market? How does it change the way we think of the relation between public and private?

Before addressing these questions directly, we need to consider the Keynesian critique of market self-regulation in some detail. A significant revision of the way we think about market economy is implied in the Keynesian critique. This revision in itself bears on central issues of political economy concerning the nature, social purpose, and therefore limits of the property system.

The Keynesian approach focuses on the instability of the process of reproduction and growth in capitalist economy.[1] For reasons we will develop in this chapter, capitalist economies incorporate processes that make their reproduction unstable and therefore uncertain. Such processes cast doubt on the appropriateness of the self-regulating market as the institution through which society should organize the production and distribution of goods.

This perception of the nature of capitalist economy has a long history. Among nineteenth-century economists, Karl Marx stands out as the most vigorous critic of the idea of the self-ordering market. Marx argued that capitalist economies have an inherent tendency toward crises involving the widespread unemployment of labor and the failure of product markets to provide adequate outlets for the existing productive capacity of capital equipment. Marx saw these crises as violent events that brought acute suffering to workers. He argued that the reproduction process of the capitalist economy, rather than proceeding smoothly, advances through a sequence of "explosions, cataclysms, crises" (Tucker, 1978:291) that arise out of contradictions inherent in an economy based on private ownership of capital and the unregulated market.

Keynes shared Marx's view up to a point. Although he did not think about the disruptions of the capitalist reproduction process in the violent language

---

[1] The Keynesian approach presented here emphasizes the work of the British neo-Keynesians and the American post-Keynesians rather than that of those economists (such as Paul Samuelson and James Tobin) who sought to place Keynesian ideas into a more neoclassically inspired analytical framework.

typical of Marx, he equally denied the ability of the market to maintain employment and smooth reproduction. Indeed, while rejecting the hypothesis that capitalism is violently unstable, Keynes concluded that left to its own devices, the capitalist economy might settle into a situation of significant underutilization of resources:

> In particular, it is an outstanding characteristic of the economic system in which we live that, whilst it is subject to severe fluctuations in respect of output and employment, it is not violently unstable. Indeed it seems capable of remaining in a chronic condition of sub-normal activity for a considerable period without any marked tendency either towards recovery or towards complete collapse. Moreover, the evidence indicates that full, or even approximately full, employment is of rare and short-lived occurrence. (Keynes, 1936:249–50)

Thus, Keynes argued against both the notion of equilibrium characteristic of late nineteenth- and early twentieth-century economics and the notion of the "invisible hand," favored by Adam Smith and the early advocates of laissez-faire.

The Polish economist Michal Kalecki came to a similar conclusion based less on a notion of chronic unemployment, and more explicitly on the implications of cyclical instability:

> Even on the average the degree of utilization throughout the business cycle will be substantially below the maximum reached during the boom. Fluctuations in the utilization of available labor parallel those in the utilization of equipment. Not only is there mass unemployment in the slump, but average employment throughout the cycle is considerably below the peak reached in the boom. The reserve of capital equipment and the reserve army of unemployed are typical features of capitalist economy at least throughout a considerable part of the cycles. (1978:131)

Thus, for Kalecki, cyclical instability implies that the economy must, aside from exceptional circumstances (the peak of the boom), fail to fully utilize the human annd material resources available to it. This failure implies a high cost in human terms resulting from high levels of unemployment.

Economists working in the Keynesian tradition accept the argument that capitalist economies, left to their own devices, will not make full use of the resources available to them. This failure necessitates government intervention. In this sense, the instability of capitalist economy casts doubt on the hypothesis of the invisible hand and therefore also on the implications that hypothesis has for political economy. It leads to arguments in favor of government policy aimed at assuring a stable process of reproduction and adequate levels of employment.

> In 1965 President Johnson was making a controversial statement when he said: "I do not believe recessions are inevitable." That statement is no longer controversial. Recessions are now generally considered to be fundamentally preventable, like airplane crashes and unlike hurricanes. But we have not banished air crashes from the

land, and it is not clear that we have the wisdom or the ability to eliminate recessions. The danger has not disappeared. The forces that produced recurrent recessions are still in the wings, merely waiting for their cue. (Okun, 1970:33–4)

Okun goes on to identify the source of the problem in the "vulnerability of the economy to cumulative movements upward and downward" (p. 34). In this chapter, we investigate those cumulative movements and the possibility that government policy may offset them.

Instability undermines the conclusion that markets regulate themselves. By so doing, instability supports the conclusion that the social and private ends whose pursuit justifies organization of our economic lives through markets also justifies restricting movements within markets through institutional changes in property relations (regulation and policy). Instability characterizes capitalist economies because processes within such economies (movements of output, investment, employment, and prices) tend to be self-reinforcing or cumulative. Limiting cumulative processes requires appropriate changes in property relations and the types of contracts agents enter into. In order to understand these changes, we first consider those features of capitalist economies that lead to cumulative movements. Fundamentally, the features are of the following kinds: (1) those having to do with the circularity of economic processes, (2) those having to do with the motivations of agents and with the kinds of information the organization of the economy makes available to agents, and (3) those having to do with the kinds of contracts agents enter into.

The desire on the part of agents to stabilize their environment has two implications with special importance for political economy: First, it sets limits to the pure property system and changes the nature of some of its most important contractual relations (including the wage contract). Second, it involves the state in regulating the production and distribution of wealth, thus reducing the scope of market self-regulation. We take up both of these implications in this chapter.

The circularity of economic processes

The classical idea of the reproduction of a social division of labor has a built-in circularity. As we saw in Chapter 2, the classical theory treats the output of each individual production process as inputs into other processes. This identity of inputs and outputs holds at the aggregate, or macroeconomic, level; it implies that the flow of inputs and outputs must return to its starting point in order to begin again. This circular process involves production and investment decisions by the individual producers (firms), it involves aggregate results of many such decisions, and it involves the way in which those aggregate results affect subsequent production and investment decisions. In

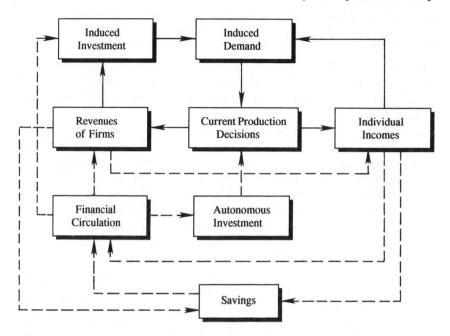

Figure 2. The circular flow without government

order to construct an image of the flow, then, we must combine individual decisions (microeconomics) with aggregate flows (macroeconomics).

Figure 2 presents a simplified image of the circular flow. It ignores both the government sector (taxation, government spending, transfer payments, and government debt) and the possibility of international trade. Without government, individuals' incomes depend entirely on the amount and kind of property they own. Property in labor services can be sold to firms for a wage. The exchange of labor for a wage (or salary) makes up the primary source of individual (or consumer) income. Property in capital also yields income in the form of interest, dividends, and capital gains.

Aside from the flows into and out of the financial sector, the circular flow consists of movements of goods in one direction and of money in the other. Flows into, out of, and within the financial circulation consist of money and financial assets (stocks, bonds, and private debt). Money plays a primary part in the circular flow when we consider its stability or instability and, for this reason, it is important to bear in mind the monetary nature of all movements within the flow.

Within the circular flow as depicted in Figure 2, the movements indicated by solid lines make up a closed circuit. They connect those aspects of the entire movement that are genuinely circular. The movements indicated by broken lines are open in the sense that the flows they represent either move out of the circuit (savings) or enter into the circuit from outside. This distinction is very important. We begin with the closed circuit.

Assume that firms make production decisions in the present based on the level of demand for their products. They may, for example, attempt to maintain a target or planned level of inventories of finished but unsold products. As inventories are sold they must be renewed with current output. When demand is higher than current levels of output, inventories fall below planned levels. This indicates a need to increase levels of production. Given levels of demand, firms maintain levels of production appropriate to planned levels of inventories.

In order to maintain appropriate levels of production, firms must purchase required inputs of labor and materials. We can assume a more or less technically determined relationship between these inputs and levels of output – that is, to produce a unit of output requires so many hours of labor and so many inputs of the various materials used to produce the specified product (see Chick, 1983:ch. 4; Pasinetti, 1977). We assume that while the amount of plant and equipment does not adapt to short-run fluctuations in demand, the existing plant and equipment can be operated at different levels of capacity utilization. Thus, the movements that concern us here are not movements of capital stock (fixed assets) but of output, demand, and working capital. Movements of capital investment in plant and equipment take us outside the "closed" part of the circular flow. In the short run, levels of capacity utilization adjust to variations in demand so that, to meet varying levels of demand, we need not carry out investment in plant and equipment.

The purchase of the productive inputs required to meet demand and maintain inventories creates revenues for suppliers: for workers who supply labor and firms who supply materials. Workers and firms use the revenues they receive for two purposes, to acquire goods and to save. Saving usually means acquisition of a financial asset (for example, stocks and bonds), about which we shall have more to say below. The act of saving removes revenue (money) from the circular flow and, in itself, acts as a drain on that flow with the potential of disrupting the circuit and adversely affecting demand, thus causing firms to reduce output and employment. We return to some of these implications of saving further on. For the moment, we focus on the spending decisions of individuals and firms.

The receipt of revenue by firms and workers induces spending, but for different reasons. Wages provide workers with their only or primary incomes. Because of this wages must be used to purchase needed means of consumption. The fact that workers depend in this way on employment and wages keeps the flow of value (money) going. Firms produce in order to make profit, and make profit in order to expand their capital and increase their productive capacity. Thus, while firms produce goods in order to make profit, they also make profit so that they can expand production. Since expansion of output (when sold) expands revenues, it induces investment in working capital and eventually in fixed capital (see Kalecki, 1978). Thus, the part of revenue spent by firms as a group generates demand for their products (materials, means of consumption, and means of production). We have termed this "induced" demand since it results from current production decisions. It has the effect of absorbing inventories and thus stimulating another round of production decisions. The circuit begins once again.

To summarize, circularity results from the following three features of market economy:

1. A link exists between income and employment. Because a market is a system of property relations, acquisition of things agents need depends on the property they own: its type, its value, and its amount. Their wants and needs send individuals and firms into the market.
2. Incomes induce expenditures for individuals.
3. Demand induces both production and investment on the part of firms.

These three conditions depend primarily on the form of economic organization. They do not result from psychological or technical conditions (although they involve such conditions). Outside of a private enterprise, private property system, individuals may still have wants and needs, and technical knowledge as embodied in means of production will still determine the extent and manner of need satisfaction. Yet, the peculiar circularity of a private enterprise market economy need not develop.

The economic cycle

The circularity of the economic flow has the important implication that changes in the level of output will tend to be self-reinforcing or cumulative. That is, an initial increase (or decrease) will lead to further increases (or decreases) rather than to continuing or stable reproduction at the higher (or lower) level. This tendency toward cumulative movement makes the economic process unstable.

The circular flow

Within the circular flow narrowly conceived (the closed circuit), we do not attempt to identify a particular determinant from among the distinct elements of the process as a whole. Instead, we treat the economic process as a system of mutual and reciprocal determination. Revenue determines spending, which determines demand, which depletes inventories and thus stimulates production, which in turn generates revenue. The investment induced within this circuit is primarily investment in working capital, which follows the movement of the process as a whole.

Investment in fixed capital (plant and equipment) poses an additional problem. Such investment is not so easily incorporated into the closed part of the circular flow (a relatively short-run phenomenon) because of its connection to the long-run growth path of the economy. In this section, we consider investment in fixed capital within the narrower time horizon of the circular flow. Some economists, such as Joan Robinson (1961), have argued that investment depends on expectations of profitability, which depend on recent profit experience. Linking investment to profit expectations and profit expectations to recent (and current) profitability, forms a circle of causation, which can generate a cumulative process. The following briefly summarizes this process.

In order to see how a cumulative process might develop, we need to understand the two-sided relation between profitability and investment. We assume that the level of current investment depends on expectations of future profit because the motivation for acquiring capital equipment is the profit we expect it to produce for us. While this assumption does not capture some important features of the investment decision, it does summarize one crucial component.

At the same time that profit expectations determine investment, investment also determines profitability. This results directly from the operation of the multiplier process (see Kalecki, 1965; Kaldor, 1960). In order to see this more clearly assume that (for whatever reason) an investor decides to purchase $1,000 worth of additional investment goods. Assuming that this stimulates the production of an additional $1,000 of such goods, the additional investment stimulates the creation of an equivalent amount of additional revenue for firms and workers. Assuming, for simplicity, that the recipients of this revenue save 10 percent, the revenue created by the new investment will stimulate additional demand in the amount of $900. This additional demand will, in turn, deplete inventories and stimulate new production and new revenues. Expenditure of 90 percent of the latter will add an additional $810 to demand, revenue, and output. Because of the circularity of the process, the initial addition to demand multiplies itself and stimulates a final growth in demand greater than the amount originally invested. Total addition to demand is the sum of a geometric series: $1,000 + $900 + $810 + $\cdots$ = $10,000. Economists refer to the mechanism that leads to the cumulative effect exemplified here as the "multiplier."

Since the purchase of commodities generates incomes, and since incomes stimulate their recipients to purchase commodities, any initial addition to demand will multiply into a series of additions to demand. Since growth in demand depletes inventories of produced commodities held by firms, the growth in demand will also stimulate investment in working capital to renew inventories; this investment will stimulate demand and revenues, which will multiply again into a series of expenditures. The circularity born of the link between incomes and expenditures breeds a tendency toward cumulative processes. The economic flow can, in principle, cumulate in either direction. An increase in investment or demand will build into a self-reinforcing growth in output, demand, and employment. A reduction in demand will lead to a self-reinforcing decline in demand, output, and employment.

Following the argument of Kalecki (1965), assume that firms sell their products at a given price that exceeds their costs by a fixed margin. This profit margin equals the difference between price (total revenue received per unit of output sold) and the cost per unit of output. At different levels of output and sales, different rates of utilization of capital imply different amounts of profit. If the rate of profit is defined to be the ratio of total profit to the value of the capital stock, that rate increases with increasing levels of output (and sales) or capacity utilization.

Higher rates of investment thus imply higher (current) profitability. If expectations of profit depend on profitability, then higher (lower) rates of investment will stimulate more (less) robust profit expectations, which stimulate further reductions in investment. Thus, in addition to the circular causation built into the closed part of the circular flow, there is also an expectational loop that incorporates investment in plant and equipment (at least up to a point). This expectational loop develops because of the dependence of expectations on current conditions. The strength of the loop, and of the cumulative processes it implies, depends on the extent to which investment decisions are made within a short-period context. It emphasizes once again the link between instability, cumulative processes, and the short-run perspective.

The capital market and instability

Induced investment results from the necessity that capital stock be kept adequate to the needs of current production to meet current levels of demand. It is induced by current demand or profitability and involves a short-period orientation on the part of the investor. Such a perspective is particularly appropriate to investment in working capital – inventories of materials and finished products. Acquisition of plant and equipment (fixed capital), by contrast, involves judgments concerning the likely levels of demand (and price) over an extended period. Such investments have a relatively long life expectancy and only pay off over a series of production cycles. Thus, whereas investment in working capital results from calculations of current (or short-run) circumstances, investment in plant and equipment results from calculation of future (or long-run) circumstances. Economists emphasize the subjective element in these calculations by referring to short-period and long-period expectations as the proximate bases for investment decisions (Chick, 1983; Robinson, 1971).

The implications of the dominance of the short-period or long-period viewpoint in decision making plays a significant part in political economy. Not the least important of these implications is for the stability of the reproduction process. For this reason, we will consider the distinction between long and short period in somewhat greater detail.

In economics, the long period refers to the planning period appropriate to investment in capital equipment. Such equipment (1) produces a stream of products over an extended series of production cycles and (2) cannot be easily sold; it therefore requires a long-run commitment on the part of its purchaser or owner. This second point deserves a brief further comment. Plant and equipment tend to be technically specific to the production of a particular product or narrowly defined and related set of products. This, together with the tendency of technical change to make existing (used) equipment uncompetitive with new equipment, narrows the market for older capital stock. Since the secondary market in such stock is poor, its purchaser must at least anticipate owning and using it over an extended period. The purchase of plant and equipment thus depends on a perception of a future made up of a series of production runs and marketing periods.

In the long run, we can contemplate adjusting to our (possibly changing) circumstances by making changes in the amount and type of our plant and equipment. In the short run, we cannot adjust in this way. In the short run, we can change the rate of utilization of plant and equipment (and our associated purchases of material and labor inputs), but our (overhead) costs remain largely beyond our control. This means that, if we adopt a short-run planning period, our plan will not involve changes in our stock of plant and equipment. An important corollary of this is that if we have little or no plant and equipment (or other overhead costs) then we will always find ourselves planning in the short run. It turns out that this conclusion plays an important part in the Keynesian argument for the instability of capitalist economies. The more agents find (or place) themselves in situations that encourage them to adopt the short-period perspective, the more unstable the market outcomes to which they contribute.

In the Keynesian view, the organization of a private enterprise economy incorporates a tension between the public good served by accumulation of capital and the reason private individuals hold their wealth in liquid form. The argument that such a tension exists sharply distinguishes the Keynesian approach from those of its predecessors. The classical economists (including

Marx) tend to assume that the end of private wealth accumulation is well served by private ownership of the means of production on the part of individuals. They assume that private wealth accumulation means the growth of society's productive capacity and thus serves a social purpose. The Keynesian argument attacks this core idea.

While the social purpose is best served by the accumulation of means of production (plant and equipment), the private ends of individuals are best served by holding wealth in a liquid form that can be easily used to acquire the things capable of satisfying their wants. Because of this, the individual's interest is not well served if he must purchase means of production in order to accumulate wealth. Yet, in a private enterprise system, the means of production must be held by someone as private property. This is the dilemma that inspires much of the Keynesian revision of earlier ideas regarding the process of the growth of social wealth and the part played by the individual property owner.

The dilemma has an institutional resolution in the development of the private corporation. The corporation owns society's capital stock as its private property. Yet its institutional ends are sufficiently distinct from those of the individual to make, under certain circumstances at least, the ownership of means of production the relevant means to its ends. The corporation thus solves the problem of who will own society's producing capacity. It simultaneously helps to solve the problem of providing the individual with a way of holding and accumulating wealth in liquid form. The individual can own shares in corporations, leaving the corporation as the owner of the means of production themselves. These shares are highly liquid and thus better serve the ends of the individual than would ownership of plant and equipment.

For the Keynesian theory, this solution to the problem of who will own society's capital stock as private property is more a shifting of the problem to a new plane than a real solution. What it does is transfer the difficulty to the realm of financial circulation. Much of the Keynesian theory explores the way this resolution of the dilemma of private ownership of means of production generates instability in the accumulation process. We will briefly explore the Keynesian argument in the following pages.

The dilemma referred to above can be restated in the language of the short run and the long run. Those who adopt a short-run perspective will need to hold their wealth in a liquid form that does not involve any long-run commitment to a particular productive enterprise.

Keynes argues that the shift from the long- to the short-period perspective significantly undermines the stability of the capitalist economy (Keynes, 1936:ch. 12; see also Levine, 1984). He attributes this shift to the development of the market in securities, which, he argues, provides investors with an increasingly attractive alternative to investment in plant and equipment.

According to Keynes, the "outstanding fact" concerning investment decisions "is the extreme precariousness of the basis of knowledge on which our estimates of prospective yield have to be made" (1936:149). This fact places a premium on investments that demand only a short-period commitment. The stock market provides investors with the alternative of investments of this type.

Profit-seeking agents face a choice of the form of their capital investments. One option, productive capital, fixes capital invested for the productive lifetime of the equipment while restricting the return to profit realized for the sale of the stream of products. This option also commits large amounts of capital to a single form and makes the return contingent on the vicissitudes of the market for a particular product (or limited product line). A second option, financial assets, fixes the form of investment (a particular stock or bond) for only so long as the investor desires. As Keynes puts it:

[T]he stock exchange revalues many investments every day and the revaluations give a frequent opportunity to the individual (though not to the community as a whole) to revise his commitments. It is as though a farmer, having tapped his barometer after breakfast, could decide to remove his capital from the farming business between 10 and 11 in the morning and reconsider whether he should return to it later in the week. (1936:151)

The ready movement of investments in financial assets from one kind to another has important implications. In particular it places a premium on short-term capital gains (the difference between the price at which the asset is bought and sold) as the source of profit rather than on the sale of produced commodities. This emphasis on capital gains in the buying and selling of easily liquidated assets encourages cumulative movements in asset prices. Professional investors devote their energies not to "making superior long-term forecasts of the probable yield of an investment over its whole life, but [to] foreseeing changes in the conventional basis of valuation a short time ahead of the general public" (Keynes 1936:154). Profit goes to those best able to anticipate "what average opinion expects the average opinion to be" (p. 156).

When profit can be made by anticipating movements in asset prices, movements in asset prices will also depend on the state of expectations concerning price changes. The more we expect prices to rise (fall), the more we act in ways that make prices rise (fall). Demand for assets increases with the expectation that their prices will rise and this same demand brings about a rise in price. Behavior of investors in such markets brings about cumulative movements in asset prices. Profit-oriented speculative behavior encourages price instability.

If this happens, the implications for the economic circuit can be severe, and for two reasons:

Money flows away from investment in productive capital and into the buying and selling of financial assets (the financial circulation). Investment in real capital falls, demand for labor falls, revenues decline, a downward spiral results.

The money flowing into the financial circulation contributes to speculative movements in asset prices. Speculation feeds instability in the financial sector, which can, if allowed to proceed beyond certain limits, harm the process of reproduction and accumulation. "When the capital development of a country becomes a by-product of the activities of a casino, the job is likely to be ill-done." (Keynes, 1936:159)

This second point increases in importance with the increasing dependence on the financial circulation as a source of funds to maintain production and finance investment. Cumulative movements within the financial circulation can disrupt the ability of financial institutions to support the activities of producers (and consumers): the supply of credit needed for acquisition of both fixed and working capital. Bank failures, credit crunches, and depreciation of financial assets can significantly disrupt the circular flow. This is the way in which cumulative processes in the financial sector mean instability for the market as a whole. (For more detailed discussion, see Galbraith, 1954; Minsky, 1975; and Kindleberger, 1978.)

The ownership of long-lived assets (productive capital) is the basis for economic well-being and security in a private enterprise economy. A private enterprise economy requires that private persons own the capital stock as their property (if only indirectly). As Keynes puts it, "there is no such thing as liquidity of investment for the community as a whole" (1936:155). The corporation, as we have seen, is a mechanism for reconciling the necessity that the capital stock be privately owned with the fact that the motivations and time horizons of private persons are inconsistent with its ownership (see Minsky, 1975:ch. 4). The corporation plays a primary role in assuring the presence in the market of an agent with a long-period view. The corporation (1) has an image of the future and of its place in that future consistent with ownership of long-lived equipment, (2) is motivated to maintain an institutional identity into the future, and (3) has purposes that are served by the production of commodities (at least normally).

Because the corporation sustains an institutional identity into the long run, it represents a stabilizing influence on the economy. By focusing its attention on making profit from the production of commodities, the firm commits itself to the work of securing an environment suitable to assuring the return on its investment over the period of its lifetime. It thus concerns itself with the stability of its market (and possibly of its market share), the stability of its work forces, and the stability of its price–cost structure. In the next section, we consider some of the larger implications of this behavior.

At the same time that firms lend stability to the market, they also contribute to the development of the market in shares (the "financial circulation") which, while ultimately tied to the success of the firm in producing and selling commodities over the long run, develops independently of that connection. The destabilizing effect of the independent movements within the financial circulation also result from the growth of corporations. Keynes and his followers (such as Minsky) focus on the destabilizing implications of the opposition between ownership of the firm and ownership of society's capital stock.

In terms of those considerations that affect the likelihood that agents will adopt a long-period perspective, the holders of shares appear decidedly different from the corporations they own. Shareholders do not value the preservation of an institutional identity tied to production and sale of commodities, a particular location (or set of locations) in the market, or more generally, a determinate and enduring location in the overall social division of labor. Instead, they value liquidity of investment and the spreading of the investment over a wide range of firms and industries (diversification). In a sense individual shareholders operate from a different and narrower definition of their private interests. The interest of the shareholder does not extend beyond his private wealth-position: The monetary value of his portfolio of financial assets at a point in time. Firms have a much broader interest in the security of their markets, the reputation of their products, the stability of their costs (including their labor costs), the value of the stocks they have issued in the past and that are now held by their juridical owners, and so on. This does not mean that firms act in the public interest (they may or may not). It means that they represent, within the sphere of private ownership and private interest, an important component of the process of social reproduction. Unlike that of shareholders, the private interest of the firm incorporates the execution of a social imperative.

The narrow commitment of shareholders can lead to behavior conflicting with the achievement of the broader ends of the corporations they own. The basis for ownership of capital equipment by the firm is the expectation that the products that equipment can produce will satisfy the wants of consumers or of other producers. The basis for ownership of shares is the expectation that they will contribute to the growth of the value of the portfolio of assets held by their owner. Such ownership always has a strong tendency to become speculative in the sense discussed previously. When this happens, the historical value of the firm as reflected in the price of its shares diverges both from the historical value of its capital stock and (of more importance) from the expected value of the returns to the productive use of that stock over its lifetime. This divergence is rooted in the private ownership of capital and in the latent and overt opposition between the logic of private ownership and the logic of large-scale production. This opposition has both beneficial and harmful effects on the circular flow.

Political economy of labor and capital markets

We can trace the peculiarities of the Keynesian approach, when contrasted with the neoclassical, to the premise that expectations of demand rather than costs of production drive investment decisions. This premise has significant implications for the argument over the self-regulating market. In this section, we explore those implications further, first with regard to the wage contract, then with regard to saving.

The labor market stands at the center of the issue posed for political economy by instability. It is central for two reasons. First, the labor market is the mechanism through which most individuals in a capitalist economy acquire their livelihood. As Lindblom puts it, in a capitalist economy "livelihood is at stake in exchange" (1977:47). Second, the wage contract links demand by products to wages and employment. As we have seen, the circularity of the economic process in a private enterprise economy results from the fact that employment both depends on and determines demand. In this section we explore this centrality of the labor contract and suggest some implications for political economy.

The success of a capitalist economy depends in part on its ability to provide individuals with their livelihoods through a series of voluntary contracts. From the side of the worker, this requires that the demand for labor be sufficient to provide employment at a wage adequate for that worker to purchase the needed consumption goods given their market prices. Economic instability endangers this outcome. It means that periodically the demand for labor will not be sufficient to provide the needed employment and therefore the needed incomes. Instability is no small matter viewed from the worker's standpoint.

This observation suggests an important question we have not so far addressed. When the demand for labor falls short of the level required to provide employment for those able and willing to work, can the unemployed make decisions and take actions likely to bring about the adjustments necessary to call forth a higher level of employment? If the answer is yes, then we will be encouraged toward a favorable judgment of market self-regulation. If the answer is no, the argument in favor of the free market will be undermined. One of the virtues claimed for the self-regulating market is that it facilitates all mutually beneficial transactions, and in so doing assures that society's productive potential will be fully exploited. Failure of the market to provide employment for those able and willing to work is a failure to exploit their potential productive contribution. When those unemployed are willing but unable to make adjustments that will call forth demand (for example, adjustments in the wage), then the market mechanism has failed to secure the full range of transactions needed to realize society's productive potential. In narrower terms, the labor market has failed to bring about the adjustment between supply and demand needed to assure an adequate level of employment.

In the neoclassical model of the economy, the responsiveness of demand to price assures that markets will clear. For this to work in the labor market, the worker must be able to influence the demand for labor by influencing its price, thus finding employment by offering to work for less. The Keynesian approach argues that workers do not have the capacity to influence employment in this way (see Keynes, 1936:ch. 19, and Kalecki, 1969).

The first limitation workers face in their attempt to increase demand for their labor by reducing its cost is their lack of control over that cost. This lack of control results from the fact that the wage bargain controls the money wage rate and not the relationship between money wages and prices. The latter, measured for example by the profit margin, indicates to the employer the impact of the wage bargain on profitability. If we think of the real wage as the money wage adjusted for changes in the price level, then changes in the real wage imply changes in the cost of labor to employers and in their profit margins; changes in money wages do not. Given that workers bargain over money rather than real wages, the impact of the wage bargain on money wages need not imply impact on the real cost of labor.

There may be no expedient by which labor as a whole can reduce its *real* wage to a given figure by making revised *money* bargains with entrepreneurs. (Keynes, 1936:13, italics in original)

If the employer treats the wage he pays as a cost of production, changes in that cost may imply changes in the price of the product. And, if this implication follows, a general fall in money wages as a part of an effort by workers to increase employment will bring down the price level rather than increasing demand for labor.

If, however, prices do not fall with wage costs so that, in Kalecki's language, the degree of monopoly or profit margin rises, a fall in money wages will lower real wages and the real cost of labor to employers. Whether this leads to an increase in employment depends on the relative impact on production and investment decisions of two factors: (1) the lower cost of production and (2) the lower level of demand for products that results from lower real wages. Thus, if lower costs do not stimulate investment, a lower real wage means that the level of demand forthcoming from current production and investment decisions will be lower. The fall in demand can, through its influence on production and investment decisions, lead to a lower level of employment. When levels of production and investment are sensitive to demand rather than costs, workers cannot influence (except perhaps perversely) their level of employment by influencing the nominal price of labor (the money wage).

If this is indeed the case, then a capitalist market economy poses a dilemma for those who depend on the wage contract for their livelihood. The failure of demand that deprives them of their livelihood is neither of their own making nor responsive to their actions. In the language of the neoclassical approach, they suffer from a negative external effect (see Baumol, [1952] 1965). Without employment, they cannot purchase the goods they need. If they cannot purchase those goods, firms cannot make profit by selling them.

It is, then, beyond the power of the parties to the wage contract, acting in their capacities as private agents, to correct the failure of the market and bring about the exchanges that would be in their interest. By doing what is rational from an individual standpoint, they create an aggregate condition that defeats their purposes. What is rational at the microeconomic level becomes irrational at the macroeconomic level.

It is in the interest of both employers and employees that something be done to stabilize the employee–employer relation to assure the livelihood of the worker, and with it adequate demand for the firm's products. Strategies arise on two levels for coping with the problem posed by the wage contract (see Piore and Sabel, 1984). At the microeconomic level, changes in the terms of the wage contract can lend stability to labor markets benefiting both employer and employee. At the macroeconomic level, demand management by the state can maintain levels of demand and employment by countering the instability born of the unregulated and uncoordinated decisions of private agents.

The Keynesian analysis of the labor market centers on the implications of the wage bargain for demand. Because of this, it sees the possibility that decisions by and contacts between agents (workers and employers) will have perverse effects. The Keynesian analysis of saving develops in a similar direction. It also highlights the potential for conflict between the rationality of the individual agent and that of the system as a whole. We turn now to a brief summary of that conflict.

In the last chapter of *The General Theory*, Keynes explores the broader implications of his ideas. This exploration of the "social philosophy" toward which the theory might lead focuses on the problem of saving and especially on the "belief that the growth of capital depends upon the strength of the motive towards individual saving and that for a large proportion of this growth we are dependent on the savings of the rich out of their superfluity" (1936:372). Keynes thought that the argument of *The General Theory* could be used to undermine one of the most fundamental and long-standing justifications for the inequalities of income and wealth we associate with capitalist economy, especially under a regime of laissez-faire:

> Thus our argument leads towards the conclusion that in contemporary conditions the growth of wealth, so far from being dependent on the abstinence of the rich, as is commonly supposed, is more likely to be impeded by it. One of the chief social justifications of great inequality of wealth is, therefore, removed. (1936:373)

Keynes goes on to note that other arguments (having to do with incentives) could support a degree of inequality, but not that degree traditionally claimed on grounds of the demands for financing investment.

In the "older" view, accumulation is limited by the supply of savings from the community (or, in the classical approach, by the magnitude of the profit or surplus). The level of savings in turn depends (in important part) on the distribution of income. Unequal distribution supports community saving. In the classical theory this inequality was structural; it was an inequality in ownership of the means of production. The capitalist class does the saving by transforming its surplus into new capital. The more profit placed into the capitalist's hands, the greater the social saving, the greater the accumulation of capital:

> Accumulate, accumulate. That is Moses and the Prophets!...Therefore save, save, i.e. reconvert the greatest possible portion of surplus-value or surplus-product into capital. Accumulation for accumulation's sake, production for production's sake: by this formula classical economy expressed the historical mission of the bourgeoisie....(Marx, 1967a:595)

In the classical model, the division of society into classes was, among other things, a mechanism for social savings. This savings was more or less automatically used to create new capital. Accumulation was understood to be constrained and determined by the magnitude of the surplus. Inequality thus plays a decisive part in economic progress.

Inequality can still play this role in the absence of the classical structural model. So long as those with higher incomes save a greater portion of their incomes and so long as inequality creates high-income groups, it will stimulate saving. And, again, so long as saving brings about investment, the argument for investment becomes an argument for saving, which becomes an argument for inequality.

The classical economists link saving to investment more or less by assumption. The class that does the saving is by nature parsimonious and eager to invest. The neoclassical economists develop their theory on a plane that leaves class differences out of account. They employ a different mechanism linking saving to investment: the rate of interest. The neoclassical economists develop an elaborate argument centering on the role of the interest rate in matching saving and investment (see Fisher, 1930). By making the interest rate a crucial determinant of the demand for new capital (the amount invested), the neoclassical economists introduced a mechanism that made investment respond to the supply of funds (saving). Put somewhat loosely, a greater supply of funds would, other things equal, imply a lower interest rate (a greater supply means a lower price). A lower interest rate implies a lower cost of investing, which implies more investment.

This line of thought parallels that applied to the labor market in the neoclassical approach. Changes in the price of labor should affect demand for labor just as changes in the cost of finance should affect demand for capital. In both cases agents respond to changes in input costs rather than demand expectation when making investment decisions. It makes a difference whether we think investment is constrained by the supply of funds (savings) or by expectations of demand for the products the new capital will produce. Prior to Keynes and Kalecki the former was the dominant view. Keynes and Kalecki argue that the interest rate and supply of savings play a relatively minor role in determining or stimulating accumulation.

If investment decisions are unresponsive to changes in the supply of savings, then encouraging saving by the community has perverse effects. The higher the level of saving out of income, the lower the level of demand for products out of that income, and, other things equal, the lower the levels of output and employment. Given the circularity of economic processes, the higher the proportion of current income saved in a Keynesian world, the lower is current demand for output; the effect on the circular flow translates into lower levels of income and therefore, perversely, a lower overall amount of savings.

In a Keynesian world, a decision to save neither implies nor stimulates a decision to purchase capital goods (that is, real investment). Where his predecessors saw the trade-off between saving and consumption as one between acquisition of means of production and acquisition of means of consumption (of the community), Keynes saw that trade-off as one between current consumption (and thus demand) and a leakage from the circular flow that did not stimulate any equivalent demand. The more the community attempts to save, the worse off it is both in the present and future. This "paradox of thrift" undermines a main support for the argument from political economy in favor of the income inequalities that result from the operations of unregulated markets.

In a capitalist economy that operates in the way the Keynesian theory predicts, both the wage bargain and the saving decision can have perverse effects. In both cases problems arise because investment decisions center on demand expectations rather than costs of production. Piore and Sabel summarize the problem well:

In a mass-consumption economy, the natural response of prices to many kinds of disturbances has the perverse effect of producing contractions of economic activity, rather than relaunching growth. Investment is not directly responsive to declining wages and interest costs as long as industry already has substantial excess capacity; and the fall in wages under the pressure of unemployment undermines the demand for consumption goods, creating exactly the kind of excess capacity that deters the revival of investment spending. Because investment is so sensitive to consumer income, it is thus possible that the mass-production economy will respond to a wage decline in a fashion precisely opposite to that of a competitive economy. (1984:77)

The idea that the demand side of the accumulation process becomes dominant in later stages of capitalist growth is also a main theme of what has come to be referred to as the "regulation theory" (for brief accounts of this theory see DeVroey, 1984, and Noel, 1987).

The regulation theory distinguishes two phases, or regimes, of capitalist accumulation on the basis of the relations between production decisions and the determinants of aggregate demand. In the first phase, wages are experienced primarily as a cost and accumulation as a process of building a producing apparatus to meet an expanding demand. In the second phase, demand becomes the dominant concern, with an implied emphasis on the sales effort and the wage as a determinant of demand. The growing concern with demand encourages the state to play a more active role in demand management. The involvement of the state at the macroeconomic level parallels growth of collective bargaining arrangements and associated changes in the nature and conduct of the wage contract. These changes can have the consequence of stabilizing incomes and demand.

Implications for political economy

The foregoing discussion of labor markets and saving underscores the broader implications of Keynesian theory for political economy. The self-regulating market cannot be relied on to secure the livelihoods of those dependent on it, or to translate the community's desire to save into the formation of the capital needed to make that saving bear fruit in the future. More damaging still is the implication that in crucial areas individual pursuit of self-interest even when based on a reasonable means-ends calculus will often be self-defeating. Workers' efforts to increase demand for labor can lead to lower levels of employment; the community's effort to save more can lead to less saving and investment. These conclusions help lay a foundation for state intervention and thus help to define the role of the state in relation to the economy. The state works to secure the macroeconomic conditions needed so that the pursuit of private interest will not have perverse effects.

Government stabilization policy focuses primarily on systemic conditions in three areas: (a) aggregate demand, (b) the financial sector, and (c) prices.

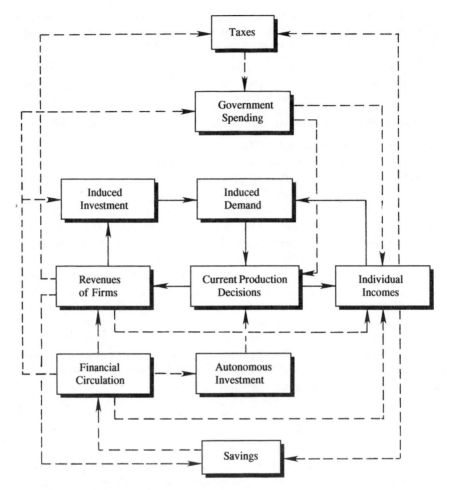

Figure 3. The circular flow with government

We will not attempt to summarize here the methods employed in these areas. We focus instead on the objectives of stabilization as they reveal important features of the understanding of the relation of state to economy.

To help understand the proximate objectives in stabilizing aggregate demand, we revise our diagram of the circular flow to take the government explicitly into account (see Figure 3). The state's ability to affect the circular flow depends on the way it is connected to that flow. This connection consists of the following points:

1. Government spending. The government uses its revenues to acquire goods from the private sector, employ labor, and provide incomes to consumers (and to various corporate entities) independently of their employment or of their providing goods and services in exchange.
2. Government borrowing. One source of revenue for the spending indicated in point (1) is borrowing from the private sector. The government issues bonds, which can be held by individuals or firms. The purchase of government bonds from the state provides revenues to fund the state budget.
3. Taxes. The state can fund its activities without borrowing either by printing money or by taxation. In the following, we ignore the former and concentrate on revenues resulting from taxes on the incomes of firms and consumers.

The proximate cause of instability in consumer demand is the link between income, employment, and consumption. This link translates fluctuations in investment into fluctuations in demand. To stabilize employment and output, the government seeks to modify this link. In order to stabilize demand, the government must compensate for fluctuations in output and employment originating in the private sector. In the following, we focus on efforts to support or maintain a level of demand and output.

Clearly, if the government, in taxing consumers, simply shifts demand from them to itself, the net effect cannot be to enhance output and employment. To achieve this end, the government must do one of two things.

1. Tax incomes that would otherwise be saved rather than spent by their original recipients and (a) spend the tax revenue directly on goods and services or (b) transfer the tax revenue to agents who will consume it (or at least consume more of it than would have been consumed by those bearing the burden of the tax).
2. Spend more than it collects in taxes by borrowing the difference from agents who would not otherwise have spent it or even received it themselves.

When the state does either of these things, it stimulates demand and employment. Either government spending directly offsets deficiencies caused by inadequate private investment (as emphasized by Baran and Sweezy, 1966) or government transfers income from employed to unemployed, either by borrowing from or taxing the former. By so doing, it increases the overall proportion of income spent on goods and services rather than saved. Economists refer to this as an increase in the overall propensity to spend. This latter can be exemplified in the following way.

Assume that consumer A receives $50,000 per year income and spends 90 percent of it. He thus uses $45,000 to acquire goods and services, $5,000 to acquire a financial asset. Consumer B has no income. The overall income of the two consumers is $50,000, which generates demand of $45,000. Now assume that the government taxes consumer A $10,000 and transfers the money to consumer B who, having a low level of income, consumes the entire $10,000. After the transfer, consumer A spends $36,000 and saves $4,000, consumer B spends $10,000, so that total spending and demand out of the $50,000 rises from $45,000 to $46,000.

If the government commits itself to income supports, then it commits itself to assuring that fluctuations in investment will not multiply their effects. When employment falls as a result of a fall in investment, incomes will not fall (or will not fall proportionately) since incomes are not so tightly linked to demand for products. Stabilization thus tends to break the link first between income and output, and ultimately between income and employment. Stabilization as pursued by firms tends to soften the impact on income from changes in current demand (see Okun, 1981; Schofield, 1978), making a larger part of the wages bill an overhead expense whose magnitude is relatively more stable in the face of fluctuations in output and investment. Stabilization as pursued by government weakens the link between income and employment (as emphasized by Offe, 1984). Stabilization modifies, and may implicitly or explicitly challenge, a central institution of private enterprise economy. It thus has profound political implications.

The pursuit of stability by government policy, if successful or even if only assumed to be successful (see Baily, 1978), changes the subjective environment within which individual and firms' decision making takes place. As we emphasized earlier, agents act differently in a stable environment; they form and act on plans oriented toward the long run. Their sensitivity to current conditions declines, and they are less likely to exacerbate short-period fluctuations by their responses to them. This fact also contributes to the stability of the economy, since it reduces the expectational component of cumulative processes. Stabilization breeds stability; but it is also perceived to breed its own set of political and economic problems. It has potentially profound political implications and thus stimulates a political agenda.

Some political implications

The approach to macroeconomic intervention briefly discussed in the foregoing has encouraged a technical interpretation of the work of the state vis-à-vis the economy. Given the objective of stabilizing a private enterprise economy, some economists attempt to treat the methods of stabilization as "tools." Political process and political judgment need not play a role. Stabilization is a technical problem best left to those having the appropriate know-how, much as we might leave car repair to a competent mechanic. In this view the less politicized the process the better (see Silk, 1984).

Treating stabilization as a technical problem fits nicely into the classical agenda of depoliticizing society. Even when we need the intervention of the political authority, we can drain politics as much as possible out of that intervention. Is stabilization an essentially nonpolitical matter? Debate over this issue has inspired a number of contributions to political economy. Here we briefly summarize two: the political business cycle and the crisis of legitimation.

One difficulty encountered by the Keynesian approach derives from limitations in its conception of the state. If we interpret the state as (or as potentially) a competent economic manager, we need not employ an explicitly political context to consider what it does. We can think of economic management as an economic activity even if that activity is undertaken by a political authority. However, if economic management impinges on the political process, and if state intervention depends on politics as well, we cannot employ the image of the state as competent manager. We cannot ignore politics in thinking about stabilizing the economy.

The political business cycle literature emphasizes one important political dimension of demand management (see Kalecki, 1971). The state of the economy has a significant influence on the outcome of the electoral process. When officeholders are held responsible for the state of the economy, their reelection will depend on whether they are blamed for recession or praised for prosperity. If the electorate has a sufficiently short memory, officeholders can improve their chances for reelection if they can manage the economic cycle in such a way as to assure that the appropriate phase of the cycle will line up with the period of reelection. Political considerations outweigh economic, and economic instability gives way not to competent management but to the so-called political business cycle.

A political dimension with even broader implications than those associated with the political business cycle is the challenge to the basic institution of the labor market. Some theorists see this challenge in the effort to stabilize the economy and protect incomes from the vicissitudes of the unregulated market (see Offe, 1984). The more functioning of the economy becomes an administrative-political matter, the weaker the hold the idea of self-regulation has over the population. The domain of commodity relations (especially in the older sense associated with more or less free markets, especially in labor) alters in ways that undermine assumptions about the legitimacy and inevitability of the dependence of livelihood on the wage contract. Thus "decommodification" of labor leads to a crisis of legitimacy that raises a political challenge to the market economy. Demand management contributes to this crisis so far as it weakens the link between income, employment, and aggregate demand. The more economic management encourages expectations regarding incomes the free market can only satisfy intermittently if at all, the more demand management undermines the legitimacy of the self-regulating market.

Thus, demand management, even if made a depoliticized (administrative) process, has politically relevant consequences. It places the issue of the configuration of public and private on the political agenda. It brings into question the underlying principles that organize a private enterprise market system. Debate over the organizing principles that configure the relation of public to private is political debate touching on the nature and limits of the market, the treatment of human capacities (labor) as a commodity, and the dependence of livelihood on exchange.

If the process of demand management alters the definition of human capacities as commodities on whose value must depend the welfare of the individual, it makes the boundaries of the market and the specification of the nature of a commodity problematic. This constitutes a lead-in to a political debate over market self-regulation. In other words, it suggests a (political) process of redefining the market as the primary social institution sustaining property relations and the pursuit of private interest.

It needs to be emphasized that this does not, strictly speaking, politicize the economy, if by that we mean making the economy a political system. Rather, it encourages collective rethinking of the nature and limits of the market. This rethinking is a political process that redefines the market, not a political process that takes the place of the market or does its work.

When some of the work of the market is taken over by a public authority, this does not in itself politicize that work. The political process can also transfer wants and their satisfaction from private to public ("reassign" them, in Walzer's language [1986]), from market relations to administrative process. If politics is the assignment process, and administration the work done subsequent to reassignment away from the market, the market is not made political.

In drawing this conclusion, we have assumed a clear distinction in nature between politics, administration, and the market. This distinction presumes a conception of politics and economics that restricts each to a domain rather than treating them as more general modes of action and interaction applicable in principle to all social domains. The conclusion drawn makes sense only when we define economics in relation to market institutions and politics in relation to struggle over and definition of the public agenda.

Even within the suggested conceptual framework for talking about politics and economics, the administrative process may not be insulated from politics. If enough discretion remains in administration of outcomes reassigned from the market to the public authority, administration can contain a political dimension. It is not inevitable that it do so; administration is not in its nature politics. But it can become politicized.

We should observe, in addition, that if we define the economic as the provisioning process, reassigning dimensions of want satisfaction from market to administration makes the economy an administrative system. Framed in this way, the economy might be politicized if the administrative process allows sufficient discretion and is made vulnerable to a struggle between contending groups. The result is not an identification of the political with the economic, but the specification of a definition of the economic and the circumstances under which the economic process is politicized. It remains relevant to note that the political-administrative process that oversees the provisioning of wants contains distinctly economic, political, and administrative aspects. That these aspects come together in practice does not mean we will understand that practice better without clearly distinguishing between them and understanding that each has its own imperatives, logic, and meaning.

6

Economic approaches to politics

Let us start with two broad definitions of economics.

Economics is a study of mankind in the ordinary business of life; it examines that part of individual and social action which is most closely connected with the attainment and with the use of the material requisites of wellbeing. (Alfred Marshall, *Principles of Economics*, ([1890] 1930:1)

Economics is the science which studies human behavior as a relationship between ends and scarce means that have alternative uses. (Lionel Robbins, *An Essay on the Nature and Significance of Economic Science*, 1932:16)

These two definitions, the former stressing material well-being and the latter efficient allocation, recall two of the three approaches to economics discussed earlier in the book. The former definition, offered by Marshall in *Principles of Economics*, conforms to the idea of economics as material provisioning to satisfy needs and wants. If we broaden Marshall's definition to include non-material means, we have an idea of the economy, or economic processes, that is concerned with wealth, its production, distribution, and consumption. The latter definition has to do with adapting means to ends. Economics here is defined more abstractly, in methodological terms. Economics does not refer to particular kinds of activities but to a distinctive way of adapting resources to ends.

It is this second definition that becomes central to this chapter. Once we abstract economics from economic activities, using the term to characterize situations of choice and scarcity, the door opens to an expanded domain of economics. As Becker puts it:

The definition of economics in terms of scarce means and competing ends is the most general of all. It defines economics by the nature of the problem to be solved, and encompasses far more than the market sector or "what economists do." Scarcity and choice characterize all resources allocated by the political process (including which industries to tax, how fast to increase the money supply, and whether to go to war); by the family (including decisions about a marriage mate, family size, the frequency of church attendance, and the allocation of time between sleeping and waking hours);

126

Table 1. *Economics and politics as method and substance*

	SUBSTANCE	
	Economics	Politics
METHODS Economics	(1) traditional economic theory; maximizing behavior in market settings, price theory, allocative efficiency	(2) application of economic method of politics: public choice
Politics	(3) application of political methods to economics; power-distributional analysis within market settings	(4) traditional political science; power-distributional analysis within political arena

by scientists (including decisions about allocating their thinking time, and mental energy to different research problems; and so on in endless variety. (1976:4)

In this chapter we introduce a new conception of how politics and economics relate to each other. In previous chapters, politics and economics were conceived in substantive terms. The subsequent theoretical task was to provide a coherent explanation of how these two domains affect each other. The economic approach to politics does not see political economy as the set of theoretical relations describing the connections between politics and economics. Instead, politics is considered economic – susceptible to analysis by economic method – insofar as political facts are characterized by choice and scarcity.

The relations between economics and politics conceived in substantive and methodological terms are illustrated by Table 1. Cells 1 and 4 refer to the traditional fields of economics and political science. Cell 1 is the intersection of neoclassical economic method and economic phenomena. It involves the rational pursuit of self-interest in perfect or imperfect market settings, the study of price movements and efficient allocation of resources. The fourth cell defines political science traditionally conceived as the study of public patterns of power and authority within the state. Cell 3 is perhaps the most difficult to describe because it is unclear whether there is a distinctive political method and, if so, what it is. Without attempting to resolve this issue, we simply note that politics has often been associated with analysis based on power and distributional transfers or with attempts on the part of a community to constitute itself (to affirm its identity, to express itself publicly).

Such attempts to isolate a political method do not succeed in achieving a degree of separation from the subject matter of politics parallel to the economic case.

The second cell is the one of direct concern to us in this chapter. The application of economic methods to politics is evident in public choice theory, game theory (when applied to political actors or issues), and economic analysis of the law and political institutions.

The economic approach to politics requires us to break with the idea that political economy involves the interaction of political and economic spheres, arenas, or subsystems. Political economy is not about "what happens" when political and economic phenomena collide; it is the application of economic reasoning to political processes. A substantive conception of the political is retained, while economics is interpreted formally as conformity to the rules of economizing behavior. After defining the economic approach to politics, this chapter discusses three examples: public choice theory, economic analysis of policy, and economic analysis of institutions.

Defining the economic approach to politics

At the heart of an economic approach to politics are rational choice and efficiency. We must first consider what economic reasoning or the economic approach is, a question that turns out not to be easily answered. The economic approach is variously identified with subjective utility, the rational pursuit of self-interest, cost and scarcity, marginal analysis, partial and general equilibrium thinking, and allocative efficiency. To a certain extent, these concepts come together as a coherent ensemble. Choice is made necessary by scarcity and in turn implies cost (opportunity cost if nothing else). Rationality, utility, and efficiency are also closely bonded in the same sense that a utility schedule is needed to motivate rational action and efficiency provides a yardstick to measure progress toward achieving goals. If a person behaves rationally in the economist's sense, it amounts to saying he or she gets what he or she wants subject to the constraints of the situation.

Whether the aforementioned elements of the economic approach must go together or whether they can be treated separately for some purposes is an important question we do not try to answer here. In the section below we deal with rationality and efficiency.

Rationality

What does it mean within the neoclassical framework to choose rationally? To answer this question, we must first introduce some subsidiary concepts: preferences (goals), beliefs, opportunities, and actions. Preferences describe the goal states of the individual with respect to the environment. Goals must be weakly ordered, affectively, for consistent preferences to exist. Second, beliefs are important too. The choosing individual must have some information about alternative goals – for example, how obtainable they are, relations between different actions and outcomes, and costs, in terms of direct expenditures of resources and forgone opportunities. Third, there are resources that define opportunities and constraints. Fourth, there are the actions themselves that are usually taken as objects of explanation.

To see why each of these terms is important for rational choice explanations, let us examine each in more detail. If the object is to explain behavioral outcomes (or simply actions), we must know what agents want, what they believe, and what their resources and constraints are. Preferences must assume a particular form. We must be able to rank outcomes, and that ranking must be transitive. In other words, we can say $a > b > c$ (a is preferred to b, b is preferred to c) and that $a > c$ (transitivity). While these requirements may seem straightforward when applied at the individual level, we will see later that the transitivity requirement is by no means easily satisfied for groups (aggregates of individuals).

The second component of the rational choice scheme is beliefs. As Elster puts it: "In order to know what to do, we first have to know what to believe with respect to the relevant factual matters. Hence a theory of rational choice must be supplemented by a theory of rational belief" (1986:1). The emphasis on beliefs implies that individuals do not act out of pure habit or emotion. They hold some beliefs about the causal structure of the world, beliefs that provide hypothesized links between alternative actions and their consequences defined in terms of utility. We may believe that avoiding eggs and eating oat bran will prolong our lives, but we may be wrong. Or, an example more to the point in a book on political economy, we may think that a federal governmental structure, involving a territorial division of political responsibility among spatially distinct units, promotes peaceful relations among different ethnic and religious groups, when in fact such divisions provide organizational resources for group conflict. Or we may believe that a policy of export-oriented industrialization is best for a less developed country, "best" defined in terms of growth of output and sectoral composition of the economy.

The third component of the rational choice paradigm concerns resources and constraints. Sometimes this factor is omitted (see Elster, 1986), not out of neglect but because it enters implicitly under preferences. Preferences and resources would seem to be distinct. What one wants and what one can get are two different things unless aspirations are completely determined by possibilities. At a given moment, it makes sense to talk as Elster does, of a "feasibility set," the set of actions that are possible, given logical, physical, and economic constraints. In doing this, resources and constraints are folded into the structure of preferences themselves and cease to operate "externally."

The fourth and final component is the actions themselves, the observed choices of agents. The aim of rational choice theory is to explain these choices. The core claim is that preferences and beliefs are exogenous and fixed and that choices respond to changes in incentives (costs) at the margin.

The essence of a rational choice explanation embodies a conception of how preferences, beliefs, resources, and actions stand in relation to one another (Elster, 1987:68). This relation can be broken down into two parts. First, there is a consistency criterion that applies to the structure of preferences and beliefs. Second, there is a series of correspondence requirements. An action is rational when it stands in a relationship to preferences, beliefs, and resources. Those actions are rational when they can be shown (*ex ante* rather than *ex post*) to be the best actions possible to satisfy the agent's preferences given his or her beliefs, that the beliefs are rational given the evidence available, and, finally, that the amount and quality of the evidence available can be justified in terms of cost/benefit ratios (Elster, 1987:68). In a fully specified account of rational choice, actions, beliefs, and the evidence on which these beliefs are based should be arrived at through rational calculation. This is another way of saying that everything is endogenous except preferences. To quote Elster once again, "Showing that an action is rational amounts to offering a sequence showing that an action is taken as given but everything else has to be justified – ultimately in terms of that desire" (1987:69).

Several points we haven't yet discussed are often the source of confusion in rational choice explanations. The first has to do with rationality and self-interest. Although the two terms are often treated as synonymous, they are distinct. As Sen points out (1989:320), the rationality criterion is purely procedural. It specifies nothing about the content of pursued goals. By contrast, the idea of self-interest at least implies a location where want, desire, or need are registered. But, in principle, there is nothing inconsistent about rational behavior that tries to advance the well-being of others (spouses, children, friends, or humanity).

The second common point of confusion concerns the methodological status of preferences. Are they to be thought of as psychological data (as mental or emotional states) or as behavioral data that conform to specified consistency requirements? Neoclassical economics has largely opted for the latter course, treating preferences as revealed through the actions of agents themselves. That is, preferences are reconstructed out of the actions in which agents engage. Agent i prefers a to b if, when both are available, i chooses a over b. While this threatens to erode some of the content of our previous remark that actions need to stand in a certain relationship to preferences, for the moment we pass over this problem.

The debate over the status of preferences is related to the broader theoretical controversy about the nature of agents engaging in economic transactions. While the very terms "rational" and "choice" suggest conscious agents weighing the costs and benefits of various alternatives, there is a substantial group of neoclassical economists who see rationality as a pattern of behavior that is adaptive or functional for the needs of certain individuals and groups. According to this view, individuals need not be rational at all in the sense of consciously calculating how best to achieve their preferences. Rational results might be achieved by a process of competitive selection similar to that which ensures adaptive results in biological evolution, as Hirschleifer argues (1985). When there are consistent selective mechanisms in the environment, adaptive behavior will occur simply as a result of winnowing and differential survival. Thus some economists (Alchian, 1950; Hirschleifer, 1985) argue for "as-if" rationality.

The third source of confusion, or at least complexity, concerns the unit to which the terms of rational discourse are applied. If the unit is a collectivity, there may be severe problems of aggregation of preferences, so much so that it is impossible to say what the social preferences are. This was the message of Kenneth Arrow's *Social Choice and Individual Values* (1951). Arrow argued that when decisions are made in groups through democratic procedures, there will not exist a social welfare function that (1) expresses the preferences of the collectivity as a whole and (2) conforms to the consistency requirements established for individual preference orderings. Thus a rational choice explanation may fail at the level of the political system either because collective agents do not behave rationally or because the very idea of what is rational for the collectivity breaks down.

Efficiency

The second major component of the economic approach is the efficiency orientation. Since economic reasoning is a means-ends calculus with available means inadequate to satisfy all ends, the economic method must assume a specifically defined condition of scarcity: Resources are inadequate to satisfy fully desires expressed in preference orderings.

Thus the general idea of efficiency has to do with the way resources are used. A firm's productive efficiency has to do with the way it uses its inputs of land, labor, and capital to produce goods and services. It is using them most efficiently if it cannot rearrange them (buy more or less of the inputs, buy different types of inputs, combine them in different proportions) so as to produce more output with the same amount of inputs. For an individual consumer, efficiency means getting the greatest utility possible within the limits of budget constraints.

There is one more efficiency concept to introduce, that of efficiency for the collectivity, or Pareto optimality. Pareto argued that economists could judge one distribution as better than another if this distribution improved the lot of at least one person without harming the condition of anyone. The core claim is that a collective allocation is optimal if resources cannot be rearranged so as to make anyone better off without making anyone worse off. Any policy that is redistributive (that takes from some and gives to others) violates the Pareto condition.

An important question arises in this framework having to do with the connection between rationality and efficiency. Given the preceding discussion, we ask whether efficiency is implied by the very idea of rational choice. If people behave rationally, do they automatically behave efficiently? Let us try to answer this question first, by making a distinction between normative and explanatory uses of the efficiency criterion and second, by examining the differences in the meaning of efficiency within market and political settings.

Efficiency may be used only as a normative yardstick, a standard by which to assess different choices, distributions, and allocations. Nothing is predicted or explained by efficiency. It does not enter as a term in theories about why decision makers allocate resources the way they do. Instead, it is simply used to evaluate the properties of allocations, however these allocations are made. On the other hand, efficiency may be thought of as an active factor in propelling economic decisions, or rather decisions economically made. In the latter event, efficiency achieves theoretical status as an operative force in the actual process of making decisions or, at the least, as part of the selective structure that determines which decisions survive and reproduce.

If efficiency is used only as a normative criterion, there is no necessary connection between it and rational behavior, at least in one sense – no prediction is made as to how individuals will behave. Yet, even here inefficiency would have to raise doubts about the rationality of agents. Individuals could do better given the resources they have, yet they don't. What is the problem? Thus the failure to behave efficiently implicates the rationality of individuals.

Departing from efficiency as a normative device, let us ask the same question: Does rationality entail efficiency? An answer to this question depends on the environment within which persons pursue their interests. Within a market setting, individuals engage in voluntary exchange. Agents decide for themselves, on the basis of their own interest, whether to participate in transactions in which they will give up their goods in return for others. For agents to engage in exchange, they must believe they will be better off: otherwise they will refuse. The capacity to say "no deal" and to "exit" is an inherent property of the market. Thus, in market settings individuals will trade until they reach the highest possible levels of satisfaction. As Wolff and Resnick put it:

> In neoclassical theory, there is a precise and necessary correspondence between a fully competitive private-property economy and an optimally efficient one. The insight of Adam Smith is retained in neoclassical economics: each individual having the power (freedom to act in his or her own self-interest) will be led as if by an "invisible hand" (the fully competitive market) to actions that produce the maximum wealth (efficiency) for a society of individuals. (1987:89)

Applications of economic theories of politics

In this section we consider three different economic approaches to politics: public choice, economic analysis of policy, and economic analysis of institutions. These are not the only approaches that could have been examined. Game theory, rent-seeking models of the political process, and the political economy of regulation could also have been included. Space limitations confine our examination to the three approaches mentioned previously.

Public choice theory

At the broadest level, public choice theory involves the application of economic methods to politics.

> [It] takes the tools and methods that have been developed to quite sophisticated analytical levels in economic theory and applies these tools and methods to the political or governmental sector, to politics, to the public economy. (Buchanan, 1984:13)

While this definition may seem straightforward, the transference of economic methods from the economy to the polity involves some complications. These complications center on the aggregation of individual preferences into collective, or "public" outcomes, the problem of coordinating individual interests and choices to achieve collective outcomes, and the interdependence of individual decisions. These three problems have been dealt with in the literatures on voting rules, collective action theory, and strategic (or game) theory.

Public choice theory is relatively new as economic theories go, deriving in part from the literature on public finance during the 1950s (Musgrave and Peacock, 1958; Musgrave, 1959), and in part from the seminal contributions of Kenneth Arrow's *Social Choice and Individual Values* (1951), Anthony Downs's *An Economic Theory of Democracy* (1957), and James Buchanan and Gordon Tullock's *The Calculus of Consent* (1962). Mancur Olson's *The Logic of Collective Action* (1965) helped to place the public choice work of economists in front of political scientists and to facilitate the conceptualization of many standard preoccupations of political science (including interest group organization, bureaucratic behavior, the organizational bases of influence, alliances) as problems of collective action.

The contributions of public choice are easily chronicled since there is a journal (*Public Choice*) and a professional society (The Public Choice Society). While the literature on public choice theory is not limited to the journal, the existence of a publication outlet, a society, and professional meetings has served to consolidate and give focus to what otherwise might be a fragmentary research program. The Public Choice Society took shape during the mid-1960s, was headquartered at the University of Virginia, and was initially called the Committee on Non-Market Decision-Making (Tollison, 1984:3). In 1966 it published a series called *Papers on Non-Market Decision-Making*. In 1968 the group changed its name to Public Choice Society and the journal title to *Public Choice*. Still, the original labels are instructive since they imply that economics as subject matter is concerned with markets and decision processes that are individual, while politics is concerned with processes (or outcomes) that are collective.

Let us see if we can sharpen the previous definition of public choice as simply the application of economic methods to politics. It is after all possible to apply economic methods to political problems that are not public, at least not to any significant degree. For example, one could analyze the efficiency properties of a redistributional program.[1] In most standard works, public choice is defined as the application of economic methods to politics (Mueller, 1979:1; Buchanan, 1984:13; Ekelund and Tollison, 1986:440) without linking these methods to outcomes that are in some sense public (for an overview, see Plott, 1976). In this regard the treatments by Stiglitz (1988:145ff.) and McLean (1987:9–11) are more helpful. Nevertheless, the public choice literature makes it clear that the relationship between public choice and public goods is a close one. If outcomes were not characterized by externalities, private decisions would do. The focus remains that of the choosing individual – his or her preferences and maximizing behavior. It is the results of private-regarding decisions that are public, collective, and indivisible. The public is not a choosing agent; indeed, it could not be so in a methodologically individualist theory.

Public choice theory sees individual actors as central, whether operating as members of political parties, interest groups, or bureaucracies, whether elected or appointed, whether ordinary citizen or chief executive:

[1] It is true that the program itself, embodied in a policy, is public, and perhaps brought into existence by authoritative action. But the redistribution itself, taxing resources from x and giving to y, is not public in the sense of either nonexcludability or nonrivalness, the two standard characteristics of public goods.

The fundamental premise of public choice is that political decision-makers (voters, politicians, bureaucrats) and private decision-makers (consumers, brokers, producers) behave in a similar way: they all follow the dictates of rational self-interest. In fact, political and economic decision-makers are often one and the same person – consumer and voter. The individual who buys the family groceries is the same individual who votes in an election. (Ekelund and Tollison, 1986:440)

Public choice theory is different from conventional economics not in its conception of the individual and the forces motivating action but rather in the different constraints and opportunities offered by the political as opposed to the market environment. In this new theory, economics (as market exchange, production, consumption) and politics (as political exchange, power, authority relations) appear as special applications rather than as distinctive subject matters. Politics simply refers to those institutions and processes through which individuals pursue their preferences when these preferences refer to goods that are interdependent or public.

In the remainder of this section we will discuss two strands of public choice theory: normative and positive. The former often has to do with issues related to political design, basic political rules, in short, with the constitutional framework within which political processes take place. The work of Arrow (1951) and Sen (1970) exemplifies the normative strand. The positive strand has to do with attempts to explain observable political behavior in choice theoretic terms. The distinction between normative and positive public choice is not airtight. Arrow's impossibility theorem can be interpreted in positive terms as predicting cycles in majorities as well as the emergence of political rules to prevent them. Nevertheless, these categories have served to organize thinking and research among adherents of public choice theory.

Normative public choice. Normative public choice deals with the analysis of desirable properties of the political system. What sorts of institutional arrangements are efficient, responsive, and fair? What types of voting rules most faithfully translate (aggregate) individual preferences into public decisions? What governmental structure is likely to prevent concentrations of power, stagnation, or instability? Will a federal or unitary system be better able to "contain" ethnic, class, and religious differences? These are representative questions consistent with a public choice viewpoint.

Buchanan and Arrow provide two examples of normative public choice. James Buchanan is interested in organizing society so as to increase the scope for free exchange, whether within economic (market) or political (state) settings. Within political settings he distinguishes between constitutional and postconstitutional politics. However, a strong contractarian position is maintained in both. The political system is judged desirable to the extent that it facilitates voluntary exchange and proportionate relations between private costs and publicly provided (but privately consumed) benefits (Buchanan, 1987, 1988). Kenneth Arrow, in *Social Choice and Individual Values* (1951), deals with voting rules that consistently translate individual preference orderings into group decisions. We will go through this example in more detail.

In 1951 Kenneth Arrow published his *Social Choice and Individual Values*, a book that was to stimulate wide interest in public choice. The basic problem was simple: In a representative democracy, where individuals vote or otherwise register their preferences in collective outcomes, how can those individual preferences be consistently aggregated so as to produce collective decisions? The word "consistently" refers to the same transitivity condition necessary for rationality at the individual level.

What Arrow discovered (or really rediscovered, the results having been known to deBorda and Condorcet in the eighteenth century) was that individual preference orderings do not in general "add up" to a consistent social preference ordering (or social welfare function). The group literally cannot make up its collective mind (Buchanan, 1984:17). Yet, as Frolich and Oppenheimer point out, for the assumption of individual rationality to be of value in explaining political outcomes, which are perforce collective, there must be a consistent link between individual and group orderings (1978:15). This is precisely what Arrow found did not, given his assumptions, exist.

Let us run through a stylized example. Suppose we have three individuals and three choices of candidates or policies. See Figure 4, where the private preferences of voters 1, 2, 3 are given for candidates or issues A, B, and C.

Now let us try to aggregate these individual orderings by having a pairwise vote among alternatives. If A is compared to B, it dominates (beats) B. Voters 1 and 2 both prefer A to B. Comparing B against C, B dominates. If A dominates B and B dominates C, A should dominate C. But this is precisely what we don't find. Instead, C is preferred to A by voters 2 and 3. Individually consistent preference orderings do not define a consistent ordering at the group level.

Arrow's result, labeled a general impossibility theorem, has met with diverse reactions. Some treat it as irrelevant (see Tullock's "The General Irrelevance of the General Impossibility Theorem," 1967) while others argue that it attacks the very logical foundations of democracy.

What Arrow seems to be saying is not only that without restrictions on the form of individual preference orderings democracies are not democratic, but that they can *not* be, at least in the sense of having voting rules for consistently translating private wants into collective decisions. A democratic procedure that produces transitive, yet nonarbitrary group choices is impossible, given Arrow's five reasonable assumptions.[2]

[2] These assumptions are as follows: nonrestriction of individual preferences, nonperversity of

Candidates/Issues

VOTERS	A		B		C		
1	A	>	B	>	C		
2 _private ordering_	C	>	A	>	B		
3	B	>	C	>	A		
collective ordering	A	>	B	>	C	>	A

Figure 4. The problem of social choice

Arrow's own solution to the problem requires us to give up the assumption of full exogeneity and autonomy of individual preferences.

[I]t must be demanded that there be some sort of consensus on the ends of society, or no social welfare function can be formed. (1951:83)

But how can we secure such a consensus without assuming that preferences are in important ways formed so as to serve that consensus? If preferences are thus shaped, they are in this sense endogenous.

Since 1951 much research, normative-formal as well as empirical, has been inspired by Arrow's problem. Arrow's theorem implies that democracies must either be unstable and experience perpetual cycling of majorities or else be characterized by arbitrarily induced equilibrium. The choices are not attractive. It is not surprising that much follow-up work was stimulated. This research attempts to find a way out of the paradox by exploring alternative voting arrangements. Some of this research only confirms and deepens Arrows's proof, as in McKelvey's "Chaos Theorem" (McKelvey, 1976, 1979), which demonstrates that unless preferences are perfectly symmetrical around

aggregation, the independence of irrelevant alternatives, citizen sovereignty, and nondicta-torship. They seem quite reasonable, indeed even weak, in that they only made explicit what most had always assumed in democratic theory. For a thorough discussion of these assumptions, see Frolich and Oppenheimer (1978:19–23).

a median point, there is a global cycle involving all choices. This result has proved to be durable and has been expressed in game theoretical terms by Schofield (1978), who shows that multidimensional voting games have empty cores, where "core" refers to the set of possible equilibrium strategies (see McLean, 1987:186). Some of this work attempts to explore the properties of majority rule with the goal being the establishment of whether or not majority rule fulfills certain normative criteria (see Rae, 1969; Taylor, 1969).

Additional work has proceeded by attempting to relax Arrow's already weak assumptions by allowing restrictions on preferences, varying intensities of preferences, and control over the agenda. While we will not discuss this research in detail here (see Mueller, 1979:ch. 3 for a discussion), a brief word is in order. Arrow's assumption that any possible array of preferences is allowable is relaxed so as to consider particular distributions of preferences, such as those which are single peaked (a point from which all other points are lower). Single-peaked distributions can result in majority equilibrium, as Slutsky (1977) has shown. Allowing for varying intensities of preferences encourages logrolling, opening up possibilities for solutions not available with preferences ordinally defined. Finally, agenda control suggests a possible solution to the cycling problem although it is not clear how this solution is nonarbitrary.

Positive public choice theory. While normative public choice deals with desirable characteristics of the rules, procedures, and institutions through which collective choices are made, positive public choice attempts to devise explanations for these rules, choice processes, and their consequences. The following questions are representative: Why and how do people establish laws, create political institutions, join groups, and vote? What factors figure in the formation and influence of groups? What conditions conduce to successful cooperation among members of cartels or classes. How (and when, under what conditions) do nation states make decisions about the provision of international public goods? What accounts for the behavior of bureaucrats, legislators, and lobbyists? Although not unrelated to normative issues, these questions are different from those concerning the equilibrium properties of majority voting procedures and whether it is possible to construct a consistent social welfare function from the ground up.

Thus, while normative public choice poses questions about how we might organize political life so that outcomes best express private (utilitarian) self-interest, positive public choice theory goes further. It assumes that citizens do in fact act on the basis of self-interest (in the economist's sense) so that actual political outcomes can be explained on that basis.

Much of the research on positive public choice has been inspired by Olson's *Logic of Collective Action* (1965). This research ranges from the experimental and simulation approaches of Axelrod (1981, 1984) to historical case studies on rational peasants by Popkin (1979), Taylor's work (1988) on revolution as a collective action problem, and Bowman's treatment (1989) of cooperation among capitalists from the same vantage point. Similarly, we can include much of the international relations literature, especially that addressed to the problem of public goods provision at the international level (Keohane, 1982, 1984; Gilpin, 1987; Gowa, 1989).

To illustrate this approach, we briefly discuss the phenomena of voting (Downs) and interest group organization (Olson). First let us turn to Anthony Downs's treatment of voting in *An Economic Theory of Democracy* (1957). Voting leads to a single outcome (electoral victory or defeat) for all, a single party in power, and a single set of policies. Electoral outcomes have some of the characteristics of public goods, most importantly the difficulty of excluding anyone from benefits and costs associated with the winning coalition. If there are any costs associated with participation, there will be an incentive to free ride.

Downs's rational analysis of voting recasts democratic political theory in economic terms. The politician is the supplier of policies and governmental services. The voter is the consumer, using his or her votes as dollars to express political demands. The politician trades services for political support. The voter trades votes for publicly provided services. It is easy to see how political advertising, campaign financing, and media consulting enter the picture. The resulting image is one of a political process where individuals, although occupying different political roles, are nevertheless motivated by self-interest, and are ready to engage in exchange to further that self-interest. The importance of ideology (for instance, belief in the New Deal) and traditional forces (such as party identification) declines in favor of interest and perceptions of utility associated with one party or another, one policy or another.

How does the voting model work in Downs's theory? There are two political parties in the model. Presumably this results from an institutional specification given outside the model. For example, a rule requiring single-member districts, with a plurality winner-take-all vote, would all but ensure no more than two parties. Voters in the electorate are arrayed along a unidimensional, liberal-conservative, continuum. Note that this avoids the Arrow problem, the distribution of voters being single peaked. Parties attempt to formulate packages of policies (programs) that appeal to a majority of voters. Parties do not offer their programs because they believe in them or have attachment to their contents. They offer them instrumentally, as a way of attaining political office.

With the preceding conditions in place, Downs is able to show that both political parties will move to the center of the continuum, toward the median

X = median
C = conservative
L = liberal

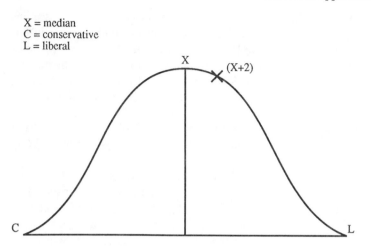

Figure 5. Political parties and the median voter

voter. Any other strategy would not be rational, for it would not be designed to win the election. Figure 5 illustrates this point.

In this figure the voters are arranged along a continuum from most conservative to most liberal. The median voter lies at point X. Exactly half the voters are more conservative; half are more liberal. If party A gears its program for the more liberal voter, say at $X + 2$, all party B has to do is to aim for all voters to the left of $X + 2$ and it is assured of victory. The median voter identifies the reference point for victory. Voters $X + 1$ (and everyone else to the left of him or her) defines a minimal winning coalition.

Underlying this prediction that parties will move toward the median voter is a conception of the individual voter and the calculations underlying the vote. There are three components to this calculation. The first is the difference in utility deriving from one or the other party being in power. The second is the probability of affecting this result – that is, the probability of making a difference. And third are the rewards associated with participating in the democratic process. Downs reasoned that the voters care about elections to the extent that they care who wins or loses. Thus a critical variable is the difference to a voter in whether one party or another wins. This difference may be high without implying much motivation to vote. The individual may calculate that the probability of affecting the outcome is very low. In effect, this probability is equal to the chances of being the critical member (the decisive member) of a minimal winning coalition. If the electorate is large or the election is forecasted to be a landslide, the probability of being the decisive member will be very small. The conditions under which an individual will count (close elections) seem to be precisely those where differences between parties reduce to zero. If parties behave rationally, they will adopt policies aimed at the median voter.

There is an unmistakable irony built into the way the utility of the party differential and probability of affecting the election result compete with each other. If the voter thinks it makes a difference who wins, the election cannot be close, since at least one of the parties must not be appealing to the median voter. On the other hand, if the parties are very close to each other in terms of the programs offered, they should also be close in electoral support, meaning that the probability of affecting the outcome is higher.

Another important area of positive public choice involves the analysis of interest groups. In *The Logic of Collective Action* (1965), Mancur Olson brought the ideas of public goods and the problem of collective action directly to the attention of political scientists. He did this by trying to show that phenomena central to politics – interest group organization and influence – were public goods.

In making his argument, Olson vigorously attacked both pluralism and Marxism for ignoring the collective action problem for groups and classes respectively. Pluralists believed, almost without question, that interest group organization was the natural expression of collectively held interests. Some argued that Marxists believed that the transition from objectively shared interests to class organization and mobilization was spontaneous. Olson saw things differently. He not only questioned the automatic nature of the transition from private interest to group organization but seemed to turn the matter upside down by arguing that it is not rational for individuals to contribute toward pursuit of collective interests. Democracy had fallen on hard times. Arrow questioned the logical foundations of democracy through his analysis of voting rules. Olson attacked the rationality of interest group organization, the primary mechanism for translating preferences into policy between elections.

But it is not in fact true that the idea that groups will act in their self-interest follows logically from the premise of rational and self-interested behavior. It does not follow, because all of the individuals in a group would gain if they achieved their group objective, that they would act to achieve that objective, even if they were all rational and self-interested. Indeed, unless the number of individuals in a group is quite small, or unless there is coercion or some other special device to make individuals act in their common interest, *rational self-interested individuals will not act to achieve their common or group interests*. (1965:1–2, italics in original)

Olson laid down the challenge to pluralism in direct terms. Some interests are never organized, some groups forever "latent," some classes forever "classes in themselves" rather than "classes for themselves." And unlike the critics of pluralism such as Schattschneider in *The Semisovereign People* (1960), who chastised pluralists for overlooking the role of wealth and resources in fostering group organization, Olson seemed to be saying that the forces shaping group organization lay elsewhere.

Since 1965 there have been numerous studies of interest groups from an economic and public choice perspective. However, the basic logic of the argument remains the same. The benefits of group organization and influence are public; the costs of excluding anyone from those benefits are high. Once the benefits are present for anyone in a group, they are available for everyone. Thus, group organization and group activities take on the characteristic properties of public goods: They are undersupplied and subject to free riding.

From a microeconomic standpoint it is the calculations of individuals that are important. An individual *i* in a large group would reason in the following way if he or she were rational, well-informed, and self-interested. Individual *i* is only one member of a large group. Any effort for the provision of public goods is privately borne, whereas benefits are jointly consumed. Furthermore, the public good (interest group organization) may be provided independently of *i*'s efforts. The larger the group, the greater the probability that *i*'s efforts will be irrelevant.

In explaining why interest groups do emerge and do provide collective benefits, Olson does not appeal to individual irrationality, collective purposes, or social norms encouraging cooperation. Instead, he tries to identify explanations consistent with his view of individual self-interest. Individuals may participate in groups because they are coerced, because they are provided with selective incentives, or because they constitute a "privileged group."

The case of coercion is not of great interest for a theory based on voluntary choice. However, Olson stresses the importance of selective incentives – that is, payments or rewards to participants beyond the public goods benefits. Selective incentives "are benefits that can be conferred upon contributors and withheld from noncontributors – insurance policies, news publications, discounts on goods and services – anything at all that individuals may value and that can be selectively conferred or withheld" (Moe, 1980:4).

A group is said to be "privileged" if there is some subset of the whole group for whom benefits exceed costs regardless of what others in the group do. If it is to the advantage of the United States to cease emitting chlorofluorocarbons into the atmosphere so as to protect the ozone layer, regardless of what all other countries do, we speak of the group as "privileged." The existence of privileged groups is important for Olson's theory. From this idea Olson argues that large groups are less likely to succeed than small ones and that concentrated groups – that is, groups with a few large members – are more likely to succeed than dispersed groups. If Olson is right, it would mean that hegemonic distribution of international power would be associated with international public goods (free trade, monetary stability) as Kindle-berger (1973, 1981) and Gilpin (1981, 1987) have argued. It also suggests that labor has more organizational difficulties than capital, consumers more than producers, small capital more than large, concentrated capital, and the numerous small countries in the United Nations Conference on Trade and Development (UNCTAD) more than the smaller organizations.

The Logic of Collective Action provides an economic theory of interest group organization and influence. As such, it is an economic theory of politics. It stresses the rational, self-interested bases of interest groups and tries to devise a theory of what group life would look like, including what groups would not exist except as aggregates of shared interest, if it conformed to the calculus of individual interest. Olson's attempt to identify the conditions that are conducive to cooperation among individuals has stimulated much research among political scientists and sociologists.

The economic analysis of policy

In a sense the economic analysis of policy is an activity that begins after the tasks of public choice analysis are either accomplished or assumed. Public choice theory concerns itself with the method of combining individual pref-erences into social welfare functions and public choices. This section assumes that preferences have already been combined, communicated to decision makers, and the task is now for decision makers to choose among alternative policies in such a way as to maximize satisfaction (of those affected by the policy – not just the decision maker). Thus, while there is a close relationship between the economic analysis of policy and public choice, the focus of this section is different.

When approaching policy choices, what kinds of questions does the econ-omist ask? What orientations are assumed? What yardsticks are used? The neoclassical approach to economic policy should help answer three broad types of questions. These questions concern the proper sphere of government, the constitutive principles of government, and the best (the most efficient) way to achieve collective goals. While most of our attention will be directed toward the third item, efficient choice, a word about the first two may be in order.

What is the proper sphere of political activity or, put differently, what is the appropriate dividing line between state and market? This is a question asked long ago by Adam Smith (1776) and by Herbert Spencer (1843). Indeed, Spencer's essay is titled "The Proper Sphere of Government." To answer this question, economists start with the individual and the market. Inside the market, individuals engage in countless exchange activities, ac-quiring and giving up goods, services, and productive factors. It is a fundamental theorem of neoclassical welfare economics that if markets are perfectly competitive, an equilibrium set of prices will exist that will allow all welfare-improving exchanges to take place. In such an equilibrium no one can improve his or her position without damaging the position of someone else. In a market society, government will be limited to doing what the market cannot do, or at least cannot do well, in other words, to cases of market failure. Market power may include the specification and enforcement of property rights, the supply and organization of military power, public goods and externalities, and the control of concentrations of economic power (Rhoads, 1985:66).

The simplest statement of the demarcation is this: The market allocates whenever it can do so efficiently; when it fails, government enters and provides through political action what could not be supplied through private initiative. This simple formula was for some time accepted, but a number of economists (McKean, 1958; McKenzie and Tullock, 1981) have pointed out that the theory of market failure must be accompanied by, and compared with, a theory of political (or governmental) failure. Now, the dividing line is not so clear. A demonstration that the market cannot provide certain goods, or cannot provide them efficiently, does not constitute proof that government can do better. Governmental action consumes resources that, presumably, have alternate uses. Interest group activities, lobbying, legislation, enforcement, regulation, and adjudication are all costly and must be compared against the resulting benefits.

The second matter concerns how government should be organized. There is an economic perspective on questions relating to basic political structure. The first principle is that government should be organized so as to maximize exchange – that is, to expand the sphere of voluntary private exchange even within government. While governmental activities must at some point involve indivisibilities, which infringe upon individual choices, the effort should be to disaggregate the political process, to "unpack" more comprehensive alternatives, and to write laws in such a way as to allow for coercion only when indivisible benefits and free riding are at issue. Thus, specific activities such as vote trading, logrolling, and tying tax payments to capturable political benefits, would be encouraged on the grounds that they free up Pareto-improving exchanges and allow intensities of preference to register in the political process.

The second principle is the Wicksellian unanimity (or near-unanimity) principle, which is the Pareto-optimal idea carried over to the political realm. In 1896 Knut Wicksell wrote a work that has come to be popular among advocates of the contractarian state and limited government. In it he attempted to devise ways in which democratic governments could organize themselves to implement policies in a consensual way. Wicksell tried to introduce concrete voting arrangements that would assure the minimum of coercion within government. Specifically, on issues related to spending and taxation, a simple majority in favor of new proposals was not adequate. Wicksell proposed 75 percent to 90 percent agreement among political representatives and urged representatives to withhold tax payments from their constituencies if the exchange was not deemed beneficial (Wicksell, 1896; Wagner, 1989:210).

Finally, once basic political structures are in place, economists can address particular policies. As Stokey and Zeckhauser point out (1978:22), economists are likely to approach policy issues with the same questions asked of private choice: What is it we want? What is it that we can get? The usual conditions are assumed: exogenous preferences, scarce resources, alternative paths of actions, beliefs about the relationships between alternatives and outcomes, and so on. The key differences are that the alternatives are policies and their outcomes affect many people; in the economist's language, they bring non-excludable costs and benefits. The economic approach to policy emphasizes the continuity of individual decision making in market and governmental contexts.

The focus on the individual is retained in both an ontological and theoretical sense.[3] Within this framework, the individual constitutes the ontological bedrock. The individual is a locus of preferences and an agent pursuing utility maximization. There are no needs or wants attached to groups, political parties, governmental agencies and bureaus, or legislatures, bureaucracies, and courts. Theoretically, political institutions and structures must be understood from the ground up, as resultants of self-interested actions.

Economic analysis of policy is grounded in individual utility. The market's idea of consumer sovereignty carries over to the popular sovereignty of politically organized individuals. True, the unequal dollars of individuals in the market contrast with the equal votes of citizens and representatives, although a parallel is found with the unequal spending (and influence) of interest groups. The basic similarities are pervasive.

When addressing policy questions, economists are most comfortable in discussing efficiency. Given that certain goals are not individually attainable, the question is how best to attain these goals collectively. In other words, what is the best (most efficient) policy?

We saw earlier that efficiency meant getting the most out of a given set of resources. What does this mean in a policy context? The effectiveness of a

[3] James Buchanan sees the focus on the individual versus the state as an entity as the primary difference between the way economists and political scientists approach the study of politics. (See Buchanan, "An Economist's Approach to 'Scientific Politics'," chapter 7 in Buchanan, 1979:143–59.)

policy has to do with whether it achieves its goal. A cost-effective policy may be one that, out of a number of policies that achieve the same goal, is the least costly. This is a truncated form of cost-benefit analysis (since benefits are assumed to be constant). A policy that is best from a cost-benefit stand-point is one that maximizes the difference between total benefits and total costs. Costs and benefits must both be explicitly included in the evaluative process and compared across the available alternative policies. This is the way the economist normally proceeds.

To illustrate the efficiency principle, let us develop an example. Assume that individuals within a political system desire both the capacity to deter external military aggression and a capacity for defense, should deterrence fail. In other words, they want to dissuade potential enemies from military incursions and to be able to fight such incursions if they take place. Military strategists generally concede a negative relationship between these two objectives. If a government wants to reduce the threat of military aggression as much as possible, it will put all of its resources into countervalue (including countercity and industrial targets) forces. This, however, leaves it with no ability to defend itself should attack occur. On the other hand, if it spends all its money on defense, it has nothing left with which to threaten an enemy (in his own homeland), which lowers the costs of a nuclear war.

While this may be a somber example, the economist approaches it in the same spirit as he or she would approach the question of how several alternative oil-drilling operations will affect oil yield and the environment. Let us assume that there are five different policies (force structures, strategies, battle plans, targeting, and so on) that attempt to satisfy the requirements of deterrence and defense. Further assume that these alternatives are equal in all respects, including costs, except for the different combinations of deterrence and defense yielded. Figure 6 illustrates the decision problem. In this figure are plotted our five policies and the amounts of deterrence and defense associated with each (using an arbitrary scale from 1 to 10).

The economist examines these alternatives in light of the desired goals. Recall that since both are desired, any policy that increases the government's capacity for both deterrence and defense is preferred. If there is a single alternative that is superior to all others, this would be the "best" policy. It would be the Pareto-superior point, a single point lying to the north and east of all other points. No such point exists.

Given that there is no single Pareto-superior point, are there any that are Pareto-efficient – points from which we cannot deviate without doing worse with regard to at least one goal? The policymaker throws out points E and D. E is dominated by C (C is northeast) and D is dominated by both A and C. Thus any policymaker who values both deterrence and defense will prefer

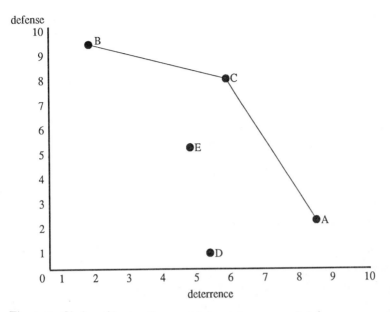

Figure 6. Choice of best policy combining deterrence and defense

C to E and C and A to D. However, among points A, B, and C there is no clear preference. All three points are Pareto-efficient. All three points lie on a possibility frontier (a Pareto-possibility frontier) (see Stokey and Zeckhauser, 1978:24–5).

Figure 6 provides a graphical illustration of the policy possibilities. In a sense, these alternatives represent the familiar production possibility frontier of neoclassical theory. They provide us with an account of what is technologically possible, but they do not speak to what is desirable, except that "more is better." However, the exact choice can only be determined from information that brings together the preferences of decision makers and available policy alternatives. If we had wanted to illustrate this "best choice" solution, we would first have connected points A, B, and C by a line indicating the possibility frontier. Then we could have drawn indifference curves in the same space.

Indifference curves describe the rates at which one is willing to give up one good in return for another. In a sense they describe the individual substitution ratios of different goods. For example, a policymaker might value both deterrence and defense, yet be willing to give up only a little (or a lot) deterrence for a lot (or a little) of defense.

The solution (the preferred point) lies where the slope of the indifference curve is just tangent to the slope of the possibility frontier, indicating that the marginal rates of transformation and substitution are equalized. The marginal rate of substitution is that rate at which one is willing to give up one good for another. The marginal rate of transformation is the rate at which one is *able* to acquire one good instead of another. When these rates are equalized, the best choice has been defined.

The illustration is based on highly simplified assumptions: two goals, unitary decision maker preferences, and fixed costs. Other cases call for a more complicated reshuffling of resources. In "Economic Reasoning and the Ethics of Policy" (1984), Thomas Schelling goes through numerous examples in which the economic logic is used to "solve" problems for which common sense often provides a different answer. Gas rationing provides but one example. If gas is in short supply, the price will rise, making it difficult or perhaps impossible for poor people to purchase it. One solution is to ration gasoline. This might seem to have desirable distributional properties since the burden would be supported by all. Schelling, invoking economic reasoning, suggests that policymakers let the price rise, tax the windfall profit, redistribute income to the poorer people, but give them the choice of spending their money on gas or some alternative. Schelling's argument is based on the presumption that, if we are concerned about the impact of high-priced gasoline on the poor, we can deal with the impact more efficiently using the market in conjunction with tax instruments than by rationing. The market can continue to do its work of reflecting relative scarcities through prices, hence encouraging substitution, while the distributional goal of providing purchasing power for the poor can be satisfied by other means.

If carried to the extreme, this approach might prove startling. Schelling's example of the case for different traffic and safety measures surrounding rich and poor neighborhoods is provocative. The poor, to be sure, might prefer to spend their money in other ways than for airline safety measures, but is this relevant? One can also imagine the Occupational Safety and Health Administration (OSHA) asking workers if they would like to give up some personal safety in return for payments to spend as they like. If so, then why not apply the same reasoning to the right to trial by jury and so on? The problem, as Levine argues (1983), is that the efficiency-cum-choice orientation fails to provide a dividing line between individual choice guided by preferences and rights. The latter refer to a realm of entitlements based either on widely acknowledged perceptions of common needs or citizens' rights, and are not allowed to exchange (that is, to be bought and sold). In discussing policy, the economist should distinguish between economic policy designed to improve choice and efficiency and policy designed to preserve or advance rights (Levine, 1983:84).

Economic analysis of institutions

While institutions are not necessarily political, political institutions are central to politics. Hence we discuss here the way that economic reasoning is used to explain behavior within institutional settings as well as to explain the changing content of institutions themselves.

First, we need some definitions. North and Thomas define an institution quite broadly, as "an arrangement between economic units that defines and specifies the ways by which these units can co-operate or compete" (1973:5). In a different source, North specifies that "institutions consist of a set of constraints on behavior in the form of rules and regulations; a set of procedures to detect deviations from the rules and regulations; and, finally, a set of moral, ethical behavioral norms which define the contours that constrain the way in which the rules and regulations are specified and enforcement is carried out" (North, 1984:8).

Note that these definitions treat institutions as constraints (or opportunities) external to economic agents. This is important because it allows the preservation of both the individual focus and the maximization hypothesis, altering only the costs and benefits of various courses of action. Now the individual maximizes subject to the distribution of endowments, technology, preferences, and given institutional arrangements. The introduction of institutions adds one more variable to the basic economic equation.

The economic analysis of institutions stresses the ways that institutions can foster instrumental cooperative behavior, reduce (or increase) transaction costs, and provide the organizational basis for production and exchange. The focus is on the relationship between institutions and efficiency – that is, the ways in which institutions facilitate or retard self-seeking.

Institutions, within this framework, are rules or procedures that prescribe, proscribe, or permit particular behavior. Political institutions, as applied to economics, may define appropriate objects of exchange, the rules guiding the exchange process, and property rights with respect to both benefits and liabilities. The political aspects of political institutions lie in their origins in the state and in the use of state power, authority, and sanctions to enforce prescribed behavior.

If the economic approach to institutions can best be understood in contrast with sociological conceptions,[4] perhaps political institutions can best be understood in contrast with markets. The pure idea of market behavior has individuals pursuing their preferences in a world of freely exchanging agents

---

[4] For a brief survey of the sociological approach to institutions, see Shmuel E. Eisenstadt, "Social Institutions," *International Encyclopedia of Social Sciences*, Vol. 14, ed. David Sills (New York: Free Press, 1968), pp. 409–29.

and alienable goods. The value of these goods is determined by the interplay of relative scarcities and relative preferences. Political institutions also establish opportunities and constraints, but they take the form of authoritative policies that alter costs. We return to this point later in the chapter.

Institutions and market behavior. The preceding discussion raises the issue of the connection between markets and institutions. There are at least three ways of conceiving the relationship. First, markets are themselves institutions. They are not simply unstructured collections of individuals freely engaging in buying and selling. The market economy is, as Polanyi argues, "an instituted process" (1957:243–70), not just in the sense that behavioral regularities are present in the market, but because rules are embedded in the market itself. These rules govern the terms of exchange and responsibility for external costs. Agreements about property rights and contract enforcement, and prohibitions against theft, coercion, and fraud are understood. These are part of the constitutive rules or conventions of the market without which exchange among individuals could hardly work (Field, 1984:684).

Second, institutions generally define the scope of market exchange. Some objects or characteristics may not exchange for personal or cultural reasons. A person may not sell a child even though it might be profitable to do so. Another person does not sell her labor for work that is considered objectionable. In addition to these individual "bans on exchange," many such bans are politically proscribed. Governments usually ban trading votes for dollars (buying votes), though the rules governing the relations between interest groups and U.S. representatives leave this question somewhat open. Governments may or may not prohibit the manufacture and sale of alcohol, pornographic magazines, and insider trading on the stock market. They may or may not establish laws to govern the sale of knowledge gained through experience in "public service" – to control whether former public servants may publish memoirs before a certain period of time out of government or establish a consulting service to advise weapons industries on the basis of a brief appointment in the Defense Department.

Banning certain kinds of exchanges alters market allocations in important ways. If the rules work perfectly, a portion of the market is suppressed and potential "gains from trade" are lost. In addition, there is the opportunity cost of making and enforcing rules. The time, energy, and resources of legislators, bureaucrats, and lawyers have alternative uses that are forgone in making and enforcing rules. These are the social costs of politics emphasized by some public choice theorists.

Third, apart from their function as prohibitions, political institutions are typically used to alter the incentives underlying market exchange. In the former Federal Republic of Germany, special subsidies and depreciation allowances were given to industries specializing in exports. In Japan the high rate of personal savings has much to do with the nature of financial institutions and the politically supplied rewards for savings. In France special subsidies are given to cutting-edge technologies and in the United States, as everywhere else, tax policies and environmental regulations are not imposed in a flat (even) way, but discriminate among various sectors, penalizing some and rewarding others. Sometimes political rules "merely" channel economic activity from some sectors to others. However, rules can also affect the balance of wealth-producing versus transfer or rent-seeking activities (Krueger, 1974; Tollison, 1984).

Economic reasoning and political institutions. Neoclassical economic theory has traditionally ignored institutions. If it recognized them at all, it treated them as constants that did not function actively in explaining allocative activity. The usual justification was that while institutions do matter in the long run, for questions concerning short-term allocative activity, they can be ignored. In recent years there has been a revival of interest in institutions, spurred in part by increasing attention to economic history, in part by a recognition that comparative economic behavior cannot safely ignore institutions.

Among those economists who examine institutions, there are two schools of thought. One school allows that institutions are important, but takes them as provided by forces outside the economic model. The chief aim here is to understand the significance of institutions for allocative behavior. This, in turn, is accomplished by exploring the comparative incentive features of different institutions. Since institutions are exogenous (yet variable), we may refer to this as the "institutionally situated rational choice approach." The second school takes institutions as endogenous; that is, institutions themselves become a variable to be explained by economic behavior. We return to this second approach shortly. Within the institutionally situated rational choice school, there is a distinction between those who do empirical and those who do analytic work. The empirical work conforms to the preceding discussion about the comparative incentive features of institutions. What difference do institutional variations make for the behavior of rational, self-interested actors? This is the central question posed.

The work of Douglass North (1981, 1984), Margaret Levi (1988), Mancur Olson (1965, 1982), and Robert Bates (1981, 1983, 1988) falls within the empirical tradition. North examines the effect of changes in property rights on economic growth. He is interested in how institutions can change to bring private and social costs more closely together (for example, by reducing externalities). Bates has written extensively in the area of economic and political development and has argued that incorporating political institutions into models of development can help explain why political and economic actors seem to behave irrationally on purely economic grounds. His work on price setting of food goods by state agencies partly explains the attitudes of peasants toward production (Bates, 1981). The incentive to produce more food may not exist in a country where the terms of trade between farm and city are established by state institutions that depend on urban areas for political support.

The analytic branch of this school asks different kinds of questions, questions that explore the logical properties of models that simultaneously incorporate terms describing exchange behavior and institutions. Is it possible to design institutions incorporating democratic voting procedures that do not have the instability properties pointed out by Arrow? How, if at all, may the introduction of specific institutional arrangements affect the stability of various voting systems (electorates, legislatures, and committees)? Do institutions "inherit" (see Riker, 1980; Shepsle, 1983) the same characteristics that preferences have? That is, are institutions unstable in exactly the same way that preferences for specific outcomes are unstable? These questions are representative of the analytic tradition.

Among those in the analytic tradition, the work of Riker (1980), Schofield (1980), Shepsle (1979a, b, 1983), and Shepsle and Weingast (1981) is particularly relevant for our purposes. Much of the research in this tradition has been inspired by Arrow. Some have been anxious to confirm or generalize the basic instability theorem; others have taken Arrow's book as a challenge and have asked à la Tullock (1981), "Why so much stability?" Riker (1980) starts from the theorem of voting instability and goes on to assess the implications for the study of political institutions. The central question he asks is whether institutions inherit the same problem of social intransitivity and cycling that characterize preferences over specific outcomes. If institutions are, as he argues, "congealed tastes," this would seem to imply that institutions are unstable too, even if these instabilities manifest themselves more slowly than specific policy instabilities.

Shepsle, a student of the U.S. legislature, starts with the point that the observable world is not as chaotic as implied by the work of Arrow and McKelvey. Why is this so? Shepsle claims that part of the answer lies in the way political institutions mediate preferences and social choices. Not just any preferences may be expressed in any particular fashion. There are rules about what preferences can be expressed, in which order, in combination with what particular other preferences – that is, which coalitions are possible (Shepsle, 1983:1–9). As Shepsle and Weingest put it:

In our view, real-world legislative practices constrain the instability of PMR [pure majority rule] by *restricting* the domain and the content of legislative exchange. The latter, in our view, is part of the problem (though by no means the only part) with PMR, not part of the solution. Throughout, then, we hope to convey what we believe is a compelling case for answering Tullock's question, 'Why so much stability?' with "Institutional arrangements do it." (1981:504, italics in original)

The work of Shepsle, of Riker, and of Fiorina (1982) in some ways returns the attention of the formal theorist to the more traditional preoccupation with the nuts and bolts concerns of political scientists. In his *U.S. Senators and Their World* (1960), Donald Matthews provides an account of the operation of the U.S. Senate that is rich in normative and institutional details. Formal theorists, starting from an abstract proposition about the instability of social choices in normatively and institutionally unconstrained settings, have (re)discovered, as Shepsle put it, "that tastes and their expression are neither autonomous nor necessarily decisive" (Shepsle, 1983:1). According to Shepsle, the actual world of legislatures, committees, and electoral systems is characterized by complex divisions of labor (not atomistic exchange), restrictions on preferences as in germaneness rules, and sequencing rules specifying how items may come up, be amended, and voted upon. These conditions place some distance between operating institutions and the pure majority rule of Arrow's world. Equilibrium is possible after all.

Finally, we come to rational choice theory with institutions as endogenous. This approach differs in important ways from the institutionally situated rational choice approach. The latter approach is a natural extension of the basic economic model simply activating a factor that almost everyone recognized in the first place. By contrast, endogenous institutional theory alters the theoretical status of institutions, shifting them to the left-hand side of the basic explanatory equation. In this approach, institutions themselves become the objects of choice, arguments in utility functions, and "outputs" to be explained in the same manner as allocative activity in general. The revised institutional model now says that variations in the form and content of institutions are explicable by appealing to exogenous changes in endowments, preferences, and technology. For example, given an exogenous increase in the labor/land ratio, property rights assignments should shift in favor of holders of the scarce resource, that is, more favorable to landowners, less so to workers.

The attempt to create an endogenous theory of institutions is reflected in the work of North and Thomas (1973), North (1978, 1981, 1984), Levi (1988), and Basu, Jones, and Schlicht (1987). For North and many of his followers, the key forces acting on institutional change have to do with the potential gains associated with innovation, production, and exchange. Forms of property rights that cut down on external benefits (that is, positive externalities), discourage rent seeking, and reduce the costs of making and enforcing contracts are central to North's analysis of institutional change. Thus the modern corporation (which limits personal liability), the stock market (which pools capital and reduces information costs), and patents (which protect income arising from innovations) are stock examples. Changes in relative prices of factors and products provide the stimulation for changes in institutions. Levi also relies to some extent on the role of institutions in reducing transaction costs, although her work is supplemented by a theory of power and bargaining (1988:17–23).

Finally, the work of Riker (1980) and Shepsle (1983), although primarily analytical, can also be interpreted as part of the endogenous institutional change movement. In commenting on Riker's work, Shepsle reflects that Riker "treats institutions like ordinary policy alternatives in an important respect: they are chosen" (1983:27). Shepsle's distinction between institutional equilibrium and equilibrium institutions attempts to capture the difference between those institutions that can provide equilibrium of policy outcomes versus those that can themselves be institutionally stable.

The effort to create an endogenous account of institutions – that is, to provide a theory of how institutions are created and how they change, is not new, but it is important. It involves an effort to resurrect a project that was central to Marxian political economy. But while Marx saw the engine of institutional change in the dialectical tension between forces of production and relations of production, the new institutionalism of neoclassical economics focuses on institutions as organizational, procedural, and rulelike responses for economizing on transaction costs and capturing the gains from innovation in production and exchange. This literature is not limited to the theory of the firm. It extends well beyond this to include efforts to understand legal changes, changes in property rights, and changes in the form and content of political institutions over long historical periods.

Conclusion

As a field of study, economics has evolved a distinctive method based on the adaptation of scarce resources to competing ends. When applied to politics, the central assumption of the economic approach is that private and public decision makers can be described in the same way. Both have goals and limited resources and pursue their goals according to a rational, self-interested calculus.

In this approach, voters are consumers choosing among different candidates and policies; politicians maximize the interests of their organizations (parties) by pursuing median voters; bureaucrats are agents whose objective functions include budget maximization, expansion or protection of personnel, and discretionary behavior. Laws are rulelike structures that affect how individual goals may be pursued as well as products of self-interested calculations themselves. As developed in economics, the overall approach is demand driven, with consumers pursuing their political goals and politicians passively supplying public goods (Buchanan, 1979:177). Models developed by political scientists (such as Levi, 1988) have allowed for a distinctive set of goals on the part of the state agents.

The economic approach to politics has forced analysts to disaggregate the state and to focus on its numerous constituent components and processes. Echoing Bentley, we might say that there is no need at all for the state as an entity. Once we have specified the relevant agents, resources, goals and rules, politics is the analysis of choice in political settings, often concerning public goods.

While focusing on particular political actors in various strategic settings is valuable, the approach does have limitations. We focus on three.

First, there is the issue of whether politics, specifically democratic politics, is better described by the ends pursued by citizens or by the modes of activity in which citizens participate. To the extent that politics can be represented by agents who have goals that can be satisfied by choosing among alternative actions, the economic approach to politics makes sense. But suppose there is something valuable about the process itself. Suppose that people do not so much "use" politics to satisfy ends as to express themselves through political institutions. What if part of the point of participation is simply to participate, rather than to secure the ends to which participation might lead?

Disagreement over the relevance of the economic approach to politics may turn in part on disagreement about the nature of politics. If politics refers to goal seeking in political environments, then the approach is clearly relevant. However, an alternative conception exists that identifies politics with processes through which individuals discover themselves, learn about their preferences, engage in debate, and shape (and are shaped by) opinions of others. The process itself (the democratic political process) shapes citizens' beliefs, especially about how they fit into a society with other individuals, and thus modifies what they might want as private agents.

A limitation of the economic approach is that it misses the transformative potential of politics. Politics is not just a process by which predetermined and unquestioned preferences are converted into policy "outputs." Individuals do not simply act on given preferences throughout the political process. As Barber put it in *The Conquest of Politics*:

The journey from private opinion to political judgment does not follow a road from prejudice to true knowledge; it proceeds from solitude to sociability. To travel this road, the citizen must put her private views to a test that is anything but epistemological: she must debate them with her fellow citizens, run them through the courts, offer them as a program for a political party, try these out in the press, reformulate them as a legislative initiative, experiment with them in local, state, and federal forums, and, in every other way possible, subject them to the civic scrutiny and public activity of the community to which she belongs. (1988:199)

The second limitation of the economic approach to politics concerns its effort to explain institutions and institutional change. We noted two different ways in which institutions can figure in economic analysis. Institutions can be taken as given (much as preferences and endowments can) and the consequences of different institutional arrangements explored. Alternatively, institutions can be treated as phenomena to be explained. The former approach "merely" specifies what has always been implicit in the neoclassical model. The task is to elaborate the comparative incentive structure of various institutional arrangements and to assess the consequences for allocative behavior. The latter approach is more ambitious in that it attempts to derive institutional changes from a model of intentional action.

Were this effort to be successful, the claim that economics rests (and must rest) on a noneconomic bottom would be challenged (Field, 1979; 1984). Institutions, or rules, refer to noneconomic phenomena that affect allocative behavior, yet cannot be (or at least have not yet been) explained by that behavior. According to this view, institutions, while ultimately changeable, confront choosing agents as historical givens, as part of the architecture defining the choice situation rather than as something to be chosen.

If institutions become the object of explanation, can the economic model logically account for them without a prior (different) specification of institutions? Neoclassical economics sees institutions largely as rules. Interpreted in this way, institutions prescribe, rule out, and permit. As such, they are relevant for the feasible set of actions, those that are possible. Thus they are relevant for explaining choice behavior, including the choice of institutions. Without an antecedent specification of rules, an explanation of consequent rules would seem impossible. This is not an argument against attempting to explain institutions with the economic model, but it does suggest that the attempt can work only to the extent that it relies on prior exogenously given rules. As Field put it, "they [rules] cannot, or at least all of them cannot, be thought of as arising as the result of previous plays of the game in which they did not prevail" (1984:684).

A third limitation of the economic approach to politics concerns institutions and preferences. If institutions, including political institutions, serve merely to facilitate (efficiency in) want satisfaction, how do wants arise? What part can our social lives play in the formation and not just satisfaction of wants? With the extension of self-interest calculation to the design of institutions, we lose any sense of an enduring social world within which persons find themselves, discover their identity, their sense of self, and the wants appropriate to that sense of self.

Institutions, in part, make up that enduring social world. Our institutions allow for a frame of reference that is not contingent on exogenous preferences. If institutions are to take on this role, self-interest cannot be exogenous to them, or at least not to all of them. At a minimum, this suggests a division between those institutions aimed at serving self-interest, and thus for which exogeneity might be a reasonable assumption, and those institutions that participate in the formation of interests, for which the exogeneity assumption is inappropriate. To the extent that political institutions fall into the second class, political economy might concern itself with clarifying the necessary distinction.

Even on the basis of an appropriate distinction between the two kinds of institutions, however, problems arise for the rational choice approach. That approach is specially tailored to address the relation of pursuit of self-interest to collective outcomes. It takes for granted the motivation implied in the notion of self-interest. Adherents of this approach often write as though their conclusions follow so long as we accept the primacy of self-interest and rational calculation (that is, instrumentally rational calculation) in individual motivation and behavior. But this is not so clear as it seems.

By accepting pursuit of self-interest as a goal in exchange (and to a lesser extent in government) we do not thereby accept the way of thinking about self-interest and rationality typical of the rational choice framework. Self-interest is not, after all, such a simple matter (see Kohut, 1977). In order to be an agent and make choices, the individual must have a cohesive self to which to refer and out of which to define his or her ends. Furthermore, the nature of that self will determine the nature of the choosing undertaken by the agent, for example whether or not it can meaningfully entail ranking of alternatives into a preference ordering. Before we too easily assume that choice and rationality are about ranking and preference, we need to look more deeply into the nature of agency itself and into the qualities that make an agent capable of choosing.

It is worth noting in this connection that the classical approach sidesteps the problems of agency and choice by focusing on pursuit of profit rather than utility maximization. This focus arises from the fact that the classical theory is primarily a theory of the growth of wealth and not of its static allocation. The classical economists do not much concern themselves with consumer choice and devote themselves instead to the implications of profit seeking for the growth of wealth. In so doing, they give less attention than they might to the role of demand in the functioning of market economy, but they also avoid the dangers of interpreting the world in terms of scarcity and rational choice.

When we make political institutions derivative of self-interest, we in effect make the self an irreducible prior condition of social interaction, and this makes it difficult to consider analytically the social determinants and institutional framework of self-interest. This observation has a bearing on one of our central themes: the link between political economy and the depoliticization of society, the displacement of politics by civil society. A claim that we consider the necessary part played by political institutions in establishing an enduring framework for want formation could place limits on the erosion of the state associated with the traditional project of political economy.

7

Power-centered approaches to political economy

The interactions between power and economic phenomena may provide an appealing focus for political economy. However, the obstacles to constructing political economy on a foundation of power should not be underestimated. These obstacles are especially difficult if economics is interpreted as market behavior (one of the definitions of economics in Chapter 1).

Markets are closely related to the idea of choice among freely contracting individuals. Markets are impersonal, dispersed structures of buyers and sellers operating independently of one another in pursuit of private goals. The number of actors is large, opportunity costs are never so high as to create strong influence networks, and no collusion exists. This view of economics – as tied to markets – deprives it of power in two ways. First, since agents face an environment characterized by voluntary choice, and since from the agents' standpoint many things are given – factor prices, technology, the distribution of endowments, and wants – there is very little to decide and a very limited range of strategic behavior. Second, no single agent has enough economic capability, in terms of capital, labor, goods, to influence any other agent. Of course, any agent may refuse to contract with another or may withdraw resources previously contracted. But here the damage done is strictly limited to the loss of the benefit derived from the exchange. A cannot hurt B more than it can help B, and withholding a benefit is not seen as power so long as alternatives for B exist.

If these properties are accepted as defining the market, economic behavior easily becomes the analysis of mutually improving exchanges. This connection is fostered by a central measure of economic welfare in neoclassical theory: the Pareto-optimality criterion. An exchange is said to be Pareto-superior to existing arrangements if it makes someone better off without making anyone worse off. If parties to the exchange are not coerced, and if the exchange is fully specified to include all relevant actors and goods, then the exchanges will be, *ex ante* at least, mutual improvements.

The Pareto-optimal standard and the neglect of power come together and reinforce one another. They are initially separate and focused on different issues; yet they connect and make each other stronger. The Pareto criterion draws our attention to cases where, by definition, no one is made worse off. If this is so, we have removed an important component of power relations, namely the threat of being worse off. In a market, one may be denied opportunities to improve, by being refused an attractive job, for example, but the floor beneath – the lowest point to which one can fall – is the *status quo ante*. The collusion between the Pareto criterion and the focus on voluntary choice reinforces the neglect of power.

For defenders of market capitalism, power does not and should not exist in the market. Its appearance is not desired; it is something to be forestalled. For critics, the power within (and of) markets is "merely" opaque. In Galbraith's terms, the market is both "an effective solvent – and concealment – of the power of industrial capitalism" (1983:119). The opacity of market power is not accidental; it is essential; or at the least very helpful, to the ideological support of capitalism.

Nothing is so important in the defense of the modern corporation as the argument that its power does not exist – that all power is surrendered to the impersonal play of the market. (pp. 119–20)

In a free market economy, individuals enter into relations (exchange) voluntarily. The free market eliminates authority-based allocation, coercive forms of labor, and so on. By replacing authority with voluntary contract, the market economy seems to eliminate power. In a sense, the market is designed to free individual initiative and self-interest while assuring that choice replaces coercion. When we think of the market in this way, the terms "economy" and "power" repel each other. And, if we link the notion of political economy to the exercise of power in the economy, we make political economy problematic.

Yet, especially in recent years, the term "political economy" has been used by a variety of authors to connote the link between markets and power. Thus, Robert Keohane asserts that "wherever, in the economy, actors exert power over one another, the economy is political" (1984:21). Even more forceful statements than this characterize the work of some radical economists who insist that the economy (particularly the capitalist market economy) is a "system of power."

Clearly, what we term here power-centered approaches to political economy challenge a central claim of economic theory. In so doing they also pose a difficult problem for themselves. How can a system of voluntary relations between freely contracting and independent persons be a system of power? We address this question in the present chapter.

Whether correct or incorrect in their assessment of the market, power-centered theories force us to come to terms with one of the most fundamental questions we could raise about market economies. In dealing with this question, much depends upon our interpretation of the term power. The concept has a number of meanings (see Lukes, 1986) and the success we might expect to have in connecting power to market economy will depend critically on which meaning we consider most appropriate. We begin, then, with a brief summary of interpretations of power.

Interpretations of power

The simplest, most general, and most intuitively appealing notion of power identifies it with our capacity to accomplish our ends in the world.[1] Power expresses the idea that in order to accomplish our ends, we must do something to affect, and thus change, the world; we must act in and upon the world. In so doing, we sometimes face resistance from nature, from other persons, and conceivably from social institutions. We may even face resistance from ourselves, although this idea introduces complexities we will largely leave aside here.

The element of resistance has been important in definitions of power. In *Economy and Society*, Max Weber defined power as "the probability that an actor in a social relationship will be in a position to carry out his own will despite resistance, regardless of the basis on which this probability rests" ([1956] 1978:53). Resistance, however, while generally present in power relations in politics, is not logically necessary for something to qualify as power. Someone may manipulate the environment of others in such a way as to make it in their interest to behave in conformity to the agent's wishes, thus removing resistance. Both persuasion and inducement are terms that normally qualify as examples of power.[2] And the effort to legitimize power relations – that is, to create structures of political authority, is marked by an attempt to create generalized acceptance of the exercise of state power.

While the idea of resistance is important in power analysis, it enters in numerous and sometimes subtle ways. It may arise simply because we intend to alter the order of things confronting us with an inherent inertia. We might think of natural resistance in this way. By contrast, the resistance of persons confronts us with competing ends. It thus raises a set of issues having to do

---

[1] We recognize that there are other starting points. Giddens, for example, argues that power, although tied to human agency, "has no inherent connection with intention or 'will' . . ." (1979:92). The most general conception of power is that of possessing "transformative capacity" (ibid.:88).

[2] Persuasion refers to the act of convincing someone that something is in his or her interest. Inducement refers to the process of changing the incentive structure itself. Inducing someone to behave in a certain way entails changing the structure of rewards and penalties. Persuasion requires verbal and symbolic intervention. The aim is to change perception of interests.

with the different ways in which we engage others in our effort to achieve our ends. Finally, the presence or absence of social and political institutions may present obstacles. Institutions may exist that frustrate our purposes. The "two-party system" may ignore or dilute extreme political views; a centrally planned economy may frustrate individual initiatives and would-be entrepreneurs; and a free-market economy may produce land-use patterns that are obnoxious and difficult to change. In all cases it is not just particular agents whose will one wants to overcome but also the roles and interlocking structures that agents occupy.

In sum, we have three types of power: power to secure ends over nature, power over others, and power with others. We exert power over nature when we accomplish our ends in the face of natural opposition (say ploughing a field or unloading a truck). We exert power either by expending our own physical energies or by devising technologies to accomplish our ends more efficiently. We exert power over others either by altering incentives so that they are positive, in which case we speak of inducement, or by making them negative, in which case we speak of power or coercion. In both cases, we are able to control others by controlling the incentives associated with various courses of action. With both inducement and coercion we make it in the interest of agents to do what we want them to do. In the former case, there is the prospect of improvement; in the latter, the threat of being worse off (both with regard to the status quo as a baseline).

The third type of power, power with others, is more complex. Individuals may not be able to achieve their ends by themselves. The successful pursuit of their goals may require collaboration. This collaboration may be ad hoc, or it may require institutions.

The absence of institutions may impede the pursuit and satisfaction of goals. Suppose that two agents (A and B) desire a certain state of affairs but because of some defect of their situation, cannot achieve it. Examples abound: Two countries prefer not to pursue a costly arms race, yet feel they must, given the decentralized structure of the interstate system. Numerous citizens would like to prevent environmental damage but do not, even though the costs of organizing are less than the prospective benefits. And many individuals would like higher wages or a public radio station. All of these goals may require institutions that do not yet exist.

In these situations, agents can be characterized as having goals that are not fundamentally in opposition to one another and where expected gains exceed expected losses. Yet, because of institutional defects (lack of centralized political authority or well-specified property rights), the aims are not achieved. We can think of the absence of institutions as providing a kind of resistance, or obstacle, to the exercise or power. While treating the absence of something (certain kinds of institutions) as a source of resistance may seem odd, it seems necessary to complete our understanding of power. The capacity to construct institutions that enable us to achieve what we otherwise could not is a distinct component of power.

All conceptions of power rest on some notion of ends or interests. When these interests are clearly within the purview of choosing agents (that is, when they consciously pursue their interests), we speak of wants, preferences, or goals. When agents are not consciously aware of the importance of various outcomes, but where those outcomes can be demonstrated to affect the welfare of persons, we speak of interests. The distinction between preference and interest opens up a number of problems that we attempt to deal with later in the chapter under "conditioned power."

Interpretations of interest

Consider the following characterization of the capitalist ethic and thus the capitalist himself (from Max Weber's *Protestant Ethic and the Spirit of Capitalism*):

Man is dominated by the making of money, by acquisition as the ultimate purpose of his life. Economic acquisition is no longer subordinated to man as the means for the satisfaction of his material needs.... ([1904–5] 1958:53)

Does the capitalist depicted in this way know his interests? Does he pursue his real interests? Does he, in the successful pursuit of his interests, as he perceives them, exercise power? If he exercises power, does this make him powerful, or does this just make him the agent of power residing in the social (or spiritual) order within which he exists? Does the slave who, believing in the virtue of and inevitability of slavery, works to protect the social order of slavery know and act upon his interest? Can we deduce what is in his interests from his actions? Or is the slave, as Lukes puts it (1974:24), the victim of a power over him that shapes "perceptions, cognitions and preferences in such a way" that he accepts his role "in the existing order of things, either because [he] seeks[s] or imagine[s] no alternative" or because he sees "it as natural and unchangeable ... divinely ordained and beneficial"? Would a slave be clearly and unambiguously better off outside of his life as a slave? These examples and questions indicate the complexity of the problem of interests in relation to power. The capitalist, particularly the successful capitalist, surely has power; and yet is Weber entirely incorrect in characterizing the capitalist as a mere "steward"? The slave can hardly find his real interest in the perpetuation of slavery. Yet, is he wrong in believing that he has no life (certainly no life as he knows life) outside of slavery?

The habit of mind of economists tends to cut through these problems. Interests translate into preferences, preferences into choices given the available options. What we observe individuals freely choosing, we can deduce to be in their interests. We know individuals choose freely when we can find no one coercing them. We will term this the direct interpretation of interest or "direct interest." It is sometimes termed "subjective" (Flathman, 1966, and Balbus, 1971) or "behavioral" (Lukes, 1974). If we satisfy ourselves with the notion of direct interest, then the slave who accepts slavery independently of the threat of coercion, who thus "chooses" slavery, acts in his interest. In this spirit, Robert Nozick argues that recognition of a right to voluntary enslavement enhances our freedom (1974:331). The capitalist who devotes his life to the accumulation of capital clearly pursues his well-defined self-interest.

The notion of direct interest works well with a simple notion of power. Successful achievement of what we deem to be in our interest indicates our power; the more powerful we are, the more of our interests we can successfully pursue. This also holds for power over others measured by the outcome of the conflict of our (direct) interest with theirs.

Whether we believe that the direct or subjective notion of interest is (1) exhaustive of meaningful interpretations of interest (as a behaviorist or a utilitarian might) or (2) unsatisfactory, we might still find the associated notion of power meaningful. When we speak of capitalists as powerful and slaves as powerless, we are speaking in an intuitively meaningful way. Doing so does not prevent us from also saying that capitalists have no power so long as we carefully distinguish two different uses of language.

The second notion of interest leaves the behaviorists and utilitarians shaking their heads. This is "real" (sometimes "objective") interest. Connolly links real interest to "self-awareness" and "fully informed choice" ([1974] 1983:68). Isaac Balbus claims that this kind of interest can be distinguished by the fact that "evidence can be marshalled to demonstrate that an individual has an interest even if he is not aware of it or even that what an individual thinks is in his interest is in fact not in his interest" (1971:152). Real interest in this sense is, in effect, imputed to the individual from his objective situation. We can, then, refer to it as imputed interest.

Individuals may find themselves in situations that prevent them from perceiving the real interests that those situations define. Such individuals are powerless in a most profound sense. Such powerlessness does not directly imply that anyone has power over anyone else. It may be fruitful to consider the possibility that a social order empowers no one, as suggested by Hannah Arendt's notion of "rule by nobody" (1969). If we believe that imputed interest (1) exists, (2) differs from direct (subjective) interest, and (3) cannot be satisfied by the social order that creates and defines it, we have a significant critique of that order based on the idea of power (or more specifically its absence).

Power and the market economy

One of the great virtues of a capitalist market economy has been its ability to bring about the growth of society's wealth. With this growth of wealth comes an expansion in the capacity of society to satisfy individual needs. To be sure, important questions arise concerning the equity with which these needs are satisfied. Regardless, however, of equity issues, the expansion of wealth necessarily means an expansion of power (in our first sense) for at least some in society. Since wealth consists of objects that satisfy (some of) our wants, wealth gives us the power to achieve (some of) our ends. The more wealth we have, the more powerful we are in this sense. Furthermore, since capitalist market economies tend to distribute wealth very unequally across persons, such economies create a stratified structure of power. Wealth measures power; the more wealthy are the more powerful.

The general increase in societal wealth increases the power of some members of society to achieve their ends. Wealth means *power to*. Does it also mean *power over* others? The remainder of this section explores three ways in which wealth may be related to the power of agents (firms, capitalists, organizations of workers or consumers) within the market. The next section advances an alternate view of power as "conditioned power."

The idea of wealth as a general category may not be helpful in thinking about power over. Wealth in general leads us to think of money, land, ownership of a house and consumption goods, and investments of diverse kinds. For our purposes it is more appropriate to think of wealth as ownership and control of productive capital. Owning a house may provide little leverage in controlling others. Owning productive capital may provide much more. We explore three areas where wealth may confer power: (1) the market power of firms, (2) the labor contract, and (3) production relations within the firm. The first two are agency-oriented views of power in which the structural bases of power are subordinate to the strategic actions of power holders. The last example – production relations within the firm – highlights the structural subordination of labor to capital and downplays agency.

Market power of firms

We have argued that in perfectly competitive markets, economic exchange and power repel each other. With numerous producers and consumers, no one is able to exert influence. However, in imperfect (concentrated) markets, economic agents may have the capacity to influence others. Markets with a few producers in particular industries are not rare. Lindblom, for example, argues as follows:

For big companies in national markets, a common pattern is oligopoly, as in the American automobile industry where four companies account for 99 percent of output or the farm machinery industry where four firms account for over half the output. Perhaps as much as 60 percent of manufactured goods in the United States are produced by enterprises that make their production plans and set their prices in light of their interaction with two or three other dominant firms in their industry. (1977:149)

Large firms in concentrated industries have greater potential power. What does this claim mean and on what basis does it rest? Potential power refers to resources and means of influence that are unexploited; that is, they have not been used. We say that these resources are potential power because they imply an ability (an asymmetric ability) to inflict damage or limit gain. A worker whose only hope lies with a job that only one employer can provide has weak bargaining potential. A labor union bargaining collectively with capital has greater bargaining power than its members would have individually.

In these examples, bargaining power rests on vulnerability, or more precisely on differential vulnerability. In any exchange system, everyone is vulnerable to some extent. Since everyone expects to gain from exchange, everyone is to some extent vulnerable. This is simply to say that everyone can lose that which is gained from exchange. When the quantity that one can lose is large, and when it is not easily replaced, vulnerability is high. An actor in this position is subject to influence attempts.

To understand the link between economic concentration and power, it may be helpful to analyze the possibility of exercising power in perfectly competitive markets. In a perfectly competitive market, there are numerous producers, consumers, and laborers. Coalitions (of firms, consumers, workers) are impossible. Market entry is easy, economic adjustments are instantaneous, and rents (above average profits) are quickly eroded by competition. Finally, firms produce homogeneous products rather than tailoring them for specializing markets.

In such a market, agents cannot affect overall economic parameters (prices, overall demand) or the behavior of other agents. The important economic variables are *data* – that is "givens." Thus technology, preferences, the output of other firms, and the initial distribution of endowments are given. What remains for the firm to decide is the level of output that it should produce.

A perfectly competitive market is characterized by diversity and numerous options, in short by choice. Yet the most striking thing about a competitive market is how little power the agents possess. Spiro Latsis says that "under conditions characterizing perfect competition the decision-maker's discretion in choosing among alternative courses of action is reduced simply to whether or not to stay in business" (1972:209). Frank Knight elaborates this basic point:

Few critics of capitalism see clearly enough that the entrepreneur in his "control" of production is relatively helpless as to what he shall produce, and where and when and by what instrumentalities and methods – and in particular as to what he shall pay for labor. Under perfect competition he would of course be completely helpless, a mere automatic registrar of the choice of consumers. (1956:92)

The basic point is clear. Competitive markets as sites of social interaction offer no scope for power over others. Indeed, in competitive markets, firms don't compete. What happens when we relax the assumption of competitive market structure and allow producer concentration?

In oligopoly, there are few producers – that is, a smaller number control larger shares of the market (in total production, sales, and so on). Oligopoly is also characterized by higher barriers to entry and sometimes by producing and selling heterogeneous products. Barriers to entry seem to be the most important feature in maintaining the privileged position of the oligopolist. These barriers may have economic origins (such as economies of scale) or they may owe their existence to political practices (such as licenses, subsidies, tariffs). In either case, firms already in the market have an advantage over those outside.

What are the implications of producer concentration for power? Firms that possess a large share of the market are said to possess "market power." This could mean a number of things. Large firms might be able to affect prices, thus affecting their terms of exchange with others (consumers and other firms). Firms in competitive markets are price takers. Firms in concentrated markets may be price makers. Power in this sense means the capacity to impose a higher price and by implication inferior terms of exchange on other economic agents than would exist under more competitive market conditions.

Large firms might also be able to affect other economic parameters, including output levels, technology, and even tastes (through allocating resources to advertising). The output level under competitive conditions is fixed by the overall demand curve and by cost considerations. Since demand and prices are fixed, the firm produces up to the point where its marginal costs equal marginal revenues. But in oligopoly, a firm may lower its production level, hence increasing prices. It can affect income per unit by controlling supply. This is an important "power" that firms do not possess in competitive markets.

Finally, firms have the power to affect other firms in oligopolistic environments. In competitive markets, a firm acts without regard to other firms. The market in general establishes the important economic parameters and any particular firm is treated as if it had no known objectives or strategy. The game-theoretic analogue is a one-person game against nature (Latsis, 1972:210). But in oligopolistic conditions, firms can, by pursuing different strategies, affect what other firms do, how much they produce, their price levels, and even whether they enter or leave an industry.

The key feature of oligopoly is the interdependence among firms. Fewness of firms facilitates but does not strictly determine interdependence. By contrast, in a competitive market each firm has a dominant strategy, regardless of what others do. Thus, appropriate behavior is determined by anonymous forces (the market – not particular competitors). Interdependence means that the best strategy for a firm is shaped (though usually not uniquely determined) not by the market but by the capabilities and strategies of rival firms. In competitive markets, firms are not rivals in any sense and do not compete. In noncompetitive markets they do.

The interdependence condition opens up a wide assortment of practices and strategies in which firms might engage. Industrial policy becomes a possibility. Receiving a subsidy from government may discourage other firms from entering the market. Predatory pricing strategies offer another possibility. A firm may lower its prices in response to the possibility of another firm entering the market, thus driving it out. And strategic policies that include retaliation (in terms of prices, market share policies), either in the domestic or international realm, may become attractive. The literature on strategic trade theory offers numerous examples of practices that firms and governments may follow attempting to gain advantage over other firms and other countries.

Thus, while perfectly competitive markets provide scope for exerting power to achieve certain aims (chiefly regarding wealth), they offer no room for power over other agents. Opportunities to acquire wealth are not "at the expense of" others except in the vacuous sense that everything (including new wealth) could have been used in other ways. Oligopoly opens up opportunities for power over others. In addition to devoting resources to wealth making, resources can be channeled toward the transfer of wealth (rent seeking). Instead of taking price and demand levels as given, they are subject to change. And instead of "deciding" anonymously, firms may devise strategies contingent upon the actions of other firms.

The labor-capital contract

In this section we examine the relations between labor and capital and explore the potential for power relations among them. Inequality of wealth under capitalism gives some the resources to hire others to work for them and requires some to sell their labor in order to acquire the means to satisfy their needs. As Adam Smith put it in 1776:

As soon as stock has accumulated in the hands of particular persons, some of them will naturally employ it in setting to work industrious people whom they will supply with materials and subsistence, in order to make a profit by the sale of their work, or by what their labor adds to the value of the materials. (1937:78)

We can look at this result in two importantly different ways. First, we can treat the buying and selling of labor (the wage contract) simply as one instance of exchange. Since the parties enter into the contract voluntarily, the opportunity to do so enhances the capacity of each to pursue private interest (one in profit making, the other in acquiring means of consumption). The wage contract enhances the power of all parties, especially when contrasted to coercive forms of labor. The wage contract, since entered into voluntarily, endows neither party with any power *over* the others. As Marx puts it, somewhat sarcastically to be sure, the labor market appears to be "a very Eden of the innate rights of man" ([1867] 1967a:167).

The view that employing a worker is an instance of free exchange is widely held in neoclassical economics. Workers desire access to capital so as to earn an income. Owners of capital want to employ workers so as to capitalize on the value of their investment. Owners of labor and owners of capital in effect hire one another on terms that are more or less favorable to each in accordance with the scarcity value of labor and capital. When an employer fires a worker from his or her job, the employer "simply" declines to continue an economic exchange:

What exactly has the employer done? *He has refused to continue to make* a certain exchange, which the worker preferred to continue making. Specifically, A, the employer, refuses to sell a certain sum of money in exchange for the purchase of B's labor services. B would like to make a certain exchange; A would not. The same principles may apply to all the exchanges throughout the length and breadth of the economy. (Rothbard, 1970:228–9, italics in original)

This way of looking at the labor market gains credibility the less dependent the worker is on a single employer (in this sense, the more competitive the market). The existence of alternative bidders for the worker's commodity (labor) makes less plausible the idea that the labor market gives the buyer power over the seller:

Those who identify market with freedom introduce a distinction. . . . Freedom is abridged only when one person can compel another to do his bidding. In a market system, no particular person compels anyone else to work. People are compelled to work only by the impersonal requirements of the system. (Lindblom, 1977:47)

This conclusion depends, as we have seen, on the freedom of the worker to pass up a job offer from a particular employer. By questioning this freedom, we open up an avenue for the exercise of power to find its way into the labor exchange. This second way of looking at the labor exchange defines an entry point for a power-centered approach to political economy.

Lindblom follows up the statement just cited with the argument that dependence of the worker on a particular employer endows the latter with power over the former:

Yet when livelihood is at stake in exchange, as it has been in all market systems so far in history, personal coercion adds to impersonal. If jobs are scarce, anyone who has a job to offer can coerce job applicants. . . . A person whose style of life and family livelihood for years have been built around a particular job, occupation or location finds a command backed by a threat to fire him indistinguishable in many consequences for his liberty from a command backed by the police and the courts. (1977: 47–8)

This sort of example leads Lindblom to a generalization concerning the exercise of power in the market. This generalization provides a criterion that markets must satisfy in order to exclude the exercise of the power of one party over another. According to this criterion "exchange best supports freedom when every party can choose among offers that do not greatly differ in value from each other or from no exchange at all" (1977:49). This criterion is met when (1) markets (especially the labor market) are competitive and (2) when livelihood does not depend on exchange.

The competitiveness of markets and the degree to which subsistence depends on exchange are complex issues. However, a brief word on each is in order. The degree of competition varies throughout different economies, by economic sector, and by region. From the standpoint of the worker, is a market competitive when he or she has numerous choices within a local geographic area (so that changing domiciles is not necessary), within the country as a whole, or within the same industry? In the United States, the places where jobs are disappearing and being created are often very distant from one another. If there is an unemployed worker from Connecticut and an open job in Arizona, should that "opening" be considered as part of the "opportunity set" for this worker?

This last question may be impossible to answer in the abstract. Yet some statements can be made about the relative advantages of capital and labor. Two things are especially important. First, owners of capital are fewer than owners of labor services. Large firms are by definition economic units bringing together large quantities of labor, capital, resources, and managerial skills. Thus the ratio of workers to employers is likely to be unfavorable to workers. If workers are unionized, so that they bargain collectively, things are of course different. Our comments are addressed to the case of atomistic competition among workers.

Second, capital is at once more separate from its owner than labor is from laborers. It is also more mobile. This provides a strategic advantage to capital. If workers increase their power over capital, for example through collective bargaining, owners may move their capital elsewhere, including outside the country where its owners reside. Indeed, many firms maintain parallel production facilities in several countries so as to place themselves in a stronger structural position with respect to labor.

Power within firms

Let us assume that labor and capital markets are competitive. Does it follow that power is not a part of economic life? Not necessarily. A related, but distinct approach to linking the exercise of power to the economy looks not into the market but into the authority relations of the productive enterprise. Marx pioneered this idea when he drew a contrast between what he termed the "sphere of exchange" and the "sphere of production." While the former might be a veritable "Eden of the innate rights of man," the latter looks quite different. Once the worker signs the wage contract he gives over to the employer the right to determine what the worker does during the duration of the contract. While the market may counterpose free and independent persons, the enterprise consists of those who do the work and those for whom they work. The latter have broad discretion to determine what the former do. From the lowest level worker to the highest level manager, the enterprise works on the basis of levels of authority and the transmission of decisions in the form of orders. As Max Weber puts it, "the great majority of all economic organizations, among them the most important and most modern ones, reveal a structure of dominancy" (1986:29). This idea forms a central theme in radical political economists' attempts to link politics to market economy (Bowles and Gintis, 1986:71–9).

Both Marxian and neoclassical political economy recognize a distinctive sphere of organized hierarchy within the economy. This sphere is set apart from the conventional model of market transactions, in which the parties "meet, exchange, and then part with their new holdings . . ." (Bowles and Gintis, 1986:77). For Marxists, there is the sphere of production, where value is created, and the sphere of exchange, where it is transmitted and realized. For neoclassical economics, there is the market and the firm. In the former, transactions take place as arm's length economic exchanges. In the latter, they take place within the command structure of the firm. As Ronald Coase put it in "The Nature of the Firm" (1937):

Outside the firm, price movements direct production, which is coordinated through a series of exchange transactions on the market. Within a firm, these market transactions are eliminated, and in place of the complicated market structure with exchange transactions is substituted the entrepreneur-co-ordinator who directs production. It is clear that there are alternative methods of co-ordinating production. ([1937] 1988:35–6)

While both Marxian and neoclassical economics agree on the existence of a sphere of hierarchical relations separate from both market and state, they theorize about these relations differently. For neoclassical economics, the firm exists because the costs of transacting in markets exceeds the costs of transacting within economic organizations, for specific types of transactions (especially those where contracts are incomplete, where information is uncertain, and where incentives for opportunism are great). Thus, the firm emerges as an island of conscious economic organization within the overall system of atomistic, free exchange. The overall approach emphasizes efficiency and the minimization of transaction costs (see Williamson, 1979).

In Marxian theory, hierarchy is interpreted differently. The focus is not on efficiency and transaction costs but on the antagonism between labor and capital and the need for a hierarchical structure to discipline labor. In his article, "What Do Bosses Do? The Origins and Functions of Hierarchy in Capitalist Production" (1974), Marglin stresses the importance of relations of power rather than efficiency and traces the origin of the firm to "its capacity to enlarge the span and degree of control of the capitalist. The firm is thus explained as an institution of power rather than one that survives due to its cost-cutting efficiency" (Hodgson, 1988:214).

What are the implications for power of recognizing a separate hierarchical sphere in the economy? In the neoclassical tradition, power is minimal. Relations among members of the firm are seen in terms of efficiency, particularly in terms of the contribution of various organizational forms to the minimization of transaction costs. Thus managers and "higher-ups" have little scope for discretion. They are agents whose task is to make and monitor contracts efficiently.

In the Alchian–Demsetz tradition (1972), power disappears. These writers deny that there is any difference between ordinary market exchange and allocation of resources within the firm. The firm is essentially a bundle of contracts where the terms of exchange, including the exchange between labor and capital, are continually negotiated. The employer orders the worker to perform certain jobs just as the worker orders the employer to pay his or her wage. Thus, the power of the firm is a complete delusion:

It is common to see the firm characterized by the power to settle issues by fiat, by authority, or by disciplinary action superior to that available in the conventional market. This is delusion. The firm does not own all its inputs. It has no power of fiat, no authority, no disciplinary action any different in the slightest degree from ordinary market contracting between any two people. . . . What is the content of the presumed power to manage and assign workers to various tasks? Exactly the same as one little consumer's power to manage and assign his grocer to various tasks. (Alchian and Demsetz, 1972:777)

At a minimum, one influential branch of neoclassical economics (transaction-cost economics) minimizes power by making efficiency the central concept. At a maximum, power disappears altogether by interpreting all intrafirm relations as free exchange. There are other viewpoints worth pursuing. Lindblom, for example, finds the implications of authority structures within firms especially disturbing:

In developing market systems, most gainfully employed people in fact spend their working hours in an authority system – typically an organized business enterprise. The consequent threat to freedom is all the more obvious in large corporations: an organization in which a few men command thousands of others in the standardized patterns of bureaucracy does not nourish freedom. (1977)

The idea here is something like the following: Assume that we enter into a labor contract and thus subordinate ourselves (for a period) to those who own and manage the enterprise in which we work. If we spend a significant proportion of our lives within an authority structure, working to achieve ends that are not our own, unable to exercise any meaningful sense of self-determination, can we successfully sustain our sense of ourselves as free persons? And if we cannot, might this threaten our capacity to be free and self-determining during the time we spend on our own, away from our place of work?

Considerations such as these bring us to the role of conditioned power in the economy, to concern for the way in which a form of economic organization might affect our perceptions of ourselves, our interests, and our choices.

Conditioned power and the economy

Earlier in this chapter we alluded to the concept of "conditioned power" and remarked that it raised special concerns for power, particularly in terms of its connection to interest. Since this type of power did not fit neatly within our general discussion, we deferred treatment of it until now. We begin with some formulations by different authors.

[C]onditioned power . . . is subjective; neither those exercising it nor those subject to it need always be aware that it is being exerted. The acceptance of authority, the submission to the will of others, becomes the higher preference of those submitting. This preference can be deliberately cultivated – by persuasion or education. This is explicit conditioning. Or it can be dictated by the culture itself; the submission is considered to be normal, proper, or traditionally correct. This is implicit conditioning. (Galbraith, 1983:24)

[T]he bias of the system is not sustained simply by a series of individually chosen acts but also, most importantly, by the socially structured and culturally patterned behavior of groups, and practices of institutions, which may indeed be manifested by individuals' inaction. . . . Is it not the supreme exercise of power to get another or others to have the desires you want them to have – that is to secure their compliance by controlling their thoughts and desires? (Lukes, 1974:21-2, 23)

This interpretation attempts an end run around the difficulty posed by the concept of power for economics. Because of this, it has special significance for power-centered approaches to political economy. The success of approaches employing the strategy suggested here depends, of course, on the interpretation of power that grounds it. Before turning directly to that strategy, we consider this interpretation more closely.

Most notably, conditioned power, unlike our initial concepts, does not require an imposition of the ends of some (the powerful) agents against resistance derived from opposing ends of other agents. Indeed, the less powerful, in working to achieve *what they perceive to be* their ends, actually serve the ends of the powerful. Thus, the less powerful both achieve their ends and in so doing work for others' ends and against themselves. This makes sense only if the less powerful have "real interests" distinct from and opposed to the interests that they perceive and that directly guide their actions. The conflict that establishes an exercise of power where to all appearances a community of interest exists opposes the explicit interests of the powerful with a hidden, but real, interest of those they have power over. As Stephen Lukes puts it, a "latent conflict" exists "between the interests of those exercising power and the real interests of those they exclude" (1974:24–5). Thus, the idea of conditioned power severs both the link between the exercise of power and an overt opposition of interests, and the link between intentions (conscious ends) and real interests (of the powerless). Thus power is exercised, in this sense, when a social order operates so as to satisfy the ends of some by misleading others into thinking that those ends are also theirs. Conditioned power exhibits the following provocative characteristics:

1. Power means the ability to achieve your real interests.
2. Those who have power correctly perceive their real interests and how those interests are served.
3. Those without power do not correctly perceive their real interests. For them conscious intentions and real interests differ.
4. Power over others means the ability of a social order to condition some into misperceiving their real interests in a way that serves the real interests of the "powerful" but works against the real interests of the powerless.

Thus, "power over" others works not directly, as in our simpler interpretation, but indirectly via the system or social order as a whole. Power over is the power of the social order over some (but not all) of its members.

The notion of conditioned power bears two importantly different interpretations. According to the first, those who accurately perceive their real interests (the powerful) design a social order that conditions others to misperceive their interests in ways serving the powerful. Power, then, means (1) power to design social institutions that (2) condition others but that (3) do not condition the powerful, who retain a true perception of their real interests. According to the second interpretation, both powerful and powerless are born into an existing social order that conditions both powerful and powerless to identify their real interests with its perpetuation. Within this (self-perpetuating) order, some benefit, others do not. The notion of conditioned power attributes power directly to the social order and indirectly to those who benefit from it. This attribution obviously raises difficulties. If successful, however, it identifies power with individuals (or corporations) without seeing them as the agents who exercise power. We return to this idea further on.

Does the concept of conditioned power in some way increase our ability to treat the market economy as a place within which power plays a vital role? Clearly, a large part of the motivation for the concept stems from the way in which market economy presents itself as a system of voluntary transactions. Even when individuals place their labor at the service of the firm, they do so voluntarily. It can even be argued that, since individuals place their labor and not themselves in the service of the firm, strictly speaking they remain free while at work. So long as persons can separate themselves from their labor, we can sustain the idea that, in all its aspects, a competitive market economy excludes the exercise of power over persons (see Levine, 1978:226–36). If we accept this way of thinking, then conditioned power may be the only recourse available for us to support the idea that the economy is a system of power.

As we saw in the previous section, the advantage of the notion of conditioned power lies in the way in which it enables us to attribute power to persons and groups without claiming the exercise of power of those individuals directly over others. This, of course, also makes the notion of conditioned power a problematic one. Important instances of use of this idea in economics include the following: in the theory of consumption, the notion of false needs; in the analysis of distribution, the critique of the legitimacy of profit and of private investment; in the theory of production, the critique of the legitimacy of the authority structure of the firm; in welfare economics, the critique of the efficiency of free markets as defined by welfare criteria.

As we suggested, a pillar of the economist's argument for free markets is that they achieve efficiency in the sense of maximizing welfare defined upon the basis of individual subjective preference. What if individual preferences, while expressing the individual's direct interest, distort (even violate) the individual's imputed (or real) interest? In this case, the capitalist economy makes the individual the victim of conditioned power acting in the service of firms bent on satisfying their need for profit by convincing consumers that they want things that they do not really need:

What is certain is the negative statement which, notwithstanding its negativity, constitutes one of the most important insights of political economy: an output the volume and composition of which are determined by the profit maximization policies of oligopolistic corporations neither corresponds to human needs nor costs the minimum possible amount of human toil and human suffering. (Baran and Sweezy, 1966:139)

If direct and imputed needs differ, then satisfaction of the consumer's direct need is not in the consumer's real interest. Consumers who go about the work of satisfying those needs are the victims of (conditioned) power.

Whether this claim about false needs (stemming from the demands of profit seeking) implies the power of the producer over the consumer depends, in part, on whether the producer's interest in profit making and wealth accumulation is real or itself conditioned by his social environment. The attempt to apply the notion of conditioned power requires us to accept the legitimacy of profit seeking as a real interest for the producer. Then, if consumers develop needs for products and workers accept the idea that the firm's profitability is in their interest, this constitutes an instance of conditioned power.

Clearly, if we accept the inevitability or desirability of a capitalist market economy, the firm's profitability may very well be in the worker's interest. One of the key points about conditioned power is that it excludes important (real) options leaving its victims with a truncated set of choices all of which support the prevailing order. Lukes calls this "the supreme and most insidious exercise of power" (1974:24). By this criterion, the market economy can very readily be considered a system of power.

In thinking this way, we still need to confront and resolve a series of difficulties including the following:

1. By what process do we distinguish real needs from false needs?
2. For us to employ the concept of power, even assuming the presence of false needs, must we identify a person or group who knowingly exercises power (thus connecting conditioned power back to our earlier notions)? Or, can we still employ the idea of a system of power when power is exercised by no one?

The answer to the first question has to do with the way in which our social condition affects the process by which we define our interests. Some authors think of real needs as those we would have outside of society, and some define real needs as those we would define for ourselves in a society capable of nurturing and satisfying such needs. A Marxian view would define this in relation to a socialist or communist society. Thus, according to Agnes Heller's account of the Marxian theory of need, a "new system of needs . . . becomes comprehensible only in relationship to the functioning of the new social body," which she characterizes, following Marx, as the "society of associated producers" within which "radical needs come to be satisfied" (1976:98). The Marxian approach thus identifies real needs with needs as they would be in a particular kind of society "where economic activity is no longer dominated by profit and sales" (Baran and Sweezy, 1966:139).

Whether we accept this conclusion or not, the idea of real needs opposed to direct or subjective needs involves a criticism of social organization and a project of defining the kind of social organization that would overcome the opposition. If individuals form, perceive, and act on real needs, then they must be autonomous, at least so far as need satisfaction is concerned; they cannot be subject to the power of others.

Even if we accept the disparity, within certain kinds of societies, between real and direct interest, we still need to establish this disparity as the result of the exercise of power. One way to do so is to argue that the beneficiaries of the disparity (under capitalism, the capitalists) actually exercise power over the institutions that govern and educate in society. This is the strategy, for example, of C. Wright Mills (1956) and G. William Domhoff (1967), who argue empirically that the dominant positions in governing institutions are held by members of a ruling elite connected, at least according to Domhoff, to corporate interests. This strategy allows us to use our simpler notion of power in the service of the argument for conditioned power. We do so by making conditioning the result of the conscious effort of a privileged group to hold power in order to preserve its privilege.

While the simplicity of this idea has its attractions, it is difficult to hold power over others with the sole and explicit purpose of making yourself (and keeping yourself) rich at their expense. What is required is a unity of purpose in maintaining the wealth and power of the wealthy. In face of this unity of purpose, the exercise of power to protect wealth becomes unnecessary:

Bereft of valid reasons to justify himself and sufficient forces to defend himself; easily crushing a private individual, but himself crushed by troops of bandits; alone against all and unable on account of mutual jealousies to unite with his equals against enemies united by the common hope of plunder, the rich, pressed by necessity, finally conceived the most thought-out project that ever entered the human mind. It was to use in his favor the very strength of those who attacked him, to turn his adversaries into his defenders, to instill in them other maxims and to give them other institutions which were as favorable to him as natural right was unfavorable to him. (Rousseau, [1762] 1983:149)

This argument for conditioned power carries a historical link to the conscious exercise of power. It finds power in the ideological education of people to the acceptance of social institutions that, once accepted, work to benefit the wealthy with no need for the exercise of power on their part. If successful, the wealthy need not also be powerful (although they may be). Indeed, the more successful conditioned power, the less the need to exercise power. The notion of conditioned power inevitably leads to paradoxical formulations of this sort. When the legitimacy of a social order that bestows significantly unequal benefits is intact, that order depends on "proper" education rather than on the exercise of power.

Is it not, then, confusing to term this a type of power, a kind we never see, that no one need ever exercise? Is it not sufficient to demonstrate that the implied disparity between direct and imputed interest also implies a profound powerlessness (if power means ability to achieve our ends, we can have no power when we cannot know our real ends)? Why call powerlessness a form of the exercise of power?

The answer to this question implicit in Galbraith's *Anatomy of Power* (1983) is that a failure to convict the wealthy of the exercise of power in acquiring and protecting their wealth necessarily justifies them in having that wealth. As Connolly emphasizes, the person wielding power is responsible for limiting choice or the ability to act upon the basis of choice. To acknowledge power "is to implicate oneself in responsibility for certain events" ([1974] 1983:97); to attribute power is not simply to describe a relationship, but to accuse. If we accept the concept of conditioned power, we can continue to accuse even if we accept the absence of any direct or apparent exercise of power. Using this concept allows us to tie benefit to responsibility for the oppression of others. Indeed, it makes oppression (and/or exploitation) a logical corollary of benefit.

Much then is at stake in deciding to accept or reject the language of conditioned power. But, in accepting or rejecting it, we must decide if it is a genuine insight or a linguistic ploy aimed at preserving the notion of responsibility where none can be found. Of course, even if we deny that those who benefit are responsible for those who do not, this need not imply acceptance of the legitimacy of a system of inequality. A system that renders most of its participants powerless is vulnerable to a fundamental critique even if no individual (or group) bears direct responsibility for that powerlessness.

Conclusion

In his review of *The New Palgrave: A Dictionary of Economics*, Robert Heilbroner notes a striking fact: In a collection that runs over 4,000 pages and has 2,000 entries, there is no entry for "power" (Heilbroner, 1988:23). We have noted some of the sources of resistance to power by neoclassical economics. Important segments of Marxian political economy also resist placing power at the center, displacing the concept of class. Resnick and Wolff take pains to distance themselves from Marxian and non-Marxian formulations that try to make power central "by counterposing power as the alternative essence of social structure and development . . . " (1987:334).

Yet the appeal of building political economy on a foundation of power and wealth is strong. How can these two phenomena not be related, the naive realist might ask. While acknowledging this appeal, a good part of this chapter examined the difficulties of melding power and some central economic concepts. From our standpoint, there are two separate difficulties of placing political economy on a foundation of power.

The first problem is whether power by itself is enough to supply the (or "a") content for politics. Suppose that our subject matter permits power actions (that is, suppose such actions are not prevented by markets). Does the existence of power by itself identify our subject matter as political? Our answer to this question is "generally no." Power may exist within the firm, between firms, within the family, school, and religious groups. While power actions in these settings may have some political content, they are not intrinsically political. Politics is not identical to all relations of power and domination. So power can exist without definitionally entailing politics. And of the three core approaches to politics explored in our Chapter 1, only one (authoritative allocation of values) necessarily involves power or makes it focal.

Those (other than the state) who exercise power within the economy do so in the pursuit of their private interests. This need not (directly) involve a political struggle over the instruments and institutions of power (government). If not, then power-centered approaches to political economy have to do with politics only in a very limited sense of the word. Unlike the other approaches to political economy, power-centered approaches do not focus on the relation between private interests and public decision making. This sets the power-centered approaches apart.

The second problem with integrating power and economics concerns the capacity for activating a discussion of power within the terms provided by neoclassical economics. We started on a note that questioned the possibility of power relations within markets. We should be clear that rational choice, maximization of utilities, and exchange theory – all central to neoclassical economics – do not provide obstacles. In exercising or attempting to exercise power, people can be thought of as having goals, pursuing them in a cost-sensitive way, and employing threats and inducements in doing so (the latter typifying negative and positive exchange). We are not arguing that power is irrational or that its exercise takes us out of the realm of intentional behavior.

The obstacles presented by neoclassical economics center on the voluntary nature of exchange and the focus on efficiency. These two concepts go together and make power analysis difficult. If exchanges are voluntary, agents enter into them "of their own free will." This in turn implies that no one expects to be worse off after the exchange. The exchange situation may have been "set up" (with choices and payoffs manipulated), or the options and constraints may be unequal, or both, but no matter. These factors are treated as parameters, as unanalyzed givens. If this accurately describes economic choice, power in the sense of "power over" is impossible to wield.

While the term "voluntary" applies to individual motivations for exchange, in neoclassical theory, efficiency applies to overall allocation. Neoclassical economists ask, given a set of agents, their preferences, endowments, and the technology available, if there are any further exchanges that will improve some (at least one) without making anyone worse off. The set of exchanges that satisfy these criteria are called Pareto-improving exchanges. They enhance efficiency. There are of course other possible exchanges, such as those that make some better off at the expense of others and some that might make both or all parties worse off.

The idea of efficiency ties economics to the first set of exchanges, those that improve the lot of some without damaging others. This deprives economics of one (some would say the crucial one) way of talking about power, namely the threat of imposing negative sanctions. This idea is rather central to politics and political science. Individuals pursue goals. Often these goals are in conflict. Sometimes agents pursue their goals "at the expense of" others; that is, they use power to threaten to make others worse off if they do not yield.

To the extent that neoclassical economics restricts its focus to efficient exchanges, it deprives itself of one way of talking about power. Other avenues are still open: the power to improve technology or the power to construct institutions within which agents can more efficiently pursue their preferences. Thus neoclassical economics retains the capacity to theorize about a substantial range of "power to" phenomena. However, it generally has not chosen to use the language of power. To the extent that neoclassical economics relinquishes its focus on efficiency, it opens itself up to "power over" thinking but ceases to become the science of allocative efficiency.

8

State-centered approaches to political economy

In the approaches to political economy we have considered up to now, the state plays a subsidiary role. In these approaches, political economy is energized by the economy, or more broadly by the system of private interests. Indeed, in these approaches, little exists that cannot be understood on the basis of private (essentially economic) interest. To the extent that these approaches concern themselves with the state, they treat it as an instrument or institution employed by individuals or groups as a way of achieving private ends. Whatever important differences exist among these approaches, one similarity stands out. The state is not essentially an active agent; it serves as an instrument of forces originating among individuals or classes. As Wolin points out, this instrumental conception of the state goes back to Locke and the case against Hobbes.

[P]olitical phenomena are best explained as the resultant of social factors, and hence political institutions and beliefs are best understood by a method which gets "behind" them to the "underlying" social processes which dictate the shape of things political. (1960:287)

This form of determination leaves the state in a derivative position. Deprived of its own logic, lacking a motivation and source of energy lying outside economy, the state is reduced to a dependent variable. First, a clear distinction is made between state and economy. Second, economy is accorded a primary place, with the wants and interests of individuals at the center. And third, the state is treated as a vehicle to satisfy wants when they cannot be satisfied privately.

In this chapter, we consider approaches to political economy centering on the idea of an active state whose agenda is not reducible to wants emerging within the private sphere. Those writers who have concerned themselves with interpreting relations between state and economy in this way often employ the term "state autonomy" to distinguish their approach. Broadly, the term state autonomy refers to the ability of the state to define and pursue an agenda not defined for it solely by private societal interests.

What we term here the state-centered approach to political economy identifies politics with the state or the agenda of the state and economics with the private sphere. In the relevant literature we often find the term "society" used to refer to the world of private interests whether of individuals or classes. This carries forward the classical idea of a distinction between state and civil society. While society, or civil society, includes more than economy narrowly defined, we will use the terms economy, society, and private sphere more or less interchangeably to refer to the system of private relations among private agents. We begin with a brief discussion of state autonomy, move to the difficulties of the society-centered approaches (including utilitarian and Marxian approaches), and subsequently take up state-centered approaches.

State autonomy

At bottom, the idea of state autonomy refers to a capacity of the state to act independently of social forces (particularly economic forces). This does not mean society is irrelevant. It just means that an arrangement of social forces does not uniquely determine particular state actions. Marxists such as Poulantzas (1969, 1973) speak of the "relative autonomy" of the state. Pluralists at least theoretically allow for state autonomy when the "vector of group pressures" is unclear (that is, when the pressures generated by societal groups do not result in clear political demands). And of course state autonomy has been a central concern of statist theorists such as Krasner (1978) and Skocpol (1985). The predominant conception of state autonomy revolves around the idea of freedom from external (societal) causal influences. This idea goes as follows. If system x (say a state structure) is autonomous, it is not driven completely by forces outside of itself. Autonomy means self-contained causality; that is, the system in question has a set of boundaries. For the moment let us overlook the problems posed by such a formulation, and see where it leads us.

The conception of autonomy as freedom from "external" influences has three corollary viewpoints. The first relates to a conception of the state "exerting leverage" or "winning out" over the pressures emanating from society. The basic idea is that state leaders have their own ends and societal interest groups have theirs. In the political battle that ensues, state leaders resist pressures from private interests and translate their will into public policy. The second viewpoint refers to state action not dictated or controlled by any one group or coalition of groups. Here it is not so much that the state is opposed to economic interests as that no clear reading of those interests is forthcoming. This is the "balance of opposing class forces" of which some Marxists speak, or the theoretical possibility that "the vector of group forces is zero" in pluralist theory. In either case the basic point is the same: The state acts because the private sector as a whole does not; that is, there is a failure to formulate a "social will." In public choice theory this condition (inability to identify a societal preference) is taken to be quite general, placing the state in democratic societies in a difficult position.

The third viewpoint turns on the capacity of the state to resist pressures and is very popular among those dealing with policymaking. This view of state autonomy is closely tied to the "strong state–weak state" literature. Strong states are those simultaneously capable of resisting pressures and generating public policy initiatives on their own. Weak states are those that "cave in" to pressures from economic interests. Implicit in this third view is the idea that the structure of interest representation may be inadequate and may systematically exclude many who have a genuine interest (in the sense of stake) in the political process. In part, this is the view of E. E. Schattschneider in *The Semisovereign People* (1960). It is only the state that stands apart from the interest group process and takes the "aerial view," assessing the interests of society as a whole. In these circumstances the state may use its privileged position to speak for excluded groups or to mobilize bias in the system.

What has made state action based on its own agenda an anomaly has to do with the way we think of political agendas deriving from social forces. Approaches that ground politics in private interests identify agendas with interests and in turn identify interests with the private circumstances of actors. To be sure, these frameworks identify the private circumstances and the actors along profoundly different dimensions. Nonetheless, the links between agendas and action, interests and agendas, and interests and private circumstances, remain tight. The theories (Marxian, pluralist, public choice, and so on) treat private circumstances of actors as their circumstances in society. In Marxism these circumstances are material and objective; in the utilitarian theories they are essentially subjective. In both cases social interaction, social institutions, and social order must be explained by action driven by private interest. It is this quality of the theory that assures that "state autonomy" appears as (1) a form of state action not determined by economic interest and (2) an anomaly for the theory. Yet, even in these "society-centered" approaches, the problem of state agenda-setting cannot be entirely avoided, and elements of a more state-centered approach emerge, if in a limited way. We begin with these intimations of the state as they appear in theories centering on economy.

Society-centered approaches

Utilitarian approaches

Eric Nordlinger's *On the Autonomy of the Democratic State* (1981) attempts to adapt the utilitarian method to states that act according to their own agendas. Nordlinger does so first by introducing a utilitarian (but non–public choice) definition of the state. The term "state," we are told, "refers to all those individuals who occupy offices that authorize them, and them alone, to make and apply decisions that are binding on any and all segments of society" (1981:11). We learn two important things about the state from this definition. First, it consists of individuals and, second, it stands apart from the society on which its decisions are binding. From this definition of the state how do we get to state autonomy? Individuals have preferences that are expressed as political claims (political demands). Similarly, individuals in authorized public offices have preferences that in turn may arise from the preferences of their constituents, their own personalities, or the structure of political authority within which they operate. State autonomy for Nordlinger, then, consists in the capacity of state leaders so defined to execute their preferences by translating them into public policy, whether or not in opposition to the preferences of nonofficeholders.

The logical determination of state autonomy is easy enough. Private individuals have preferences. Individuals holding public office have preferences. Sometimes they conflict, and when they conflict, sometimes holders of public office win. When they do we have state autonomy. Nordlinger presents the problem of state autonomy as a straightforward empirical claim (who succeeds in translating preferences into policy?) along with an underlying decisional conception of power. The state is autonomous when it succeeds. However, several large questions involving the distinction between state and economy are unresolved by this approach. Nordlinger tries to establish this difference by reference to the nature of the offices held. The state is a state because it has offices that make binding decisions on any and all private agents. The private sphere lacks components capable of making such binding decisions. But the problem with this demarcation line is that it embodies no criterion relevant to the content of state decision makers' preferences and how these are distinguished. Since state and nonstate preferences are assumed to be similar in form (even if opposed to each other), it is impossible to deduce the state from the distinctive content of the goals pursued by state leaders. These goals may be essentially of a private nature (expansion of agency budgets, maximization of influence, extension of private benefits to constituents) or they may have a genuinely public character to them. The content of state preferences is open, that is to say, contingent, and may be exactly the same as the content of individual preferences in society.

The lack of a substantive distinction between state and nonstate spheres places the issue of state autonomy on uncertain grounds. If agents of the state and private persons are identical with regard to the content of their preferences, state autonomy is reduced to a tug of war between competing private claims, rather than between claims rooted in private goals and a rival conception of public interest.

Finally, consider the pluralist variant of the utilitarian approach. As we have seen, pluralism ascribes a facilitative role to the state. Faced with often conflicting societal pressures, the state mediates and coordinates conflicting group claims, fosters compromises, and assures that the rules of the game are adhered to by all participants. The state is both an arena and umpire (Connolly, 1969), a place where societal conflict is played out, and a set of governing rules. After the societal forces express their demands, the state as procedural guarantor gives way to the state as implementor of policy.

It is easy to see how pluralism as social theory relegates the state to a minor position. Arthur Bentley, the father of the theory of pluralism in the United States, remarked:

My interest in politics is not primary, but [derives] from my interest in economic life. . . . (1908:210)

And:

The "state" itself is, to the best of my knowledge and belief, no factor in our investigation. . . . (1908:263–4)

The quotes from Bentley are relevant not only for the content of his own work but also for the subsequent half-century and more of pluralist research on the state. If pluralist theory is taken seriously, it is difficult if not impossible to entertain autonomous state action. State policies reflect the resultant of group pressures in society. Indeed, the presumed stability of pluralist systems is tied to the proposition that political outcomes reflect the balance of power among groups in society (Connolly, 1969:4). If there is deadlock among groups, if the vector of group forces approaches zero, the possibilities of independent state action increase. But it is not clear if state action in these circumstances constitutes autonomy or is more akin to discretion that surrounds the ambiguities of stalemated group life.

State autonomy emerges as an empirical anomaly for pluralist theory. In numerous cases the facts of political life do not seem to fit that theory. As Skocpol points out, the world that unraveled after World War II "rendered society-centered views of social change and politics less credible" (1985:6). The Depression of the thirties ushered in a new period of interventionism and macroeconomic policy making, and public expenditures soared in almost all liberal democracies. Perhaps even more important to Skocpol was the fact that by the seventies, both Britain and the United States were under severe strain from international economic competition (Skocpol, 1985:6). Their societies, no longer strong enough to assure economic superiority, were now more prepared to accept an activist state.

Other examples are relevant. The work of Peter Evans (1979) on the Brazilian state as, in part, a "state for itself," in addition to a state responsive to domestic and international capital, comes to mind. The project of creating state enterprises in Brazil involved more than organizational adaptation. It included the creation and manipulation of the very socioeconomic base that was to serve as the foundation of state power. In this case it seemed that Bentley had been turned on his head. Evidence concerning the importance of autonomous state power is not limited to examples of activist state polices. The autonomy of the state has structural roots that give it broad scope for independent initiative. Stepan, in *The State and Society: Peru in Comparative Perspective* (1978), argues in detail that the Peruvian state is proactive in many cases. The state is highly interventionist, reaching into society to structure the conditions under which groups organize and pressure political institutions. Finally, the corporatist literature (Schmitter, 1977) points out that groups do not always "freely combine" to "spontaneously reflect new social realities." In many democratic systems, groups are licensed and chartered by the state itself and then brought into the state structure. The result is that the foundational demarcation line between the realm of the private (societal-based, self-seeking interest groups) and the public (nonprivate, state institutions) is erased, or at the least, blurred.

Marxian approaches

The problem identified in the previous section with utilitarianism arises also for Marxism. Why reach beyond the idea of the state as a creature of private interest in order to conceptualize the problem of state autonomy? The Marxian answer to this question is in some ways more complicated. Because of this it reveals something important about the shared effort to think about the state as a creature of private interest.

First, we should observe that the instrumental notion of the state as a creature of the private interests of the capitalists themselves (doing their bidding, so to speak), while visible in Marxian theory, was never considered a satisfactory resting place for that theory so far as its more sophisticated adherents were concerned. In different ways, twentieth-century theorists in the Marxian tradition (especially those often called "structural Marxists") have devoted themselves to the problem of treating the state as an agent of class interest without reducing the state to a creature of the interests of the capitalists taken individually or collectively (see Gramsci, 1971; Poulantzas, 1973; Jessop, 1982).

Explicitly, the most vexing problems raised by the instrumental approach to the state are the following: (1) Do we identify the interests of the capitalist class with the interests of the capitalists who compose that class or with an objective interest that we can impute to them on the basis of their class position? (2) Given that the state acts in the interests of the capitalist class (in one of the two previous senses), and given that (in either sense) that interest conflicts with the interests of workers, how can the state command the allegiance of the "majority" of the population as it must in a capitalist democracy? The ideas of hegemony (Gramsci) and of "relative autonomy" (Poulantzas) speak to these two problems.

The two issues identified in the previous paragraph point to the same problem. Civil society, understood as the system of private relations between juridically independent agents, sets persons in opposition one to another. This opposition appears within the capitalist class between factions of capitalists, among the workers, and between the capitalists and the workers. Furthermore, in the Marxian view, civil society in a sense educates participants to a narrow view of themselves and of their relations to one another. This education is an instance of the way in which their social condition forms the consciousness of persons rather than vice versa as in the utilitarian theories. But this education to the narrow standpoint of private self-interest stands in the way of action directed at maintaining the system within which the narrow view thrives. It endangers the pursuit of private interest precisely by obscuring the restraints on private interest needed to assure that the overall structure of self-seeking will sustain itself over time.

In order to protect the real interests of the capitalist class in preservation of the social institutions that allow it to pursue its work of amassing private accumulations of wealth, the state must (1) identify itself not with the private interests of individual capitalists but with interests it imputes to them according to the imperatives of the preservation of their class position as a whole (see Poulantzas, 1973:54, 190–3) and (2) educate both capitalists and workers to the virtues of protecting that imputed class interest. Thus, while the state is not autonomous of class interests – it is still the creature of private interest – it must be autonomous of the interests of individuals and must not succumb to their narrow views. In this sense, the state, if it is to succeed, must have the appropriate "relative autonomy."

Thus, in the Marxian theory the concept of relative autonomy of the state constitutes a repudiation of the idea that the state acts as the agent of particular persons (namely capitalists) and their given interests or preferences. It gives the interest of the state a decidedly ideological stamp since this interest is deduced from an understanding of the structure of society and from the implied requirements of social cohesion around the objective of the ongoing and long-term accumulation of wealth in the form of private accumulations of capital (see Lukacs, 1971:51). We can see here, as we will with Krasner, how the leap to state autonomy carries with it a movement from a material and individualistic conception of interest to an ideological concept of interest. This movement accounts both for the importance of state autonomy and for the difficulties which that concept creates.

If we adopt the view that the interest of the capitalist class is an interest imputed to it from its objective situation and not the interest capitalists actually pursue individually or collectively, this raises problems concerning the relation of the state to private interest. Both for Gramsci and for Poulantzas, the interest pursued by the state is an interest in the maintenance of a particular social order. The state does not maintain that order because it makes individual capitalists wealthy but because, for the state, the preservation of a favorable political and social order is its distinctive business. The state concerns itself with the assurance that the social order is, after all, a particular kind of society with space for pursuit of particular kinds of private interest.

What important themes arise within the utilitarian and Marxian analyses of the state and its relation to society? One theme concerns the problem of social order. Societies (at least national societies) are composed of millions of individuals occupying countless roles, yet relating to one another in complex, coordinated (not to say harmonious) ways. If individual interests and goals are subjective and undetermined (as in utilitarian theory) or defined by forces which are conflictual (as in Marxian theory), how is social order possible? For utilitarian theory we can ask: Can society emerge as a result of the separate pursuit of socially undetermined goals? For Marxian theory we ask: Is a social order possible given the division of society into conflictual classes? The narrow treatment of interest as material (Marxian) or subjective (utilitarian) interest places limits on the development of a full theory of the state.

Both utilitarian and Marxian theories take note of this problem, if in different ways. Utilitarian theories recognize the necessity for consensus on the basic "rules of the game" or principles of social order as an underlying condition for allowing a clash of interests within society. Since the state must take responsibility not only for assuring that these norms prevail but also for education in the norms, utilitarianism cannot rest with its own instrumental theory of the state since the purely instrumental state could never survive. Utilitarianism allows through the back door what it refuses to acknowledge as a legitimate analytical starting point. Marxian theory recognizes the same difficulty when it notes the inconsistency between the narrow material interests of the capitalists and the work that must be done by the state to maintain social order. In both cases, the concept of interest cannot support a theory of the state adequate to account for and maintain a society within which those narrow interests prevail.

Statism

Statist approaches to political economy reverse the causal flow associated with society-centered theories. In the latter, the causal flow runs from private preference (or material circumstance in Marxian theory) through organized political demands (such as interest groups, parties) to the state. The state is asked to respond in some way, to translate the aggregate of private preferences into coherent policy. Statist approaches go about the matter in a different way. These approaches are likely to begin with a state agenda not reducible to private interest and may go so far as to examine how state actors cultivate the very constituencies they are to serve. In this section, we briefly explore the contribution of Stephen Krasner to statist theory. We recognize that state-centered approaches include many other authors and issues. We focus on Krasner for illustrative purposes.

Stephen Krasner presents a distinctive and provocative view of the state and its relationship to the private sphere. He explicitly conceives of the state as "a set of roles and institutions having peculiar drives, compulsions, and aims of their own that are separate from the interests of any particular societal group" (1978:10). By beginning with roles and institutions rather than persons, Krasner sets the stage for identifying the state with goals and ends of a genuinely public rather than private character. And he proceeds to argue along these lines. Not only is it "a fundamental error to identify the goals of the state with some summation of the desires of specific individuals or groups," but, on the contrary, state objectives "refer to the utility of the community and will be called the nation's general or national interest" (pp. 11–12).

Krasner goes to some length to argue that the utility of the community must not be confused with a sum or other aggregate of private utilities of its members. Indeed, the utility of the community depends on values "assigned by the state" (p. 12). This last argument requires a sharper and more restrictive notion of the state than that of the sum total of public offices or of officeholders. For the purposes of foreign policy analysis, Krasner does indeed work with such restriction. While the restriction introduced (to the executive and state department) is justified more on empirical than analytical grounds, it is clearly necessitated by Krasner's (largely implicit) theory of the state. That Nordlinger criticizes Krasner for introducing this restriction (1981: 124–5) simply reveals the fundamental difference in conception between the two.

In a sense, Krasner defines the state in terms of the national interest. The state is the institutions (or set of institutions) responsible for assigning those values used to determine the utility of the community. This means that Krasner begins neither with empirical-historical institutions (the state consists of whatever organizations make up the "public sector" in a given society) nor with preferences of persons. He begins with the idea of the national interest. The state defines the national interest, but the capacity to define (and defend) the national interest defines the state. If there is no national interest there is no state.

The circularity of this approach will no doubt cause discomfort. We need to know the national interest in order to identify the state; thus a concept of national interest must be developed (at least in principle) independently of (prior to?) the deliberations of given state institutions. Yet, the state defines the national interest. Does this mean that the national interest is whatever the state defines it to be?

Krasner's empirical method and discussion seem to follow the latter movement. In so doing, Krasner retreats from his initial statement. He seems driven by the dilemma identified above to an inductive view of the national interest which brings in the preferences of policymakers: "Here the national interest is defined inductively as the preferences of American central decision makers." The aims of these decision makers "range from satisfying psychological needs to increasing wealth, weakening opponents, capturing territory, and establishing justice" (1978:13–14), clearly a varied assortment. Not too much further along, this list narrows to one more in line with the limitations of a national interest perspective when the goals of the state are associated with "power and the general interests of society" (p. 33). And, by the end of the book, Krasner moves the national interest a significant distance from the world of private preferences (of citizens or policymakers) searching instead into "the realm of ideology, of vision for a persuasive explanation of American foreign policy" (p. 338).

Two observations seem relevant here. First, this is a distinct method for thinking about the state. It requires a clear notion of national interest and a concept of the state that is not simply organizational-empirical. Second, in order to resolve the tension built into this method, Krasner retreats into a more purely utilitarian-empirical view by starting out from a (seemingly) arbitrary organizational definition of the state and then using that (those) organization(s) to define the national interest.

To what extent does Krasner's approach help us to clarify the relationship between polity and economy? However uncertain the rooting of the concept of national interest, it clearly suggests a ground for the distinction between the state and the economy. By definition the state pursues the national interest as its end, and only the state does so. The state defines and defends the national interest. The private sphere does not.

It is striking to discover that Krasner's statist approach does not allow the state-society opposition to parallel the public-private opposition. Of course, it should have been obvious from the outset that once we restrict the state to the executive and state department, much of government becomes part of society. This would be less true if we widened the notion of national interest to include aspects of domestic policy. But, even if we do so, the problem remains: A significant part of government and of our "public" will be outside the state.

This might seem to establish state autonomy, but whether or not it does depends on the relation between national interest and private interest. This is a bit tricky. When the national interest conflicts with private interests we have a strong case. But cases of this type force us to identify the national interest with those things private persons might not have any interest in and this is surely problematic. Surely (especially in a democratic society) we expect private citizens to perceive and value the national interest (when we think there is such a thing). What would we make of a theory that has the national interest disappear when citizens make it their own? The items Krasner includes in the national interest are clearly of this type: to "maximize the competitive structure of industry and thereby reduce prices," to "increase security of supply," and to "secure foreign policy objectives" (p. 331).

Where does this leave us? Perhaps Krasner (together with Poulantzas and Gramsci) takes us as far as we can reasonably travel within the theoretical and methodological frameworks of private interest-based approaches to the determination of state action. He does so by explicitly tying state action to ideology, and although he also makes the effort to connect ideology to private interests (indeed, preferences), the connection cannot be considered very strong. Theories of state autonomy teach us much about the limits of the underlying methods for thinking about the relation of state to society, and something also about the changes that must be made in the conception of private interest to sustain the possibility of an active state. To understand the state as an actor, however, we must give up significant elements of the underlying method used by the approaches considered so far.

A transformational view of the state

Up to this point, the term "state autonomy" has been identified with two things: first with a distinctive state agenda, one not simply derived from private interests of particular persons in society, and, second, with the capacity of the state to pursue and execute its will. In other words, state autonomy entails the idea of competence in forming objectives and bringing about desired effects.

According to this formulation, sources of causality are partitioned into two categories, those sources internal to the state and those external to it. State autonomy exists when the causal sources of its behavior are not external. While this view of autonomy is prevalent in the literature, we argue that it raises difficulties.

In defining state autonomy in terms of causal superiority of state over economy, the autonomous state is placed in an uncomfortable position in several ways. First, it is difficult to avoid the conclusion that the autonomous state violates certain principles of democracy. One core democratic principle involves a relation of responsiveness between ruler and ruled. To the extent that this responsiveness is damaged by autonomous state action, democracy is compromised. There are ways to circumvent this conclusion, for example, by arguing that the state is the only agent capable of identifying the interests of society as a whole. But, by and large, the less responsive the state is to private interests, the more suspect it is on grounds of democratic theory.

Second, the issue of state autonomy raises troubling questions of a general theoretical and methodological nature. What does it mean for the state to be autonomous in the limit? If the state forms its preferences and executes them apart from society, is it not autistic? How can the state behave purposively unless it gauges its own actions on the basis of societal conditions and modifies that behavior on the basis of feedback? A state that takes little account of society would have to present its own actions as pure willfulness, as preferences arbitrarily formed and not socially grounded.

These two difficulties suggest that more serious problems may exist in the conception of state autonomy and especially in the way it requires us to think about the relation between state and economy. In this section we explore an alternative conception of the state we refer to as transformational. While the idea of "state as transformer" is not often explicit, it finds implicit, partial expression in the work of Theda Skocpol, Peter Katzenstein, and Peter Gourevitch. Skocpol develops an historical-organizational understanding of the state, identifying it with "a set of administrative, policing and military organizations headed, and more or less well-coordinated by, an executive authority" (1979:29). These organizations are formed out of social and political forces coming together under particular historical conditions. Since the state is a historically specific structure, it must affect policy in the following sense: Differences in organizational structure of states must affect policy outcomes even when initiatives come from the private sphere. At a minimum, the state refracts those initiatives as its organizational structure transforms them into policy. At a maximum, the state creatively transforms even the subtlest of private forces. Apart from these extremes, the state organization affects the agendas (conceptions) of groups and "state structures help to inspire the very demands that are pursued through politics" (Weir and Skocpol, 1985:118).

The preceding argument that state structures make a difference provides a different foundation for the conclusion that the state is autonomous. The state is not apart from the private sphere, nor does it necessarily exert leverage against it. But neither does the economy exist as a fully formed entity, as a fundamental given existing prior to the state. The state enters into the constitution of society just as society contributes to the constitution of the state. Also, since policy outcomes depend in important ways on the nature of state organization, this requires that we treat the state as "a structure with a logic and interests of its own, not necessarily equivalent to, or fused with, the interests of the dominant class in society or the full set of member groups in the polity" (Skocpol, 1979:27). In a sense, Skocpol deduces state autonomy from the identification of the state with historically specific organizational structures. To clarify this, we can draw an analogy with the relation between the particularity of persons and their biographies. One of the primary determinants of who a person is, is the set of relations and experiences that make up that person's biography. The personality structure that emerges out of that biography determines the person's capacity for accomplishing (and defining) certain goals, developing in particular directions, and so on. This structure is a force that refracts influences upon it. Similarly, a state is always a historically specific structure resulting from the relations and events that form it. Each state has its own biography that defines its capacities, interests, and goals. These, together with the forces acting upon it, shape its further development.

If this analogy has relevance, then we would need to adapt our sense of state autonomy to it. Persons are autonomous when they make the outcome of such external influences acting upon them unique to them (their own result). So too with state autonomy. In Skocpol's sense, state autonomy cannot mean the inability of society to influence policy (and significantly so). It must mean (at least in part) that each state processes those influences in unique ways as it also contributes (just as persons do) to what sort of influences it experiences. Clearly Skocpol's approach does not allow us to reduce state actions to personal preferences (either of officeholders or others). She explicitly rejects the idea of the state as an "arena" for social conflict (1979:25). If the state has any organizational structure other than that adequately and correctly designed to aggregate-transmit preferences of interests (see public choice theory), then state structure affects policy. The state is not autonomous since it is influenced and formed by social forces; neither is it simply an arena or mechanism for the operation of those social forces since it has its own determinate structure, its own capacities that act upon and contribute to the making of the societal forces acting upon it.

In addition to Skocpol's work, that of Peter Katzenstein and Peter Gourevitch has relevance for this idea. Although Katzenstein does not typically use the vocabulary of state autonomy, his idea of policy networks fits with the general thrust of this alternative idea of autonomy. By a policy network, Katzenstein refers to groups and institutions in state and society that come together to engage in policy making (1978:19). The central question posed by Katzenstein in *Between Power and Plenty* is "Why does a common challenge such as the oil crisis elicit different national responses in the international political economy?" (1978:3). The answer in very general terms is that domestic structure is the critical intervening variable between international economic stimuli and domestic strategies and policies.

The significance of Katzenstein's placing of domestic structure between environmental input and policy result is clear. Domestic structure makes a difference and it does so not because policy networks triumph over society – indeed, parts of society are definitionally present in the concept of policy network – but because these networks energize and give creative direction to the demands and disturbances emanating from society (even if transnational society). Perhaps a part of the different policy outcomes across the countries examined can be attributed to differences in the substance of demands themselves – for example, West Germany's "preference" for policies bringing low inflation rates versus Sweden's "preference" for full employment. But even with these factors taken into account, there is a hard-core residue attributable to political structure variables.

Peter Gourevitch (1986) continues this line of thought. Gourevitch is explicit from the start that the autonomous state is not one that stands apart from or in opposition to society. First of all, the state participates in creating its own social base, indeed, "its interventions frequently require the complicity of forces it seeks to regulate or direct" (1986:230). Second, the idea of state autonomy is connected more to the highly active state, one that takes initiatives and defines creative possibilities in times of crises. Crises refer to moments when important alternatives exist (or are made) and where decisive action can, quite literally, "change history." By contrast, state autonomy is not linked to insulation from society or to causal power over society. Indeed, if this approach has merit, it may be better to leave aside the language of state autonomy altogether because it sets up a relation of state to society different in spirit from that suggested here.

Does the notion of national interest play a part in this organizational-structural approach? Only with difficulty. As Rueschemeyer and Evans point out, when we tie state action to the national interest this "contradicts the state's role as an autonomous corporate actor, since it presumes that the goals of state activities are not generated inside the state apparatus but are dictated by the general interests of civil society" (1985:47). If, of course, the state defines the national interest (as Krasner claims) this need not be the case. But, if to be effective, the state must define a national interest appropriate to the type of society it represents and defends then, a narrow notion of autonomy cannot be sustained.

What are the implications of the historical-structural approach for the conceptual distinction between state and economy, public and private? Here we enter somewhat speculative territory. The basic conceptual framework for thinking about the state derives from Max Weber. It emphasizes organizational structure joined to the instruments, power, and agents of legitimate force. Under this view, organizations whose decisions carry the authority of law and the backing of legitimate force together with their coercive agencies constitute the state. The private sphere consists of agents and organizations whose decisions bear no such authority. In a strict juridical sense, "society" consists of voluntary associations. Although power can also play a role in the formation of such associations (or relations), legitimate force cannot; and illegitimate force cannot rule for long without endangering both state and society. The practical difference between state and economy has, then, to do with the kind of force that stands behind and realizes decisions made in each.

The key to this whole construction is the idea of legitimacy. Can force be legitimate simply because it belongs to the state? Or is there a sense of what is legitimate that the state must embody and to which the state must adhere? The second alternative threatens the autonomy of the state since it subjects states to externally given canons of legitimate behavior. In this case, the concept of legitimacy disrupts the structural approach while in some sense being necessary to its concepts of the state. Although legitimacy has an historical aspect (carrying different connotations in different societies), it is not primarily historical. The term requires us to relate state action to an ideal. This ideal is the mainspring of legitimacy. It is neither (1) in society (in the sense of being a private interest) nor (2) reducible to historically evolved state structure. In other words, the concept of legitimacy marks out a dimension of the problem not clearly amenable to resolution within the historical-organizational methodology.

The idea of legitimacy connects the state to a sense of public purpose or interest and requires us to consider more closely the relation between the state and the economy in connection with the relation between public and private, a connection not explicit in the historical-structural approach. Within that approach, the state takes on a quasi-private character. Thus Skopcol observes: "Any state first and fundamentally extracts resources from society and deploys these to create and support coercive and administrative organizations" (1979:29). This tends to make the state an actor within society (the system of competition for resources). Such a tendency develops more or less inevitably out of the identification of the state with specific historical-empirical institutions.

While states are historically formed organizations that (among other things) facilitate the pursuit of private interest, these qualities do not suffice to ground an adequate theory of the state. By themselves, they leave us without its vital *differentia specifica*. Treating the state as just another organization concerned with the struggle for resources blurs important distinctions between the state and civil society. We do not deny that the state participates in the struggle for resources, or that it is like interest groups in some respects. We do argue, however, that the state has a capacity for more than self-interested behavior with its role in preserving the structure and norms underlying both society and the state itself. To bring the state back in, we need to take seriously the work of the state in setting the ideal (or ideological) underpinnings of social order. We can see an awareness of this necessity in the various theories considered in this book: in the pluralist notion of "training in the norms," in Arrow's notion of "consensus," in Lukacs's notion of "class consciousness," in Gramsci's notion of "hegemony," in Parsons's emphasis on socialization and common values, and in Krasner's notion of "national interest."

The idea links with observations made by leading pluralist and utilitarian thinkers concerning the limits of application of their methodology. Kenneth Arrow insists that there must be "some sort of consensus on the ends of society, or no social welfare function can be formed" (1951:83). Robert Dahl claims that the "extent to which training is given in [the] norms [of democratic process] is not independent of the extent of agreement that exists on choices among policy alternatives" and that "polyarchy is a function of consensus" on the norms (1956:76–7). The needs of consensus limit the range of private interest. In utilitarian language they concern notions related to those expressed in the Marxian theory under the heading of hegemony and relative autonomy.

All of these terms allude to work the state does that we cannot subsume under the heading of satisfying private needs (see Elkin, 1985). In a sense this constitutes a kind of theoretical work undertaken by the state.

9

Justice-centered theories

One definition of economics ties it to the market. In so doing, it makes the notions of property rights definitive of economic action. This notion demarcates the economy, distinguishing it from the other spheres of social life, including the political. If we attempt to address the problems of political economy on this basis, we do so by exploring the nature, specification, and limits of property rights.

The concept of justice refers to social ordering principles we can use to define rights (including property rights) and the market system. These principles follow from an idea of personhood, especially of the integrity of persons. Justice-centered theories of political economy judge market institutions against the demands of personhood. But, these demands vary for differing conceptions. In particular, the demands of personhood vary with the concreteness and richness of the idea of the person advanced in the different justice-centered theories. Some theories define personhood at the most abstract level, virtually identifying it with the purely formal condition of legal personality. The person is the legally recognized locus of property ownership and capacity to contract. Other theories define personhood in more concrete terms, identifying the capacities that underlie legal personality with varying degrees of richness. In this chapter, we consider a set of justice-centered approaches. We begin with those insisting on the most formal, and least concretized, notion, and proceed to theories incorporating a more determinate idea of personal integrity. We will attempt to indicate how the concreteness of the notion of personhood carries implications for the meaning, scope, and limits of the market.

Justice-centered approaches to determining the proper relation of public decisions to private affairs employ criteria viewed as antecedent to the welfare of individuals, the interests of classes, the needs of the state, and the relative power of persons. These criteria stem from conceptions of justice and of the just (or well-ordered) society. In the most general terms, justice-centered theories are distinguished by two related assumptions about the kinds of institutional arrangements appropriate to a well-ordered society. Such institutions must respect the equal liberty of citizens and the inviolability of persons.

Each person possesses an inviolability founded on justice that even the welfare of society as a whole cannot override.... [I]n a just society the liberties of equal citizenship are taken as settled; the rights secured by justice are not subject to political bargaining or to the calculus of social interest. (Rawls, 1971:3–4)

In justice-centered theories, the basic principles for judging institutions precede political deliberation and economic calculation.

The ideas of inviolability of persons and equal liberty focus our attention on individual rights. In a positive sense, rights define the circumstances under which individuals can act on their own initiative, molding themselves and their environments in accordance with their wants and aspirations. In a negative sense, rights limit the ways in which others can intrude on us. They thus protect the integrity of persons. Rights also limit the ways in which the state relates to citizens (see Dworkin, 1977). Because of this, a justice-centered theory can use the specification of rights (especially property rights) to determine the boundaries between market and state.

In Chapter 4, on neoclassical theories of political economy, we encountered a treatment of property right that made it depend on a welfare calculation. While a utilitarian approach may incorporate rights in this way, because it subordinates rights to the calculation of welfare, it is not a justice-centered approach in the sense used here. As one utilitarian puts it:

The concept of justice as a *fundamental* ethical concept is really quite foreign to utilitarianism. A utilitarian would compromise his utilitarianism if he allowed principles of justice which might conflict with the maximization of happiness.... As a utilitarian, therefore, I do not allow the concept of justice as a fundamental moral concept, but I am nevertheless interested in justice in a subordinate way, as a *means* to the utilitarian end. (Smart, 1978:104, italics in the original)

Indeed, respect for rights may lead us away from welfare maximization. The two criteria not only differ, but can be in conflict. Rights-based considerations "can be inconsistent even with Pareto optimality – perhaps the mildest utility-based condition and the most widely used welfare criterion in economics" (Sen and Williams, 1982:7).

From a utilitarian perspective, justice-centered approaches make the welfare of the individual and of the community vulnerable. Equally, however, because welfare-oriented arguments make rights contingent on the service they do in enhancing our material well-being, they make our rights vulnerable. A demonstration that the limitation or violation of rights enhances group welfare can justify abrogating those rights. If, in fact, a centrally planned economy without markets and private property can be shown to grow more rapidly and provide more (even substantially more) wealth to individuals, then arguments centering on material welfare become arguments against (a broad interpretation of) property rights.

For some theorists, this is a disturbing outcome. These theorists consider rights irreducible. While our material welfare may improve when our rights are limited, this does not imply an improvement in our well-being if that depends on the security of our persons, our freedom to define and pursue our own goals (including our self-interest), and the general requisites of individual integrity and self-determination. We create confusion when we try to separate the idea of individual right from the ideas of individual initiative, self-determination, and integrity. Retaining the connection between these ideas can lead to an interpretation of welfare that dominates interpretations centering on material provisioning, utility maximization, or choice.

In this chapter we explore three justice-centered approaches: the libertarian, contractarian, and Hegelian. The first builds an argument against state intervention into economic life on the basis of a strong identification between justice and property rights. Because a market economy consists of a system of property relations, the broader and more uncompromising the conception of private property right, the less room for state involvement. The second approach builds an argument capable of supporting government involvement by locating justice not primarily in defense of property, but in the terms of collective judgment regarding a just social order. Property right plays a role but only as one part of the construction of just institutions. The third approach emphasizes the social determination of persons. It connects rights and justice to the mutual dependence of persons, especially in the recognition of their personhood. Hegelian approaches judge economic intervention according to principles of equal opportunity and equal regard.

A libertarian argument

Assume that we can agree on a reasonably clear and morally compelling definition of property right, one with sufficient breadth to cover the primary ways in which persons need to have disposal over things. Doing so may be no easy matter.[1] But, if we succeed, important consequences follow. We can now refer questions concerning the use of wealth to its owner, whose property right means the right to determine its disposition. The only problems society must address with regard to wealth are the interpretation and application of established rights. These problems center on the following question: Were the arrangements by which property came into the hands of those who possess

[1] Defining rights is not necessarily a simple matter (see Dworkin, 1977; Gewirth, 1982; and Finnis, 1980).

it consistent with respect for property rights? Voluntary transactions (exchange, gift) respect property right; coerced transactions (theft, fraud, enslavement, and so forth) do not. This approach makes questions concerning distribution, insofar as they arise at all, juridical rather than political. Answering these questions need make no reference to political economy.

Assume, for example, that we can find a way to define all property as unambiguously the property of particular individuals:[2] All things are owned by particular persons; no social or communal property exists other than the joint or shared property created by voluntary decisions of otherwise independent persons.[3] In the words of Robert Nozick: "Things come into the world already attached to people having entitlements over them" (1974:160). Assume, further, that any subsequent change of ownership results from voluntary agreement between the original owners. Assume finally that property right bestows widespread power of disposal over things (limited only by respect for rights of others). Then, it follows that the problems of the ownership and use of wealth are resolved by individuals (concerned, for example, with their self-interest).

Nozick divides this idea into two parts: justice in acquisition and justice in transfer (1974:151). Justice in transfer means acquisition from a previous owner by voluntary agreement (gift or exchange). Justice in (original) acquisition refers either to an original appropriation that does not impair the situation of others or to production:

A process normally giving rise to a permanent bequeathed property right in a previously unowned thing will not do so if the position of others no longer at liberty to use the thing is thereby worsened. (p. 178)

And:

Whoever makes something, having bought or contracted for all other held resources used in the process (transferring some of his holdings for these competing factors), is entitled to it. (p. 160)

This view provides one of the strongest arguments for a state that restricts itself to the defense of property (and by extension defense of the nation) and to the administration of justice (as defined on the basis of individual rights). The presence or absence of laws of political economy makes no difference to the state. Markets will likely play the primary role in facilitating the production and circulation of wealth. But the ability of markets to secure efficient allocation and full utilization of capital (and labor) does not concern the state.

[2] This may not be easily done (see Ackerman, 1977:27).
[3] This evades some important issues concerning the natural environment (see Mack, 1983 and references therein).

The state does not concern itself with securing the "proper" functioning of markets for the following reason. It can do so only by violating property rights and bringing about a redistribution of property by illegitimate means. First, the state makes a judgment that the private decisions of individuals concerning disposal of their property must be corrected because they lead to a lower overall level of well-being. In order to correct these decisions the state takes on the responsibility of redetermining the use of existing property through taxation and spending, for example. In so doing, it places a judgment of material welfare above individual property rights.[4] Nozick goes so far as to equate taxation (necessary to government fiscal policy) with forced labor (p. 169).

Adam Smith argues against any extensive state involvement in economic affairs on the grounds that the state can only bring about an outcome less desirable than that resulting from unregulated self-seeking. Smith's argument can be evaluated by judging the logic of his assumptions (for example, full utilization of capital) and his deductions (for example, that private entrepreneurs direct capital into the most profitable and the most desirable lines of industry). The libertarian argument depends on no such reasoning about economic relations. Economic outcomes brought about by the state are by definition less desirable.

While the state has no purpose with regard to economic regulation, this does not make it inactive. On the contrary, a libertarian state may be very active in ways that affect our economic lives profoundly. The state's concern with the security of the property system requires it to assure that property is, in fact, in the hands of those who have acquired it by legitimate means. Otherwise, the state must rectify past and current violations of property right (Nozick, 1974:152). The principle of rectification allows for a kind of redistribution of property. Such a redistribution is not, however, in accordance with any principles of just distribution other than those outlined above. Thus, the state in rectifying past abuse of rights does not impose a political judgment concerning the distribution and use of wealth. The state seeks to achieve an outcome defined for it by the principle of private property. Nozick criticizes arguments in favor of redistribution aimed at achieving justice defined in any way other than repeated application of the principles of justice in acquisition, justice in transfer, and the rectification of past injustice.

What should we make of this method for resolving the problems of political economy? For one thing, we might organize our society along libertarian lines and it might not "work." That is to say, however just in principle the

---

[4] Under certain circumstances, the state can correct market failure without redistributing income. The state can raise the overall level of spending without increasing taxes and thus stimulate the production of output that would not otherwise exist.

institutional arrangements, those living within such institutions may find
them less than satisfactory. John Rawls, whose theory we discuss in the next
section, introduces this constraint on a well-ordered society in the following
terms:

A just society must generate its own support. This means that it must be arranged
so as to bring about in its members the corresponding sense of justice, an effective
desire to act in accordance with its rules for reasons of justice. Thus the requirement
of stability and the criterion of discouraging desires that conflict with the principles
of justice put further constraints on institutions. They must be not only just but
framed so as to encourage the virtue of justice in those who take part in them.
(1971:261)

Clearly, if we believe in the intrinsic justness of a libertarian order such
as outlined here, we ought to be able to communicate our conviction to others
and thus help them to embrace the principles of justice centered on rights.
But more is at stake than this. We must also establish the viability of a society
so ordered, its capacity to maintain the virtue of its principles in the eyes of
its citizens.

This might be a problem if, for example, a society ordered along libertarian
lines led to so many and frequent violations of the demands of economic
interdependence (as captured in the classical notion of a social division of
labor) that justice could survive only where such interdependence is minimal.
The less our dependence on the market for our basic needs, the less does a
failure of the market undermine our commitment to it. The prospect of
market failure may force us to choose between a just society and a society
of significant economic interdependence. Whether we must make such a
choice depends in part on the validity of the claims for the self-regulating
market made especially by the classical economists (and, as we have seen,
criticized by Marx and Keynes among others).

Mutual dependence poses serious problems for the libertarian argument.
The idea of property right implies a limitation in the like rights of others.
My right to use my walking stick according to my own determination en-
counters a limit in your person whose integrity would be violated by a too
close encounter with my stick. So much is clear. But what is implied about
rights when my decision to smoke my cigarettes pollutes your lungs or my
decision to pour waste into a river on my property pollutes water on yours?
Does my right to use my audio equipment as I see fit include a right to
impose the resulting sound (whether music, noise or both) on you? What
implications might these externalities (to use the neoclassical term) implied
in interdependence have for the libertarian argument? What might be further
implications of the dependence of persons on the market for their livelihood?

If what we do does not infringe on others except when they choose to allow
it to, the scope for applying libertarian reasoning can be broad enough to

make it relevant in thinking about the appropriate relation of state to economy. Otherwise, the presence of involuntary interdependence undermines the relevance of the libertarian approach. This tells us something important about the libertarian vision of the world. At a fundamental level, that vision incorporates a way of thinking about the separateness of and connection between persons. The libertarian understands the separateness of persons to mean a capacity to sustain and be themselves without the larger context provided by social institutions and the system of persons. Nothing about being a person necessarily or immediately entails any connections with others. This, then, means that the impinging of the actions and projects of one person on another is not implied in being a person. Put another way, no special effort, interconnection, or institutional context is demanded of us if we are to be and act as persons.

We can make the same point with reference to the notions of personhood and integrity introduced at the beginning of the chapter. For the libertarian, integrity is not socially determined and socially sustained. Thus, our capacity to hold property and enter into contracts with others does not come to us from our social existence; we bring it into that existence as a prior endowment. Nor, then, is society responsible for that capacity, although it may be responsible for preventing others from doing some of the things that could erode our capacities.

This makes persons separate in a very strong sense. It defines autonomy in a way that links it to the absence of interdependence. Given this sense of the separateness of persons, we do not need others in the strong sense of the term, nor do our lives inherently involve or impinge on others.

If this is in fact the state of affairs, then we should find externalities the exception rather than the rule. Further, it should be possible to escape from whatever external effects we experience. If someone's use of cigarettes or automobiles pollutes our air, we can remove ourselves from the kind of proximity to such persons that affects us in this way. Escape (exit) is not possible when our survival depends on others or when participation in a system of interdependence is necessary for us to be fully human. When escape is not possible, the libertarian vision is a poor guide for thinking about the relation of state to economy.

A libertarian might choose to give up mutual dependence rather than freedom. In so doing, the libertarian (naturally enough) places the integrity of the individual (which he equates with individual rights) above that of the society of individuals. The latter exists only to protect and advance the former. The former exists on its own, but in a vulnerable state.

The difficulty that we sometimes have with libertarianism is that it seems to demand that we give up much that we hold valuable and depend on: our sense of being in society and of the obligations that our dependence on society creates. What we get in return is independence and a kind of liberty that, however appealing in certain respects, seems lacking in richness of content and perhaps more than a little asocial.[5] While the libertarian does not directly demand such a sacrifice in exchange for liberty, he does insist that we reconstitute our social dependence as the result of arrangements entered into voluntarily. A well-ordered or just society is one organized in this way. It is as rich or empty as we individually or jointly choose to make it.

If we wish to deploy the notion of justice in support of arguments that allow a greater role for interdependence, we must think about the constitution of social institutions in a way distinct from that favored by libertarians. How can we conceive a just society that both respects the inviolability of the person and assures that the needs of persons arising within society will be met? The contractarian theory outlined in the following section takes us a step in this direction.

A modern contractarian argument

John Rawls has proposed a justice-centered approach different in important ways from libertarianism. His approach differs first in the way he goes about determining the basic principles of justice, and second in the resulting principles themselves. His theory is broad-ranging and not specifically focused on issues relevant to political economy (although these are given serious attention). The theory has been subject to extensive comment and criticism.[6] The following brief summary should convey a sense of the distinctive solution proposed to the problem of defining the relation between economics and politics.

When economic justice means nothing more than respect for (private) property, free market outcomes and only free market outcomes are just (by definition). For a justice-centered theory to allow for other outcomes, it must judge the distribution of income and wealth on criteria that, although they may include property right, are not limited to it. The alternative to justice as respect for individual rights proposed by Rawls is justice as fairness. Rawls summarizes the basic principle of justice as follows:

All social values – liberty and opportunity, income and wealth, and the bases of self-respect – are to be distributed equally unless an unequal distribution of any, or all, of these values is to everyone's advantage. (1971:62)

In the following, we focus our attention on the implications of this way of thinking for the distribution of income and wealth.

---

[5] For critical assessment of Nozick's argument dealing with these and other concerns, see Cohen (1978) and the articles collected in Paul (1981).
[6] See Sandel (1982) and the articles collected in Daniels (1975).

According to Rawls's principle of justice, it would be unfair to have an unequal distribution that did not benefit both those with more and those with less. This means that inequality must benefit the worst off. Rawls refers to this requirement as the "difference principle." Because he assumes that goods satisfy wants and more goods satisfy more wants, he assumes (roughly speaking) that having more income and wealth makes us better off than having less. The principle of justice then raises two important questions relevant to political economy: (1) How can having less make those with less better off? (2) Why would inequality that does not benefit the worst off be intrinsically unfair and therefore unjust? We begin with this second question.

Our answer centers on our judgment concerning a principle we found articulated by Nozick: that all goods "come into the world already attached to people having entitlements over them." This principle suggests that any inequalities arising in a just society actually originate outside what we can properly think of as society. If we think of society narrowly as the system of voluntary transactions by which we transfer property to and share it with others, then all that society does is recirculate the property persons bring into it. If persons have different amounts of property, it is because of their actions (for example, production) outside of society. To put this notion in the strongest terms: Society has nothing to do with the distribution of wealth. Rawls speaks as though this is not the case. The goods we make our property result from our agreement to work together in society (see, for example, Rawls, 1971:112). In some meaningful sense we owe this benefit to society. Indeed, we enter into an agreement to constitute our society precisely in order to gain such benefits. The agreement, or contract, to enter into or jointly create a society precedes (logically at least) any production and appropriation of goods. Society creates the income and wealth used by persons to satisfy their wants. Because of this priority of the contract and of the society it creates, we cannot treat wealth as something whose distribution among persons is already given. The contractualist approach makes distribution a problem that society must try to solve.

As we have seen, principles of justice are principles of the inviolability of persons and of equal citizenship. This would seem to imply equality of distribution of income and wealth. If, for example, we all participate equally in the production of wealth, we should share equally in its consumption. Or, if we participate unequally, our shares might be in proportion to our participation. Rawls does not directly appeal to either of these two principles. Instead, he argues that inequalities are just if they benefit the worst off. Under circumstances where this is the case, he argues, equal citizenship and individual integrity are consistent with inequalities of income and wealth.

This result depends on the definition of equal citizenship and on the definition of the inviolability of the person. With regard to the latter, Rawls assumes that our personal integrity is not necessarily upset when we have less wealth than others (as it might be if we had fewer votes for example). Rawls is mistaken, however, if the unequal distribution of wealth implies that those who are poorer are also deemed inferior persons. If we do not accept his premise, we cannot conclude that unequal distributions are consistent with a just society. If we do accept his premise, we can conclude that inequality need not undermine the integrity of persons.

Rawls further seeks to demonstrate the consistency of the difference principle with the principle of equal citizenship by showing how citizens would choose to govern their lives by such a principle if given the opportunity to do so. Rawls requires that we choose under conditions that assure our particular circumstances (what we have to gain or lose) will not affect our choices. In choosing, we must not know how well off we will be as a result of our choice. Rawls argues that, on this assumption, we would choose to protect our prospective positions by assuring that the worst prospective outcome is as good as it can be. Thus the difference principle would be chosen by participants in the contract. Since chosen by participants, it conforms to the principle of equal citizenship.

On this interpretation, justice allows for inequalities that benefit all (especially the worst off). But why should inequalities benefit those who end up with less? Political economy advances an argument to support this conclusion (see Levine, 1985). Roughly speaking, the argument runs as follows.

If the distribution of wealth places it disproportionately into the hands of those committed to investment rather than consumption, or if inequality otherwise stimulates a more productive use of wealth, it will lead to a growth in the overall amount of wealth. If this growth in overall amount enhances the incomes of the least as well as most wealthy, all benefit by it. Clearly, when those receiving high incomes use it primarily or exclusively for private consumption, it is difficult to argue that inequality benefits anyone but them. By contrast, investment of wealth can increase productivity, employment, and incomes. This view treats inequality as an incentive to socially productive works and as a way of financing those works.

In a way the argument makes inequality a mechanism for social savings, especially viewed from the standpoint of lower income groups. Income distribution restricts current consumption in the interests of capital formation and future consumption. Being better off is also a matter of the time frame in which we see our situations. Inequality of this type makes everyone better off eventually, not immediately. Much depends on how far off eventually is and how much better off we will be at that time.

For justice to be served, the inequalities implied in this regime must not only assure a higher overall level of income, they must be necessary to it. Otherwise the inequality does not make the worst off better off. A strong argument for the necessity of inequalities appeals to the idea of private incentives. If capital formation works best, or exclusively, when driven by the motive of private gain, then social organization can best enhance the welfare of all by rewarding the pursuit of private interests. Income inequality harnesses self-interest to the general benefit (the well-being of all). If correct, an argument such as this can marshal support for a regime of private accumulation (though not necessarily pure private enterprise).[7]

If correct, such arguments establish the fairness of inequality. They contribute something important to our thinking about the kind of economic system we might favor in that they tell us which kinds of economies conform to the principles of justice. This indicates an important point of contact between political economy and the theory of justice:

An economic system regulates what things are produced and by what means, who receives them and in return for which contributions, and how large a fraction of social resources is devoted to saving and to the provision of public goods. Ideally all of these matters would be arranged in ways that satisfy the two principles of justice. (Rawls, 1971:266)

Economics, presumably, can assist us in determining which kinds of inequality will likely benefit the worst off. It might also help us to discover whether those inequalities resulting from the unregulated operation of markets accord with the principles of justice and what limits on the market might make it more just.

The debate in economics over the Keynesian arguments against the self-regulating market has a relevance for a contractarian which it does not have for a libertarian. One of the important questions addressed by Keynes was that of the extent of inequality needed to stimulate growth (see Chapter 5, "Keynesian Political Economy"). Keynes's argument that saving can be detrimental to welfare works against a part of the classical argument for inequality. The contractarian approach works well with the Keynesian argument providing an ethical framework capable of enhancing its relevance. Thus, in contrast to the libertarian world, within this contractarian regime, economics becomes relevant and the problems of political economy have potentially complex solutions.

In a broad sense, government plays an active role in relation to the market, adjusting free market outcomes to the demands of justice. In this respect, politics enters into the functioning of the economy. Yet much is removed in principle from the political arena. Basic solutions to economic questions –

---

[7] Certain forms of market socialism and worker-management may well be consistent with the principles of justice and provide incentives for investment.

how much of what goods are produced, how they are produced, and how they are distributed – derive from the logic of economic affairs and the principles of justice. These are not political solutions. We remain within a framework favoring the application and administration of justice over politics. Rawls expresses this exclusion as follows:

> The intuitive idea is to design the social system so that the outcome is just whatever it happens to be. . . . Suppose that law and government act effectively to keep markets competitive, resources fully employed, property and wealth (especially if private ownership of the means of production is allowed) widely distributed by the appropriate forms of taxation, or whatever, and to guarantee a reasonable social minimum. Assume also that there is fair equality of opportunity underwritten by education for all; and that the other equal liberties are secured. Then it would appear that the resulting distribution of income and the pattern of expectations will tend to satisfy the difference principle. In this complex of institutions, which we think of as establishing social justice in the modern state, the advantages of the better situated improve the condition of the least favored. Or when they do not, they can be adjusted to do so, for example, by setting the social minimum at the appropriate level. (pp. 85–7)

Thus there is much for government to do, but little left for politics (at this level).

The contractarian approach stresses political liberty and agreement on the basic structure of society as embodied in laws (Rawls, 1971:221–8). It allows and requires (political) deliberation in setting the legal framework but does not make the specific outcomes of the operation of the resulting institutions political outcomes. To do so would be inconsistent with the idea of justice.

This treatment of politics echoes a main theme of political economy going back to its classical origins. Neither of our justice-centered approaches seeks to bring politics into the economy.[8] Each seeks to define the appropriate institutional framework within which need satisfaction takes place. The just-ness of the institutions assures the justness of the outcomes of economic activities. Justice is served so long as laws consistent with its demands are respected.

The approach summarized here follows the tradition of depoliticization of the economy originating with the classical economists. Use of the terms "justice" and "rights" places us broadly within a tradition emphasizing the separation of politics from civil society (and thus economy). Civil society exists within and is established by a system of justice. It may be just or unjust; it is not political.

In a context of social interdependence, the contractarian argument takes us further than the libertarian. Yet it continues important themes of the libertarian approach. In particular, the contractarian judges economic and

---

[8] If the contractarian approach allows for worker-managed firms, then by one definition of politics it allows for a politicized economy (see Mason, 1982:ch. 1).

political arrangements by their consistency with principles that command (at least notional) agreement. We choose the principles that ground the laws by which we are governed. By interpreting the principles grounding institutions in this way, the contractarian approach incorporates the idea (albeit somewhat attenuated) that persons are antecedent to social institutions and to the system of interdependence taken as a whole. The agent to the contract must have a capacity for judgment and for identifying appropriate criteria for judgment independent of the relations with others that develop within a social order. Since institutions retain an instrumental purpose, implied in the notion of a contract, the method opens the door for those intent on applying economic reasoning to the interpretation of institutions. The justice-centered approaches so far considered go only a limited distance in conceptualizing political economy within a context of social determination of persons.

An alternative justice-centered approach

The notion of a socially determined individual normally points away from rights-based thinking and toward some idea of community, a communitarian ethic of the good life, and communal identity:

On the rights-based ethic, it is precisely because we are essentially separate, independent selves that we need a neutral framework of rights that refuses to choose among competing purposes and ends. If the self is prior to its ends, then the right must be prior to the good.

Communitarian critics of rights-based liberalism say we cannot conceive ourselves as independent in this way, as bearers of selves wholly detached from our aims and attachments. They say that certain of our roles are partly constitutive of the persons we are – as citizens of a country or members of a movement or partisans of a cause. But if we are partly defined by the communities we inhabit, then we must also be implicated in the purposes and ends characteristic of those communities. (Sandel, 1988:115)

In this view, a full account of the social determination of persons takes us away from a justice-centered approach.

A defining characteristic of justice-centered approaches is their refusal to identify a common good or to subordinate citizens' private conceptions of the good life to the collective. As Charles Taylor puts it:

The ethic central to a liberal society is an ethic of the right, rather than the good. That is, its basic principles concern how society should respond to and arbitrate the competing demands of individuals. (1989:164)

Dissatisfaction with such a restrictive notion of the ends of public life inspires a communitarian critique of the justice-centered approaches (Sandel, 1982). Clearly, the ethic of rights, especially in the hands of the theorists so far considered, stands against the effort to find anything more in the mission of public life than the administration of justice, particularly adjudication of conflict in the private sphere.

The communitarian strategy is not, however, the only one available to those dissatisfied with the conception of the public-private relationship typical of justice-centered theories. In this section, we consider an alternative that seeks to incorporate the idea of social determination into a conception centering on notions of right and justice. This alternative has its inspiration in Hegelian social theory.[9] In the *Philosophy of Right* (1821), Hegel attempts to make political economy one element, or moment, of a systematic conception of society. In so doing, he argues for making economy part of an ethical order founded in the rights of persons. The notions of right and contract play a central role. Yet the approach is not contractualist, nor does it judge the ethical standing of social interaction exclusively on grounds of its consistency with a formal notion of private property.

Hegel criticizes Rousseau's contractarian approach for treating the individual as something antecedent to the ethical order as a whole, arguing instead that it is only as a member that "the individual himself has objectivity, genuine individuality, and an ethical life" ([1821] 1952:156). Comments such as this, especially combined with Hegel's emphasis on the corporate identity of persons (pp. 133 and 152–4), encourage a corporatist if not communitarian interpretation. Yet, while incorporating the idea that individuals depend on the whole, Hegel's ethics center on the idea of an order grounded in justice and right. He attempts to make ethical order and individual right two aspects of a single conception.

Hegel makes self-determination his starting point without making the individual autonomous in the libertarian sense or antecedent to the ethical order in the sense of the contractarians. The difference is rooted in Hegel's claim for the constitution of self-determination within the relations of reciprocity. An appropriated, constituted set of political and economic institutions can create and sustain the self-determination of persons. Within this system, persons do not give up their autonomy to the whole or find their individual identity in a communal mode of life. The mutual recognition of personhood within a well-ordered society of persons makes autonomy the result of the individual's social condition. We can only be independent persons in society. A society makes us independent. But this holds true only for the appropriate kind of society, the one Hegel refers to as an ethical order. We depend on society to provide the goods and relationships needed to be self-determining. This dependence places obligations on society. Society must

---

[9] For more contemporary discussion of Hegel's social theory, see Avineri (1972), Pelczynski (1984), and Winfield (1988).

respect and protect our rights (otherwise we lose our independence). Rights are preeminent. But our dependence on society can define more obligations than protection of rights (in the libertarian sense). This complex system of dependence and independence sets a framework that defines the appropriate relation of state to economy.

Consider property and contract within this framework of thinking emphasizing the social recognition of individual self-determination. For Hegel the significance of property lies in its manner of connecting persons or making explicit their implicit social connectedness. Exchange is, for Hegel, no mere instrument for achieving private ends; it is a mode of social constitution of persons. Thus, Hegel argues against an instrumental understanding of contract and makes it, in part, an end in itself. To own property is to express one's status as a property-owning person. To enter a contract is to establish oneself as a bearer of rights and of the capacity for contracting, and thus as a person. We make contracts not simply to acquire the things we need, but to establish and show that we are persons. Thus, Hegel makes the central concepts of the justice-centered approach – right, property, contract – part of the social construction of persons. They make persons as much as they are made by them.

This means that the system of property relations (including the economy) carries for Hegel a different ethical significance than it does for the other justice-based theories. The responsibilities borne by persons, and the responsibility of the public authority for persons, differ for Hegel with the difference in the nature of persons' social dependence. How might questions of political economy, especially economic justice, be posed and answered within this framework? Nozick resolves questions of economic justice by referring to the principles of private property and exchange. Rawls resolves them by referring to equal opportunity and the difference principle. What principle or principles might anchor a justice-centered approach that conceives of individuals as socially determined in the sense emphasized by Hegel?

Hegel does not develop a systematic answer to this question. The principle he favors is implicit in his judgment of the responsibility of the public authority for the poor:

Not only caprice, however, but also contingencies, physical conditions, and factors grounded in external circumstances may reduce men to poverty. The poor still have the needs common to civil society, and yet since society has withdrawn from them the natural means of acquisition and broken the bond of the family . . . their poverty leaves them more or less deprived of all the advantages of society, of the opportunity of acquiring skill or education of any kind, as well as of the administration of justice . . . the public authority takes the place of the family where the poor are concerned. . . . ([1821] 1952:148–9)

Hegel advances the important claim that a market economy makes its members dependent on it for their livelihood without in any way assuring that they will be able to acquire that livelihood according to the rules of the market. Society, then, is responsible for the poor because society deprives them of their livelihood. Yet Hegel makes his point in a peculiar way (Winfield, 1988:185–7). According to Hegel (market) society deprives the poor of their "natural means of acquisition" and their recourse to the family. Society is responsible because of its differences from earlier forms of connectedness and mutual dependence. It is as though we have a natural right to premodern dependence, which the public authority must take on once the older familial bonds are broken. It must "take the place of the family."

However moving this argument, it does not sit well within a rights-based approach. The form of social dependence and connectedness it refers to as justification for intervention, that of the family, is not based on the rights of independent persons. Nature and family are not integrated by concern for justice, and the effort to derive rights from their organization runs into serious problems. The question remains, then, how the failure of market economy supports a claim of rights to public welfare within a Hegelian rather than contractualist framework.

Richard Winfield answers this question in the following way:

What supplies the requisite justification of the public administration of welfare is the fundamental connection between right and duty that Hegel emphasizes throughout his analysis of the different spheres of right. Because economic right, like any other right, consists of an exercise of the freedom to which all agents are entitled, it equally entails the universal duty to respect the same exercise of freedom by others. . . . This respect, which all bearers of right are obligated to pay as well as entitled to receive, consists not just in a theoretical recognition, but in a practical commitment to curtail particular actions of one's own when necessary to permit others to exercise this right. . . . Applied to the economic right to satisfy self-chosen needs through actions of one's own choosing, the connection between right and duty signifies that market agents are duty-bound to restrict their economic activity in conformity to whatever partial regulation is necessary to extend equal opportunity. (1988:187)

Winfield's version of the justice-centered approach proposes recourse to a principle of equal opportunity in laying a foundation for public economic intervention. A principle of equal opportunity is also central to Rawls's contractarian theory, although Rawls arrives at the principle in a somewhat different way. Winfield's argument is of interest because it connects equal opportunity to an argument centering on rights and treats equal opportunity as implicit in the rights of persons. Winfield is able to arrive at his conclusion regarding the limits of the market because, in contrast to Nozick, he treats rights within the framework of the social determination of persons. The meaning of individual rights is the mutual and reciprocal constitution of persons and not their isolation one from another.

An alternative strategy within a Hegelian justice-centered approach follows Ronald Dworkin's (1977) emphasis on the principle of equal regard. The principle of equal regard follows from the premise that our personhood comes into existence in its social recognition. Our claim to be regarded (and thus treated) as persons presumes a society of persons whose regard constitutes our personhood. Unless we recognize the personhood of others, they cannot recognize ours: Thus the central place of reciprocal recognition in the Hegelian theory. The ideas of reciprocity and mutuality become the framework for a justice-centered theory once that theory incorporates the social determination of independence. Equal regard expresses this idea in the form of a principle relevant to defining the limits of market economy (the sphere of property and contract). It leads to and subsumes the principle of equal opportunity. Levine employs this principle as part of an argument for limitations on private ownership of capital:

The demand that people be treated with equal regard limits property rights to capital in much the same way that the right to life limits property rights to objects such as weapons specifically designed to deprive people of their lives. . . .

If we have a right to equal regard, and if the use of capital as private property creates a hierarchy of differential regard, then the use of capital for private ends violates rights. (1988:131–2)

This argument rests on two premises: first, that we can claim a right to equal regard in this strong sense and second, that ownership of capital by private persons as their personal property creates (and is intended to create) hierarchies of wealth and status. If these premises hold, then the justice-centered argument takes on more radical implications than generally allowed in its contractarian forms.

The justice-centered argument can be pushed in this direction only when placed within the framework of the social determination of persons (associated earlier in this discussion with the Hegelian social theory). It assumes that our integrity and capacity for self-determination are part of our social condition rather than qualities we have prior to being in society. The dependence of our integrity on our social condition as emphasized by Hegel makes society responsible for the conditions that assure that integrity and autonomy will be sustained, including those associated with the regard we might expect to receive as persons.

Equal regard does not of course mean sameness, equality of talent and achievement, or the like. It means only that we are treated equally as persons. The principle of equal regard excludes any exercise of right that challenges or violates that status. In some ways, the principle of equal regard must animate any justice-centered theory. The theories differ less in whether they appeal (implicitly or explicitly) to the principle than in the concrete meaning it takes on for them. The same can be said, of course, about equal opportunity.

A form of equal opportunity and equal regard exists in the stark landscape of the libertarian theory. Property rights are equally respected and what rights we have, we all have equally. We are all equally regarded as (potentially) property-owning persons, agents of our own destinies, centers of initiative. The demands equal opportunity and equal regard place on us here are, however, minimal. Most of what we need to develop and maintain our integrity as persons we have independently of our intercourse with others. We are not dependent on others unless we choose to be and they (individually and collectively) bear no responsibility to secure the concrete conditions that will facilitate the success of our life projects.

No theory, of course, insists that society (especially the public authority) take responsibility for assuming that each member's life projects will succeed. To do so would, so far as it is possible at all, necessitate an intrusion into the person's private life inconsistent with any reasonable notion of individual integrity. Still, those theories that claim a greater dependence of the individual on the social condition also make society bear a greater responsibility for at least assuring, so far as possible, each individual's capacity to develop and realize a life project of her own. Clearly Rawls goes much further in arguing for such responsibility than do the libertarians. His commitment to equal opportunity and the difference principle justifies a significantly greater degree of intervention into the private sphere than libertarians would sanction.

The justice-centered theories considered in this last section go further in conceptualizing the social determination and thus social dependence of persons. In this framework, being a person is a social condition, a status attainable only within a society of persons capable of constituting personhood through recognizing it. Recognition occurs in a variety of contexts, but those linked to equal opportunity and equal regard have special importance for political economy. Thus the justice-centered theory in this form supports more extensive economic intervention because it claims a deeper sense of social dependence of persons.

The communitarian critique of justice-centered theories emphasizes the thinness of the conception of the social connectedness of persons in those theories. In this chapter, we considered variants of the justice-centered approach with special consideration for their ability to encompass social interdependence. We found considerable variation along this dimension. For contractarian and especially Hegelian theories, social determination is not excluded when justice is made the central concept of the theory.

Social justice and political economy

Utilitarian theories do not define the limits of the market according to a notion of individual integrity that transcends the logic of market relations. For utilitarian theories, the limits of the market are defined by the logic of the market. We only need have recourse to nonmarket relations when the market fails.

We can make this point in another way. For a utilitarian, the matter of the limits of the market is quantitative. If nonmarket allocation or regulation will lead to greater individual satisfaction, then nonmarket methods dominate. The line separating market from government does not distinguish between kinds of needs and what is appropriate to their satisfaction, but between degrees of want satisfaction.

Justice-centered thinking begins with a notion of individual integrity. This notion defines the purpose and limits of the market. It is not a matter of degree of satisfaction, but of what is required to protect and ensure the integrity of the individual. These requirements vary, as we have seen, for the different justice-centered approaches. But, in each case, they determine the meaning and limits of the market.

In justice-centered approaches, the conception of the person is most important. The more abstract that conception, as in the libertarian approach, the wider the scope of the market. Indeed, in the libertarian approach, the scope of the market is generally wider than it would be for a utilitarian. The more concretely defined the concept of the person, the more circumscribed the domain of the market.

In each case, however, the market has a domain of its own defined by the requirements of personal integrity satisfied by market relations. This means that justice-centered approaches distinguish between domains of social life according to (1) the mode of interrelatedness characteristic of each, and (2) the requirement of personhood linked to that mode of relating. Hegel refers to these as "moments" of the conception of ethical order.

Thinking this way has important implications for the relation of politics to economics. First, it protects the market from the kinds of incursion of politics suggested by reference to merger of the political and economic, or the economy as a political system. Justice-centered approaches insist on the integrity and separability of the economy.

Second, thinking in terms of spheres or domains defined qualitatively rather than in terms of market failure prevents economic reasoning, or the logic typical of the market, from dominating in nonmarket relations. The latter also have their own integrity linked to a qualitatively distinct social purpose. Politics, then, is not the pursuit of economic efficiency by other means; it is the pursuit of ends distinctly relevant to the political process.

For this to make sense, persons must have different kinds of ends; or, more accurately, they must have the need to enter into different kinds of relationships that characterize different social domains. Pursuit of the largest available measure of satisfaction does not characterize all that we do (it can also be debated whether it characterizes anything we do, of course). Justice-centered approaches focus our attention on the differences in kind among our human ends, and on the differences in kind among the processes and relationships by which we pursue those ends. In doing so, it makes it possible to consider those relations and processes ends in themselves. In the concluding chapter, we explore this idea more fully.

Conclusion

The main purpose of this book has been to examine and develop the theoretical core of various approaches to political economy. Where possible, we began with a recognized body of theory in either economics or politics. More often than not, extant theories addressed only part of the story – either economics or politics – leaving the linkages largely undeveloped. As a result, our task was not only to describe, but also to draw out the theoretical connections between economics (however defined) and politics (however defined). Thus the book represents in part a survey of existing approaches and in part an active theoretical construction of political economy.

The emphasis of the book is on the diversity of approaches rather than their similarities. We have tried to identify the distinctive marks of each approach and to draw out their significance. We have not tried to integrate approaches, for instance by absorbing them into larger categories or by showing how the concepts of several approaches are special cases of a more general theory.

What do we mean by diversity of approaches? In general we mean that the theories examined have different key assumptions, different actors, and different explanatory and interpretive tasks. To synthesize these approaches, or to assimilate some into others, risks confusing more than is clarified. The summary following reviews each theory, highlighting its important characteristics and distinctive senses of political economy.

Summary

The classical economists use the term "political economy" to refer to a system of want satisfaction exhibiting two related qualities. First, it extends beyond the family, constituting a structure of mutual dependence (division of labor) among the people of the nation rather than the members of a family. Second, a political economy is held together by exchange contracts between legally independent property owners; it is a market economy.

217

Beyond this, the economy of the classical theory may or may not demand the attention of the public authority, and thus be subject to a political process. In classical political economy the term comes more and more to refer, paradoxically, to depoliticized society. Political economy is part of the erosion of politics and the rise to dominance of a largely autonomous private sphere.

If the economy is political for classical theory, it is in the sense that its boundaries are established institutionally. The economy's locus is within the boundaries established by the state. Thus the arena within which economic transactions take place, and within which the problems of production and distribution across classes are considered, is defined by the state. While classical economics broke its ties with mercantilism, it still relied to a large extent on the national state as the container of economic activity.

In his understanding of political economy, Marx is very much a classical economist. He thinks of political economy as the study of the "anatomy of civil society." Thus, the subject matter of political economy is the nonpolitical society of the market. Marx attempts a radical critique of this nonpolitical society, less for being unpoliticized than for its failure to provide most participants with the civilized life it promises. In doing so, Marx seeks to use political economy to support, or even create, a political agenda. Even more, he seeks to demonstrate that the development of capitalist economy inevitably engenders a political challenge to it and a struggle over its most basic institutions.

Marxism suggests different routes for connecting the political with the economic. In Chapter 3 we discussed several possibilities, including revolutionary action to change the political structure, social democratic politics, and Marxian state theory. The first approach is the most radical. Politics does not refer to policies designed to compensate for limitations of market society, but instead to large-scale changes in the political structure itself. Since such changes are not likekly to come about peacefully, revolutionary action is called for.

The route of social democratic politics proceeds differently. Political practice requires participation in established institutions, compromise, electoral strategies, and so forth. Participation in established institutions requires workers to accept extant institutions as tools by which to pursue labor's goals.

Marxian state theory starts from the assumption that economic society is polarized into separate classes. Different classes represent different objective interests that cannot be compressed into a policy that pleases everyone. Unlike in pluralism, Marxian state theory emphasizes the partiality rather than inclusiveness of the state. The issue of state autonomy emerges as a way of responding to some of the paradoxes faced by the capitalist class, particularly between individual and collective interests.

Marxian political economy houses an important tension between politics and economics. On the one hand, Marxism provides a radical critique of the organizing principle of liberal society, the self-regulating market. On the other hand, this critique is accompanied by a view of economic agents as primary. The focus on economic classes and their political significance is an example of the primacy of economics.

The end of the classical period and the rise of neoclassicism (marginalism) in the 1870s marks new departures in economics and, hence, in conceptions of how economic and political phenomena relate. The rise of neoclassical economics represents a move away from class categories toward the individual who pursues utility within the arena of consumption and profits within the productive arena. The self-seeking behavior of individuals is analyzed within market settings, both perfect and imperfect. To the extent that markets allow for individual satisfaction, politics is not implicated.

As discussed in Chapter 4, "Neoclassical Political Economy," politics enters via the concept of market failure. It enters in response to an inability of the market to satisfy private wants. Thus the predominant conception of political economy within the neoclassical system has to do with extending the idea of self-seeking into nonmarket institutional domains, particularly the state. The state may provide public goods, correct externalities, and solve collective action problems through coercion.

From our standpoint, the contribution of Keynes that is most significant for political economy is his demonstration of the limitations of the self-adjustment mechanisms of a market economy. In other words, market economies do not fully exploit their productive potential. They often do a poor job of bringing wants and means together. The depression of the 1930s suggested that persistent unemployment could occur. Keynes's model of unemployment shows that the self-correcting market mechanism can break down.

A change in our collective judgment concerning the market's capacity for self-adjustment places a number of vital issues on the political agenda. The most notable of these involve the role of government in securing incomes and investment. The Keynesian critique illuminates the way in which the organization of labor and capital markets becomes contested terrain.

Chapter 6, "Economic Approaches to Politics," considers an extension of neoclassical ideas, particularly rational self-interest, into the political domain. Individuals are seen as goal-seeking and choosing creatures operating in different environments. When the goods in question are public and the rules are provided by political institutions, the arena is by definition political. Joining the tools of rational choice analysis with individual behavior within political settings provides one version of political economy. The method is economic. The field of activity – the arena – is political.

The economic approach to politics culminates a methodological principle embodied in neoclassical economics. The idea of rational self-interest becomes focal and is harnessed to the analysis of politics. The neoclassical approach and its offshoots attempt to alter our way of understanding economics and politics. Neoclassical political economy, with its focus on the state's role in market failure, offers a way to complete the liberal project in one direction. To the extent that markets do not foster the satisfaction of private wants, the state enters. The role of the state is derivative. Its scope and content depend on the efficacy of market behavior.

What is economic in neoclassical political economy is the market, or more precisely, voluntary exchange within market settings. What is economic in the economic approach is rationality. The political content in both cases is supplied by a particular arena, institutional setting, or way of organizing – by the state or public organization (rather than by the market and private exchange). Politics and economics do not refer to qualitatively different objects. Instead they reflect comparative institutional specializations in markets and states and methods and subject matters.

The last three approaches – power-centered, state-centered, and justice-centered, take some further steps in the direction of establishing the autonomy of politics, though not without significant limitations. In all three approaches, the political is more central, more autonomous, less capable of being derived from the economic or societal.

Power approaches see relations of power and domination in the market, between the market and the state, and within the state itself. Economic agents (firms, pressure groups) may exert their power (through votes or lobbying) over the political process or over other economic agents (other firms), or over consumers in imperfectly competitive markets.

In a broad view of power, power is nearly everywhere. The problem is not where to find it but what to ignore. How does one draw the boundary between the political and nonpolitical if power is always present? This problem is often solved in an ad hoc way by limiting the scope of power analysis to settings involving the state or processes intended to affect state policy.

State-centered approaches take political institutions, especially authoritative central political institutions, as pivotal in the definition of politics. Politics is what goes on within the state, or between the state and society. What kinds of political economy flow from this conception? There are numerous possibilities centering on interrelations between the state and the economy: regulation of the economy and economic actors, the effect of economic actors on state policy, distributional effects of policy on economic resources, and traditional macroeconomic policy along Keynesian lines. State-centered approaches need not treat politics as primary, or even autonomous. The focus on the state may be central at the same time that the causal forces driving state action are located in society.

The justice-centered approach goes the furthest in turning the tables on economy-centered approaches. The starting point is justice and rights rather than self-seeking and efficiency. Justice does not emerge out of the "natural" self-seeking forces within society. The state plays an important role in establishing justice and determining the boundaries of the political and economic. If the economic realm is identified with self-seeking, with what can be freely traded by economic agents, rights and obligations impose limits to the scope of free exchange. Thus the very act of determining what is political and what is economic is political. This approach shifts our attention away from political economy defined as interaction between politics and economics toward political economy as the political processes shaping the proper scope of economic action.

The diversity of approaches

Respecting the diversity of approaches means that we have not been sympathetic to "totalizing missions," whether emanating from economics or politics. Two such missions involve power and individual rationality. According to the first conception, power is everywhere, particularly in economic relations. The economy is presented as a "system of power" masquerading as voluntary exchange. People and firms enter the market not as abstract, equal individuals but as property owners with access to vastly different amounts of capital, raw materials, labor, and technology. Furthermore, implicit rules (for example, residual product goes to the capitalist) benefit some more than others. From the starting point of inequality of assets, rules, and outcomes, the conclusion is drawn that the economy is through and through a system of power.

A second approach, derived from neoclassical economics, attempts to show that economics and politics can be accommodated within a single decision-making principle of human behavior, one based on individual rationality. If individuals can order alternatives within market settings, surely they can do the same for politics. The individual is a goal-seeking entity in both cases. What is different are the constraints and opportunities of political and market settings. Politics and economics become unified in the sense that both are assimilated into a single behavioral principle – not in the sense that politics and economics are theorized as causally related.

There are numerous problems with the imperial visions of both power and individual rationality. The greatest share of economic theorizing, from Adam Smith to modern neoclassical thought, has concerned legally voluntary exchange to improve conditions among economic agents. Since power as typically conceived involves threats to make agents worse off, power and voluntary exchange do not go together easily. The exchange approach can be made consistent with the power focus by substituting "power to" for "power over." The accommodation is achieved, however, by a conceptual stretching that renders the concept of power virtually useless. The focus on individual rationality achieves political economy in a formal way. It passes over the distinctions between economics and politics and reduces its own motivation to take up the challenge of how the two spheres are related.

Having rejected these unification attempts, where does this leave us? We argue that economics and politics differ not only in method or institutions (market, state), but also in terms of the objects and processes central to each.

For the sake of illustration, let us focus on markets. Markets are arenas within which voluntary exchange takes place. Here individuals come together as owners of property. They relate to one another as opportunities for personal satisfaction. The market is often defended on the grounds that it is the realm of freedom. Within the market, individuals are allowed to pursue their wants subject to constraints of property rights and initial ownership. Belief in the theorem that market institutions foster efficient allocation leads some economists to argue for expansion of the market. Thus, publicly owned factories, schools, prisons, and public lands are all open to free-market scrutiny of their efficiency.

The distinction between private and public goods is important for assessing the limits of the market. However, drawing this distinction according to the technical criteria favored by neoclassical economists (for example, the criterion of excludability) is deeply problematic. Even some goods that are technically excludable may resist placement within the market. We do not mean that activities concerning such goods *cannot* take place within the market. Rather, there may be normative and political objections to so doing. We have in mind three kinds of goods: those where "buying and selling" are corrosive of the good itself; those where goods are too connected to persons and identity, that is, integral; and those that are in some sense linked to shared values and collective provision.

The mechanism of buying and selling allows individuals to pursue consumption and profit with a minimum of political-legal interference, subject mostly to the constraints given by the distribution of assets, information, and technology. Individual agents are free to pursue goods without arbitrary intervention by political authority and without being pressed to explain or justify their wants. Whether a person wants a red Porsche convertible or a gray Volvo station wagon is not the business of the selling agents. The market offers great scope to individual autonomy.

However, certain goods are not readily adaptable to the market provision. There are some goods where "buying and selling" tend to undermine the enjoyment of the good, even how we think about it. Can one really buy compliments, love, friendship, and respect? In the extreme case, market provision may be logically inconsistent with how we think and feel about these goods. Thus, "paid compliments" may be an oxymoron if one views authenticity and sincerity as critical. Similarly, what troubles some people about purchasing intimate phone conversations is that intimacy means something more than quiet, suggestive conversation between perfect strangers. To be clear, we do not suggest that the state is the proper arena for these goods either. Indeed, the dichotomy between market and state is clearly inadequate to accommodate the full range of human interaction, as Walzer (1986) and others argue.

A second category of resistant goods relates to the integrity of persons and the different norms governing relations among friends or family on the one hand, and economic agents on the other. The integrity of persons is seen most clearly in cases of sale of sexual favors (prostitution), "renting a womb" to carry a fertilized egg, or selling one's labor to the highest bidder in circumstances where the outcomes matter in some moral sense. The lawyer or academic consultant who works for a cause he or she does not believe in not only sells his labor, he also relinquishes his identity.

Finally, market-provison is distinct in that it fosters a particular orientation to others and a particular method of expressing dissatisfaction with buyers and sellers. The mode of orientation is voluntary exchange. This principle is closely related to the standard mode for expressing dissatisfaction, namely "exit" (Hirschman, 1970; Anderson, 1990: 184). If the consumer dislikes price, quality, or mere existence of a commodity, he or she exercises the power to search elsewhere. Aggregate consumer decisions to buy commodities are seen as "votes" for certain products and producers. The option of dialogue, argument, or persuasion hardly exists as an independent form of influence. Consumers communicate with producers indirectly, through casting and withholding their dollars, rather than through direct verbal communication and persuasion.

Politics and markets differ in numerous ways in addition to their respective specializations with respect to public and private goods. Consider the kinds of goods most appropriate to state provision. In addition to goods implicated by market failures, there are goods that are in principle divisible and excludable that may be assignable to the state sector. For example, think of the arguments for publicly provided medical care, government-run prisons, and public education. Individuals may want the government to guarantee medical care to all persons in a society. Membership in a political system (citizenship) rather than property holding in a market becomes the crucial condition for consumption. Those who believe in the superiority of public provision may make their case in terms of need and entitlement rather than want and efficiency.

The previous example raises two issues. One issue relates to the debate between those who argue that wants are wants, more or less intensely felt, and those who see classes of qualitatively different wants. For the former, the intensity continuum runs from the faintest preference to the most deeply felt need. The second issue relates to who shall enjoy benefits – those with money to pay or those in a particular membership category (citizens). The two issues are usually linked in that those who recognize classes of wants have to consider modes of satisfaction appropriate to each. This generally, though not necessarily, includes state provision.

Politics and the state sector are also marked by different modes of orientation. Coercion is often at the basis of compliance. In the market, people comply because it is in their interest to do so. It would not do well to renege on contracts since reputation counts in the long run. In politics people may have an incentive to free ride on a public benefit, or what is often lost sight of, they may resist a policy because it represents a loss for them.

However, there is more to politics than coercion. Through politics people also relate through collective expression of shared ideas such as care for the disabled, certain expressions of world order, and minimal and uniform conditions for criminals. In this sense, care for the environment, the destitute, and criminals is more appropriately assigned to the state sector than to the market. Since a clean environment is something that a society as a whole may stand for, government should provide for it out of public monies. Rather than depend on the collection of contributions by Greenpeace canvassers, the state should express society's convictions on such matters.

The question whether prisons should be privatized or not raises another issue, that related to justice and standard conditions for criminals. If a prison is privatized it becomes an economic entity, a firm operating within an environment of competitive accumulation. Pressures to cut back on expenses for food, recreation facilities, guards, and nonproductive physical plant may increase. Some prisons may become more efficient, in the sense that they will manage a given number of inmates at lower costs. But whatever their crime, prisoners are not merely property. Certain minimum standards should be met and this is better assured with public provision.

Finally, while market exchange is assessed by criteria relating to the pursuit of utility, the political system is more complicated. There are ideas of justice, minimum provision, equality (before the law), and democratic participation. Rights and obligations engender different norms than do preferences. Thus, there are bans on trading rights even if such trades are Pareto-superior. In addition, civic participation is not only an instrumental activity, designed to achieve goals outside of itself (Elkin, 1985). It may also be valued in its own right, as expression of the shared values in which society's members participate.

The foregoing considerations point up the need for political economy to deal with the categorical distinction between politics and economics, and to take that distinction seriously. The distinction clearly has a normative grounding and normative implications. It corresponds to the classification of wants into qualitatively different groups, and to a distinction between private and public more complex than usually employed. Developing the classification of wants (and needs), the normative grounding for a theory identifying the tasks appropriate to different institutions, and a more complex and meaningful distinction between public and private should be made an important part of the agenda of political economy.

The burden of this book has been to identify and develop the differences among political economy traditions. Our project is based on a foundation that sees politics and economics as not reducible to one another. It also respects distinct understandings within politics and economics. The different approaches analyzed have broad points of contact, but they do not reduce one to another, nor are they easily assimilated into more general approaches. We hope we have added something to the clarification of the approaches discussed, and we look forward to the debates ahead.

Bibliography

Ackerman, Bruce. 1977. *Private Property and the Constitution*. New Haven, Conn.: Yale University Press.

Alchian, Armen A. 1950. "Uncertainty, Evolution, and Economic Theory." *Journal of Political Economy*, 58, no. 3: 211–221.

Alchian, Armen A., and Harold Demsetz. 1972. "Production, Information Costs, and Economic Organization." *American Economic Review*, 62, no. 5: 777–95.

Alt, James E., and K. Alec Chrystal. 1983. *Political Economics*. Berkeley: University of California Press.

Anderson, Elizabeth. 1990. "The Ethical Limitations of the Market." *Economics and Philosophy*, 6, no. 2: 179–205.

Arendt, Hannah. 1958. *The Human Condition*. Chicago: University of Chicago Press.

[1969] 1986. "Communicative Power." From *On Violence* (Florida: Harcourt Brace, 1969), reprinted in *Power*, ed. Steven Lukes. New York: New York University Press, pp. 59–74.

Arrow, Kenneth. 1951. *Social Choice and Individual Values*. New Haven, Conn.: Yale University Press.

Avineri, Shlomo. 1969. *The Social and Political Thought of Karl Marx*. Cambridge: Cambridge University Press.

1972. *Hegel's Theory of the Modern State*. Cambridge: Cambridge University Press.

Axelrod, Robert. 1981. "The Emergence of Cooperation among Egoists." *American Political Science Review*, 75, no. 2 (June): 306–18.

1984. *The Evolution of Cooperation*. New York: Basic Books. Macmillan.

Baily, M. N. 1978. "Stabilization Policy and Private Economic Behavior." *Brookings Papers on Economic Activity*, no. 1.

Balbus, Isaac D. 1971. "The Concept of Interest in Pluralist and Marxist Analysis." *Politics and Society*, 1, no. 2: 151–77.

Baran, Paul. 1957. *The Political Economy of Growth*. New York: Monthly Review Press.

Baran, Paul, and Paul Sweezy. 1965. *Monopoly Capital*. New York: Monthly Review Press.

Barber, Benjamin R. 1988. *The Conquest of Politics: Liberal Philosophy in Democratic Times*. Princeton, N.J.: Princeton University Press.

Basu, Kaushik, Eric Jones, and Ekkehart Schlicht. 1987. "The Growth and Decay of Custom: The Role of the New Institutional Economics in Economic History." *Explorations in Economic History*, 24: 1–21.

Bates, Robert H. 1981. *Markets and State in Tropical Africa*. Berkeley: University of California Press.

[1983] 1987. *Essays on the Political Economy of Rural Africa*. [Cambridge: Cambridge University Press]. Berkeley: University of California Press, paperback.

1988. "Macro-Political Economy in the Field of Development." Duke University Program in International Political Economy, working paper no. 40, pp. 1–69.

Baumol, William J. [1952] 1965. *Welfare Economics and the Theory of the State*. 2d ed. Cambridge, Mass.: Harvard University Press.

Becker, Gary. 1976. *The Economic Approach to Human Behavior*. Chicago: University of Chicago Press.

Beer, Samuel H. 1955. *The Communist Manifesto* (with selections from *The Eighteenth Brumaire of Louis Bonaparte* and *Capital*). New York: Appleton-Century-Crofts.

Benhabib, Seyla. 1989. "Liberal Dialogue versus a Critical Theory of Discursive Legitimation." In N. Rosenblum, ed., *Liberalism and the Moral Life*. Cambridge. Mass.: Harvard University Press.

Benjamin, Roger, and Raymond Duvall. 1985. "The Capitalist State in Context." In Roger Benjamin, ed., *The Democratic State*. Lawrence: University of Kansas Press, pp. 19–57.

Bentley, Arthur. 1908. *The Process of Government: A Study of Social Pressures*. Chicago: University of Chicago Press.

Bettelheim, Charles. 1985. "Reflections on Concepts of Class and Class Struggle in Marx's Work." In Stephen Resnick and Richard Wolff, eds., *Rethinking Marxism*. Brooklyn, N.Y.: Autonomedia, Inc.

Bhagwati, Jagdish N., and T. N. Srinivasan. 1980. "Revenue-Seeking: A Generalization of the Theory of Tariffs." *Journal of Political Economy*, 88, no. 6: 1069–87.

Bobbio, Norberto. 1979. "Gramsci and the Concept of Civil Society." In C. Moufee, ed., *Gramsci and Marxist Theory*. London: Routledge & Kegan Paul.

Booth, Douglas E. 1978. "Collective Action, Marx's Class Theory, and the Union Movement." *Journal of Economic Issues*, 12, no. 1: 163–85.

Bowles, Samuel, and Herbert Gintis. 1986. *Democracy and Capitalism: Property, Community, and the Contradictions of Modern Social Thought*. New York: Basic Books.

Bowman, John R. 1989. *Capitalist Collective Action*. Cambridge: Cambridge University Press.

Buchanan, James. 1954. "Individual Choice in Voting and the Market." *Journal of Political Economy*, 42, no. 4: 334–43.

1979. "An Economist's Approach to 'Scientific Politics.'" In Buchanan, *What Should Economists Do?* Indianapolis: Liberty Fund.

1984. "Politics without Romance. A Sketch of Positive Public Choice Theory and Its Normative Implications." In James M. Buchanan and Robert D. Tollison, eds., *The Theory of Public Choice – II*. Ann Arbor: University of Michigan Press, pp. 11–22.

1987. "The Constitution of Economic Policy." *American Economic Review*, 77, no. 3: 243–50.

1988. "Contractarian Political Economy and Constitutional Interpretation." *Papers and Proceedings of the American Economic Association*, 78, no. 2: 135–9.

Buchanan, James, and Gordon Tullock. 1962. *The Calculus of Consent*. Ann Arbor: University of Michigan Press.

Carnoy, Martin. 1984. *The State and Political Theory*. Princeton, N.J.: Princeton University Press.

Chick, Victoria. 1983. *Macroeconomics after Keynes*. Cambridge, Mass.: MIT Press.

Coase, R. H. [1937] 1988. "The Nature of the Firm." In R. H. Coase, *The Firm, the Market, and the Law*. Chicago: University of Chicago Press.

Cohen, G. A. 1978. "Robert Nozick and Wilt Chamberlain: How Patterns Preserve Liberty."

In J. Arthur and W. H. Shaw, eds., *Justice and Economic Distribution*. Englewood Cliffs, N.J.: Prentice-Hall.

Coles, Robert. 1986. *The Political Life of Children*. Boston: Houghton Mifflin.

Connolly, William E., ed. 1969. *The Bias of Pluralism*. New York: Atherton Press.

[1974] 1983. *The Terms of Political Discourse*. 2d ed. Princeton, N.J.: Princeton University Press.

Cox, Robert W. 1986. "Social Forces, States, and World Orders: Beyond International Relations Theory." In Robert O. Keohane, ed., *Neorealism and Its Critics*. New York: Columbia University Press, pp. 204–54.

Crick, Bernard. [1962] 1964. *In Defense of Politics*. London: Weidenfeld and Nicolson. Middlesex, England: Penguin Books, rev. ed.

Dahl, Robert A. 1956. *A Preface to Democratic Theory*. Chicago: University of Chicago Press.

Daedalus. 1979. *The State*. Special issue, 108, no. 4.

Daniels, Norman. 1975. *Reading Rawls*. New York: Basic Books.

Dasgupta, A. K. 1985. *Epochs of Economic Theory*. New York: Basil Blackwell.

DeVroey, M. 1984. "Inflation: A Non-Monetarist Monetary Interpretation." *Cambridge Journal of Economics*, 8 (December).

Dewey, John. 1927. *The Public and Its Problems*. New York: Henry Holt and Co.

Diesing, Paul. 1982. *Science and Ideology in the Social Sciences*. New York: Aldine.

Dobb, Maurice. 1936. *Political Economy and Capitalism*. London: Routledge.

1973. *Theories of Value and Distribution since Adam Smith*. Cambridge: Cambridge University Press.

Domhoff, G. William. 1967. *Who Rules America?* Englewood Cliffs, N.J.: Prentice-Hall.

Downs, Anthony. 1957. *An Economic Theory of Democracy*. New York: Harper & Row.

Dworkin, Ronald. 1977. *Taking Rights Seriously*. Cambridge, Mass.: Harvard University Press.

Easton, David. [1953] 1981. *The Political System: An Inquiry into the State of Political Science*. Chicago: University of Chicago Press.

1965. *A Systems Analysis of Political Life*. Chicago: University of Chicago Press.

Eckstein, Harry. 1979. "On the 'Science' of the State." *Daedalus*, 108, no. 4: 1–20.

Edwards, R., M. Reich, and D. M. Gordon, eds. 1973. *Labor Market Segmentation*. Lexington, Mass.: D. C. Heath.

Ekelund, Robert B., Jr., and Robert D. Tollison. 1986. *Microeconomics*. Boston: Little, Brown.

Elkin, Stephen. 1985. "Economic and Political Rationality." *Polity*, 18, no. 2: 253–71.

Elster, Jon. 1986. "Introduction." In Jon Elster, ed., *Rational Choice*. New York: New York University Press, pp. 1–33.

1987. "The Possibility of Rational Politics." *Archives Européennes de Sociologie*, 28, no. 1: 67–103.

Engels, Friedrich. [n.d. originally published] 1984. *The Origin of the Family, Private Property, and the State*. New York: International Publishers.

Evans, Peter B. 1979. *Dependent Development*. Princeton, N.J.: Princeton University Press.

Evans, Peter B., Dietrich Rueschemeyer, and Theda Skocpol, eds. 1985. *Bringing the State Back In*. Cambridge: Cambridge University Press.

Ferguson, Adam. 1773. *An Essay on the History of Civil Society*. London.

Field, Alexander. 1979. "On the Explanation of Rules Using Rational Choice Models." *Journal of Economic Issues*, 13. no. 1: 49–72.

1984. "Microeconomics, Norms, and Rationality." *Economic Development and Cultural Change*, 32: 683–711.

Finnis, John. 1980. *Natural Law and Natural Rights*. Oxford: Oxford University Press.

Fiorina, Morris P. 1982. "Legislative Choice of Regulatory Forms: Legal Process or Administrative Process?" *Public Choice*, 39: 33–66.

Fisher, I. 1930. *The Theory of Interest*. New York: Macmillan.

Flathman, Richard E. 1966. *The Public Interest*. New York: John Wiley and Sons.

Friedrich, Carl J. [1937] 1968. *Constitutional Government and Democracy*. Boston: Ginn.

Friedman, Milton. [1962] 1982. *Capitalism and Freedom*. Chicago: University of Chicago Press.

Friedman, Milton and A. Schwartz. 1963. *A Monetary History of the United States*. Princeton, N.J.: Princeton University Press.

Frolich, Norman, and Joe A. Oppenheimer. 1978. *Modern Political Economy*. Englewood Cliffs, N.J.: Prentice-Hall.

Galbraith, John Kenneth. 1954. *The Great Crash*. Boston: Houghton Mifflin.

1983. *The Anatomy of Power*. Boston: Houghton Mifflin.

Garegnani, Piero. 1984. "Value and Distribution in the Classical Economists and Marx." *Oxford Economic Papers*, 36, no. 2 (June): 291–325.

Gewirth, Alan. 1982. *Human Rights*. Chicago: University of Chicago Press.

Giddens, Anthony. 1979. *Central Problems in Social Theory*. Berkeley: University of California Press.

Gilpin, Robert. 1981. *War and Change in World Politics*. New York: Cambridge University Press.

1987. *The Political Economy of International Relations*. Princeton, N.J.: Princeton University Press.

Godelier, Maurice. 1972. *Rationality and Irrationality in Economics*. London: New Left Books.

Goldthorpe, John H. 1978. "The Current Inflation: Towards a Sociological Account." In Fred Hirsch and John Goldthorpe, eds., *The Political Economy of Inflation*. London: Martin Robertson.

Gourevitch, Peter. 1986. *Politics in Hard Times: Comparative Responses to International Economic Crises*. Ithaca, N.Y.: Cornell University Press.

Gowa, Joanne. 1989. "Rational Hegemons, Excludable Goods, and Small Groups: An Epitaph for Hegemonic Stability Theory?" *World Politics*, 41, no. 3: 307–24.

Gramsci, Antonio. 1971. *Selections from the Prison Notebooks*. Tr. Q. Hoare and G. N. Smith. New York: International Publishers.

Greenstein, Fred I. 1965. *Children and Politics*. New Haven, Conn.: Yale University Press.

Habermas, J. 1973. *Legitimation Crisis*. Boston: Beacon Press.

Hardin, Russell. 1982. *Collective Action*. Baltimore: Johns Hopkins University Press.

Hegel, G. W. F. [1821] 1952. *Hegel's Philosophy of Right*. Tr. T. M. Knox. Oxford: Oxford University Press.

Heilbroner, Robert. 1988. "Economics without Power." *New York Review of Books*, 35, no. 3 (March): 23–5.

Heller, Agnes. 1976. *The Theory of Need in Marx*. New York: St. Martin's.

Hirschleifer, Jack. 1985. "The Expanding Domain of Economics." *The American Economic Review*, 75, no. 6: 53–68.

Hirschman, Albert O. 1970. *Exit, Voice, and Loyalty: Responses to Decline in Firms, Organizations, and States*. Cambridge, Mass.: Harvard University Press.

1977. *The Passions and the Interests*. Princeton, N.J.: Princeton University Press.

Hodgson, Geoffrey M. 1988. *Economics and Institutions*. Philadelphia: University of Pennyslvania Press.

Hyneman, Charles S. 1959. *The Study of Politics*. Urbana: University of Illinois Press.

Jessop, Bob. 1982. *The Capitalist State*. New York: New York University Press.

Jevons, William S. [1871] 1970. *The Theory of Political Economy*. Harmondsworth, England: Penguin Books.

Kaldor, Nicolas. 1960. *Essays on Value and Distribution*. Glencoe, Ill.: Free Press, ch. 10.

Kalecki, Michal. 1965. *Theory of Economic Dynamics*. London: George Allen and Unwin.

  1969. *Studies in the Theory of Business Cycles 1933–1939*. New York: Augustus Kelly.

  1971. *Selected Essays on the Dynamics of Capitalist Economy*. Cambridge: Cambridge University Press.

Katzenstein, Peter J., ed. 1978. *Between Power and Plenty: Foreign Economic Policies of Advanced Industrial States*. Madison: University of Wisconsin Press.

  1978. "Introduction: Domestic and International Forces and Strategies of Foreign Economic Policy." In Katzenstein, ed., *Between Power and Plenty*. Madison: University of Wisconsin Press, pp. 3–22.

  1978. "Conclusion: Domestic Structures and Strategies of Foreign Economic Policy." In Peter J. Katzenstein, ed., *Between Power and Plenty*. Madison: University of Wisconsin Press, pp. 296–336.

Keohane, Robert O. 1982. "The Demand for International Regimes." *International Organization*, 36, no. 2 (Spring): 325–55.

  1984. *After Hegemony*. Princeton, N.J.: Princeton University Press.

Keynes, J. M. 1936. *General Theory of Employment, Interest and Money*. New York: Harcourt, Brace and World.

Kindleberger, Charles P. 1973. *The World in Depression, 1929–1939*. Berkeley: University of California Press.

  1978. *Manias, Panics, and Crashes: A History of Financial Crises*. New York: Basic Books.

  1981. "Dominance and Leadership in the International Economy." *International Studies Quarterly*, 25, no. 3: 242–54.

Knight, Frank H. [1956] 1966. *On the History and Method of Economics*. Chicago: University of Chicago Press.

Kohut, Heinz. 1977. *The Restoration of the Self*. New York: International University Press.

Koopmans, Tjalling C. 1957. *Three Essays on the State of Economic Science*. New York: McGraw-Hill.

Krasner, Stephen D. 1978. *Defending the National Interest*. Princeton, N.J.: Princeton University Press.

Krueger, Anne O. 1974. "The Political Economy of the Rent-Seeking Society." *American Economic Review*, 64: 291–303.

Latsis, Spiro J. 1972. "Situational Determinism in Economics." *British Journal of Philosophy of Science*, 23: 207–45.

Lasswell, Harold D. 1936. *Politics: Who Gets What, When, and How?* New York: Whittlesey House.

Lenin, V. I. 1932. *State and Revolution*. New York: International Publishers.

Levi, Margaret. 1988. *Of Rule and Revenue*. Berkeley: University of California Press.

Levine, David. 1978. *Economic Theory*, Vol. 1. London: Routledge & Kegan Paul.

  1981. *Economic Theory*, Vol. 2. London: Routledge & Kegan Paul.

1982. "Macroeconomic Policy: Redefining the Problem." Unpublished, Denver.

1983. "How Economists View Policy." *Democracy*, 3, no. 3: 83–93.

1984. "Long Period Expectations and Investment." *Social Concept*, 1, no. 3: 41–51.

1985. "Political Economy and the Argument for Inequality." *Social Concept* 2, no. 3 (September): 3–69.

1986. "A Note on Wage Determination and Capital Accumulation." *Journal of Post-Keynesian Economics* 8, no. 3: 463–77.

1987. "Political Economy: Mapping the Terrain." Unpublished, Denver. 29 pp.

1988a. *Needs, Rights, and The Market.* Boulder, Colo.: Lynne Rienner Publishers.

1988b. "Marx's Theory of Income Distribution." In *Theories of Income Distribution*, A. Asimakopulos, ed., Boston: Kluwer Academic Publishers.

1989. "The Sense of Theory in Political Economy." *Rethinking Marxism* 2, no. 1 (Spring): 29–48.

Lindblom, Charles E. 1977. *Politics and Markets.* New York: Basic Books.

Locke, John. [1689] 1955. *Of Civil Government*, Second Treatise. Chicago: Gateway Editions.

Lukacs, George. 1971. *History and Class Consciousness.* Cambridge, Mass.: MIT Press.

Lukes, Steven. 1974. *Power: A Radical View.* London: Macmillan.

1986. Introduction. In Steven Lukes, ed., *Power.* New York: New York University Press.

Mack, Eric. 1983. "Distributive Justice and the Tensions of Lockeanism." *Social Philosophy and Policy* 1, no. 1: 312–50.

MacPherson, C. B. 1973. *Democratic Theory: Essays in Retrieval.* New York: Oxford University Press.

Maier, Charles S. 1987. Introduction. In Charles S. Maier, ed., *Changing Boundaries of the Political.* Cambridge: Cambridge University Press, pp. 1–24.

Mansfield, Edwin. 1982. *Micro-Economics: Theory and Applications.* 4th ed. New York: W. W. Norton Co.

Marglin, Stephen. 1974. "'What Do Bosses Do?' The Origins and Functions of Hierarchy in Capitalist Production." *Review of Radical Political Economy*, 6: 60–112.

Marshall, Alfred. [1890] 1930. *Principles of Economics.* 8th ed. London: Macmillan.

Marx, Karl. [1859] 1904. *Contribution to the Critique of Political Economy.* Tr. N. I. Stone, Chicago: Charles Kerr.

1964. *The German Ideology.* Moscow: Progress Publishers.

[1867] 1967a. *Capital*, Vol. I. New York: International Publishers.

[1894] 1967b. *Capital*, Vol. III. New York: International Publishers.

1977. *Karl Marx: Selected Writings*, ed. D. McLellan. Oxford: Oxford University Press.

Marx, Karl, and Friedrich Engels. [1848] 1955. *The Communist Manifesto*, with selections from *The Eighteenth Brumaire of Louis Bonaparte* and *Capital*. Ed. Samuel H. Beer, New York: The Modern Library.

Mason, Ronald M. 1982. *Participatory and Workplace Democracy.* Carbondale: Southern Illinois University Press.

Matthews, Donald. 1960. *U.S. Senators and Their World.* Chapel Hill, N.C.: University of North Carolina Press.

McKean, Roland J. 1958. *Efficiency in Government through Systems Analysis.* New York: John Wiley and Sons.

McKelvey, R. D. 1976. "Intransitivities in Multidimensional Voting Models and Some Implications for Agenda Control." *Journal of Economic Theory*, 12: 472–82.

1979. "General Conditions for Global Intransitivities in Formal Voting Models." *Econometrica*, 47: 1085–111.

McKenzie, Richard, and Gordon Tullock. 1981. *The New World of Economics*. 3d ed. Homewood. Ill.: Irwin.

McLean, Iain. 1987. *Public Choice: An Introduction*. New York: Basil Blackwell.

Meek, Ronald L. 1973. *Studies in the Labour Theory of Value*. 2d ed. London: Lawrence and Wishart.

Mill, John S. 1848. *Principles of Political Economy*. London.

Mills, C. Wright. 1956. *The Power Elite*. New York: Oxford University Press.

Minsky, H. P. 1975. *John Maynard Keynes*. New York: Columbia University Press.

Moe, Terry M. 1980. *The Organization of Interests*. Chicago: University of Chicago Press.

Morgenthau, Hans J. [1948] 1960. *Politics among Nations*. New York: Alfred Knopf.

Mueller, Dennis C. 1979. *Public Choice*. Cambridge: Cambridge University Press.

Musgrave, Richard A. 1959. *The Theory of Public Finance*. New York: McGraw-Hill.

Musgrave, R. A., and A. P. Peacock, eds. 1958. *Classics in the Theory of Public Finance*. New York: St. Martin's Press.

Nell, Edward. 1967. "Theories of Growth and Theories of Value." *Economic Development and Cultural Change*, 16: 12–26.

Nettl, J. P. 1968. "The State as a Conceptual Variable." *World Politics*, 20 (July): 559–92.

Noel, A. "Accumulation, Regulation, and Social Change: An Essay on French Political Economy." *International Organization*, 41, no. 2 (Spring 1987): 303–33.

Nordlinger, Eric A. 1981. *On the Autonomy of the Democratic State*. Cambridge, Mass.: Harvard University Press.

North, Douglass C. 1978. "Structure and Performance: The Task of Economic History." *Journal of Economic Literature*, 16, no. 3: 963–78.

1981. *Structure and Change in Economic History*. New York: W. W. Norton.

1984. "Transaction Costs, Institutions, and Economic History." *Journal of Institutional and Theoretical Economics*, 140: 7–17.

North, Douglass C., and Robert Paul Thomas. 1973. *The Rise of the Western World*. Cambridge: Cambridge University Press.

Nozick, Robert. 1974. *Anarchy, State and Utopia*. New York: Basic Books.

Offe, Claus. 1981. "The Attribution of Public Status to Interest Groups: Observations on the West German Case." In Suzanne D. Berger, ed., *Organizing Interests in Western Europe*. Cambridge: Cambridge University Press, pp. 123–58.

1984. *Contradictions of the Welfare State*. Cambridge, Mass.: MIT Press.

1987. "Challenging the Boundaries of Institutional Politics: Social Movements since the 1960's." In Charles S. Maier, ed., *Changing Boundaries of the Political*. Cambridge: Cambridge University Press, pp. 63–105.

Okun, Arthur M. 1970. *The Political Economy of Prosperity*. New York: W. W. Norton.

1975. *Equality and Efficiency: The Big Tradeoff*. Washington, D.C.: Brookings Institution.

1981. *Prices and Quantities*. Washington, D.C.: Brookings Institution.

Olson, Mancur, Jr. 1965. *The Logic of Collective Action*. Cambridge, Mass.: Harvard University Press.

1969. "The Relationship between Economics and the Other Social Sciences: The Province of a 'Social Report'." In Seymour M. Lipset, ed., *Politics and the Social Sciences*. New York: Oxford University Press, pp. 137–62.

1982. *The Rise and Decline of Nations*. New Haven, Conn.: Yale University Press.

1984. "Indivisibilities and Information Losses." Unpublished (mimeo.), College Park, Md.

Orbell, John M., and L. A. Wilson II. 1978. "Institutional Solutions to N-Prisoners' Dilemma." *American Political Science Review*, 72: 411–21.

Pasinetti, Luigi L. 1977. *Lectures on the Theory of Production*. New York: Columbia University Press.

Paul, Jeffrey, ed. 1981. *Reading Nozick*. Totowa, N.J.: Rowman and Littlefield.

Pelczynski, Z. A. 1984. *The State and Civil Society*. Cambridge: Cambridge University Press.

Piore, M. J., and C. F. Sabel. 1984. *The Second Industrial Divide*. New York: Basic Books.

Pizzorno, Alessandro. 1987. "Politics Unbound." In Charles S. Maier, ed., *Changing Boundaries of the Political*. Cambridge: Cambridge University Press, pp. 27–62.

Plott, Charles R. 1976. "Axiomatic Social Choice Theory: An Overview and Interpretation." *American Jounal of Political Science*, 20, no. 3: 511–96.

Polanyi, Karl. 1944. *The Great Transformation*. Boston: Beacon Press.

1957. "Aristotle Discovers the Economy." In K. Polanyi, C. Arensber, H. Pearson, eds., *Trade and Market in the Early Empires*. Chicago: Gateway Editions.

Popkin, Samuel. 1979. *The Rational Peasant*. Berkeley: University of California Press.

Poulantzas, Nico. 1969. "The Problem of the Capitalist State." *New Left Review*, no. 58: 67–78.

1973. *Political Power and Social Classes*. Tr. by T. O'Hagan, London: New Left Books.

Przeworski, Adam. 1985a. *Capitalism and Social Democracy*. Cambridge: Cambridge University Press.

1985b. "Marxism and Rational Choice." *Politics and Society*, 14, no. 4: 379–409.

Rae, Douglas. 1967. *The Political Consequences of Electoral Laws*. New Haven, Conn.: Yale University Press.

1969. "Decision Rules and Individual Values in Constitutional Choice." *American Political Science Review*, 63: 40–56.

Rawls, John. 1971. *A Theory of Justice*. Cambridge, Mass.: Harvard University Press.

Reich, Robert B. 1983. *The Next American Frontier*. New York: Penguin Books.

1988. *The Power of Public Ideas*. Cambridge, Mass.: Ballinger.

Resnick, Stephen A., and Richard D. Wolff. 1987. *Knowledge and Class*. Chicago: University of Chicago Press.

Rhoads, Steven E. 1985. *The Economist's View of the World*. Cambridge: Cambridge University Press.

Ricardo, David. [1821] 1951. *The Principles of Political Economy and Taxation*. In *Works and Correspondence of David Ricardo*, Vol. I, ed. P. Sraffa. Cambridge: Cambridge University Press.

Riker, William H. 1980. "Implications from the Disequilibrium of Majority Rule for the Study of Institutions." *American Political Science Review*. 74: 432–47.

Robbins, Lionel. 1932. *An Essay on the Nature and Significance of Economic Science*. London: Macmillan.

Robinson, Joan. 1962. *Essays in the Theory of Economic Growth*. New York: St. Martin's.

1971. *Economic Heresies*. New York: Basic Books.

Roemer, John E. 1978. "Neoclassicism, Marxism, and Collective Action." *Journal of Economic Issues*, 21, no. 1: 147–61.

1988. *Free to Lose*. Cambridge, Mass.: Harvard University Press.

Roll, Eric. 1953. *A History of Economic Thought*. Englewood Cliffs, N.J.: Prentice-Hall.

Rothbard, Murray. 1970. *Power and Market*. Kansas City, Kans.: Sheed Andrews and McMeel.

Rousseau, Jean-Jacques. [1762] 1983. "Discourse on the Origin of Inequality." In *On the Social Contract*, tr. Donald A. Cress. Indianapolis: Hackett.

Rueschemeyer, Dietrich, and Peter B. Evans. 1985. "The State and Economic Transformation: Toward an Analysis of the Conditions Underlying Effective Intervention." In Peter B. Evans, Dietrich Rueschemeyer, and Theda Skocpol, eds., *Bringing the State Back In*. Cambridge: Cambridge University Press.

Sahlins, Marshall. 1972. *Stone Age Economics*. Chicago: Aldine Press.

Sandel, Michael. 1982. *Liberalism and the Limits of Justice*. Cambridge: Cambridge University Press.

1988. "The Political Theory of the Procedural Republic." In R. Reich, ed., *The Power of Public Ideas*. Cambridge, Mass.: Ballinger.

Sartori, Giovanni. 1973. "What Is Politics?" *Political Theory*, 1, no. 1 (February): 5–26.

Schattschneider, E. E. 1960. *The Semisovereign People: A Realist's View of Democracy in America*. New York: Holt, Rinehart, and Winston.

Schelling, Thomas C. 1984. "Economic Reasoning and the Ethics of Policy." In Thomas C. Schelling, *Choice and Consequence*. Cambridge, Mass.: Harvard University Press.

Schmitt, Carl. 1976. *The Concept of the Political*. Tr. by George Schwab, New Brunswick, N.J.: Rutgers University Press.

Schmitter, Philippe C. 1977. "Modes of Interest Intermediation and Models of Societal Change in Western Europe." In Schmitter, ed., *Corporatism and Policy-Making in Contemporary Western Europe*, special issue of *Comparative Political Studies*, 10, no. 1: 7–38.

Schofield, Norman. 1978. "Instability of Simple Dynamic Games." *Review of Economic Studies*, 45: 575–94.

1980. "Formal Political Theory." *Quality and Quantity*, 14: 249–75.

Schubert, Glendon. 1960. *The Public Interest: A Critique of the Theory of a Political Concept*. New York: Free Press.

Schumpeter, Joseph. 1942. *Capitalism, Socialism and Democracy*. New York: Harper and Brothers.

Sen, Amartya. 1970. *Collective Choice and Social Welfare*. Edinburgh: Oliver and Boyd.

1989. "Economic Methodology: Heterogeneity and Relevance." *Social Research*, 56, no. 2: 299–329.

Sen, Amartya, and Bernard Williams. 1982. Introduction. In Sen and Williams, eds., *Utilitarianism and Beyond*. Cambridge: Cambridge University Press.

Sennett, Richard. 1978. *The Fall of Public Man: On the Social Psychology of Capitalism*. New York: Vintage Books.

Shepsle, Kenneth A. 1979a. "Institutional Arrangements and Equilibrium in Multidimensional Voting Models." *American Journal of Political Science*, 23: 27–59.

1979b. "The Role of Institutional Structure in the Creation of Policy Equilibrium." In Douglas W. Rae and T. J. Eismeier, eds., *Public Choice and Public Policy*. Beverly Hills, Calif.: Sage Publications, pp. 249–83.

1983. "Institutional Equilibrium and Equilibrium Institutions." Center for the Study of American Business, Washington University, St. Louis, Working paper no. 82, pp. 1–54.

Shepsle, Kenneth A., and Barry R. Weingast. 1981. "Structure-Induced Equilibrium and Legislative Choice." *Public Choice*, 37: 503–19.

Shepsle, Kenneth A., and Barry R. Weingast. 1984. "Political Solutions to Market Problems." *American Political Science Review*, 78, no. 2: 417–34.

Silk, L. 1984. *Economics and the Real World*. New York: Simon and Schuster.

Singer, Peter. 1981. "The Right to Be Rich or Poor." In *Reading Nozick*, ed. by Jeffrey Paul. Totowa, N.J.: Rowman and Littlefield.

Skocpol, Theda. 1979. *States and Social Revolutions*. Cambridge: Cambridge University Press.

ed. 1984. *Vision and Method in Historical Sociology*. Cambridge: Cambridge University Press.

1985. "Bringing the State Back In: Strategies of Analysis in Current Research." In Peter B. Evans, Dietrich Rueschemayer, and Theda Skocpol, eds., *Bringing the State Back In*. Cambridge: Cambridge University Press, pp. 3–37.

Slutsky, S. 1977. "A Characterization of Societies with Consistent Majority Decision." *Review of Economic Studies*, 44 (June): 211–25.

Smart, J. C. C. 1978. "Distributive Justice and Utilitarianism." In J. Arthur and W. H. Shaw, eds., *Justice and Economic Distribution*. Englewood Cliffs, N.J.: Prentice-Hall.

Smith, Adam. [1776] 1937. *The Wealth of Nations*. New York: Modern Library.

Sowell, Thomas. 1972. *Say's Law*. Princeton, N.J.: Princeton University Press.

Spencer, Herbert. [1843] 1981. "The Proper Sphere of Government." In *The Man Versus the State: With Six Essays on Government, Society, and Freedom*. Indianapolis: Liberty Fund.

Sraffa, Piero. 1960. *Production of Commodities by Means of Commodities*. Cambridge: Cambridge University Press.

Steindl, Josef. 1952. *Maturity and Stagnation in American Capitalism*. Oxford: Blackwell.

Stepan, Alfred. 1978. *The State and Society: Peru in Comparative Perspective*. Princeton, N.J.: Princeton University Press.

Steuart, [Sir] James. [1767] 1966. *An Inquiry into the Principles of Political Economy*. Edinburgh: Oliver and Boyd.

Stiglitz, Joseph E. 1988. *Economics of the Public Sector*. 2d ed. New York: W. W. Norton.

Stokey, Edith, and Richard Zeckhauser. 1978. *A Primer for Policy Analysis*. New York: W. W. Norton.

Sweezy, Paul. 1942. *The Theory of Capitalist Development*. New York: Monthly Review Press.

Swift, Jonathan. [1726] 1941. *Gulliver's Travels*. Oxford: Basil Blackwell.

Taylor, Charles. 1982. "The Diversity of Goods." In Amartya Sen and Bernard Williams, eds., *Utilitarianism and Beyond*. Cambridge: Cambridge University Press, pp. 129–44.

1989. "Cross Purposes: The Liberal-Communitarian Debate." In Nancy Rosenblum, ed., *Liberalism and the Moral Life*. Cambridge, Mass.: Harvard University Press.

Taylor, Michael J. 1969. "Proof of a Theorem on Majority Rule." *Behavioral Science*, 14 (May): 228–36.

1987. *The Possibility of Cooperation*. Cambridge: Cambridge University Press.

1988. "Rationality and Revolutionary Collective Action." In Michael Taylor, ed., *Rationality and Revolution*. Cambridge: Cambridge University Press.

Therborn, Goran. [1970] 1982. "What Does the Ruling Class Do When it Rules?" *Insurgent Sociologist*, 6, no. 3. Reprinted in A. Giddens, ed., *Classes, Power and Conflict*. London: Macmillan.

Tollison, Robert D. 1984. "Public Choice, 1972–1982." In James M. Buchanan and Robert D. Tollison, eds., *The Theory of Public Choice – II*. Ann Arbor: University of Michigan Press, pp. 3–8.

Tullock, Gordon. 1967. "The General Irrelevance of the General Impossibility Theorem." *Quarterly Journal of Economics*, 81 (May): 256–70.

1981. "Why So Much Stability?" *Public Choice*, no. 37: 189–202.

Tucker, R. C., ed. 1978. *The Marx-Engels Reader*. New York: W. W. Norton.

Wagner, Richard E. 1989. *To Promote the General Welfare: Market Processes vs. Political Transfers*. San Francisco: Pacific Research Institute for Public Policy.

Walras, Leon. [1874] 1954. *Elements of Pure Economics*. Tr. W. Jaffe. London: Allen and Unwin.

Walsh, Vivian, and Harvey Gram. 1980. *Classical and Neoclassical Theories of General Equilibrium*. New York: Oxford University Press.

Walzer, Michael. 1986. "Toward a Theory of Social Assignments." In Winthrop Knowlton and Richard Zeckhauser, eds., *American Society: Public and Private Responsibilities*. Cambridge, Mass.: Ballinger, pp. 79–96.

Weber, Max. [1904–5] 1958. *The Protestant Ethic and the Spirit of Capitalism*. Tr. Talcott Parsons. New York: Charles Scribner's Sons.

[1956] 1978. *Economy and Society*, Tr. by G. Roth and C. Wittich from German 4th ed. Berkeley: University of California Press.

1978/1986. "Domination by Economic Power and Authority." In *Economy and Society*, Berkeley: University of California Press. Reprinted in Steven Lukes, ed., *Power*. New York: New York University Press.

Weintraub, E. Roy. 1979. *Microfoundations*. Cambridge: Cambridge University Press.

Weir, Margaret, and Theda Skocpol. 1985. "State Structures and the Possibilities for 'Keynesian' Responses to the Great Depression in Sweden, Britain, and the United States." In Peter B. Evans, Dietrich Rueschemeyer, and Theda Skocpol, eds., *Bringing the State Back In*. Cambridge: Cambridge University Press, pp. 107–163.

Weisskopf, Thomas E., Samuel Bowles, and David M. Gordon. 1985. "Two Views of Capitalist Stagnation: Underconsumption and Challenges to Capitalist Control." *Science and Society*, 49, no. 3: 259–86.

Wendt, Alexander, and Raymond Duvall. 1989. "Institutions and International Order." In Ernst-Otto Czempiel and James N. Rosenau, eds., *Global Changes and Theoretical Challenges*. Lexington, Mass.: Lexington Books, pp. 51–73.

Whynes, David K., and Roger A. Bowles. 1981. *The Economic Theory of the State*. New York: St. Martin's Press.

Wicksell, Knut. 1896. "A New Principle of Just Taxation." *Finanztheoretishe Untersuchungen*. Jena, Germany.

Williamson, Oliver E. 1979. "Transaction-cost Economics: The Governance of Contractual Relations." *Journal of Law and Economics*, 22: 233–61.

Wilsford, David. 1989. "Tactical Advantages vs. Administrative Heterogeneity: The Strengths and Limits of the French State." In James A. Caporaso, ed., *The Elusive State: International and Comparative Perspectives*. Newbury Park, Calif.: Sage Publications, pp. 128–72.

Winfield, Richard. 1988. *The Just Economy*. London: Routledge.

Wolff, Richard D., and Stephen A. Resnick. 1987. *Economics: Marxian Versus Neoclassical*. Baltimore: Johns Hopkins University Press.

Wolin, Sheldon. 1960. *Politics and Vision*. Princeton, N.J.: Princeton University Press.

Index